The Dinah Shore
AMERICAN KITCHEN

The Dinah Shore AMERICAN KITCHEN

Homestyle Cooking with Flair

DOUBLEDAY

New York   London   Toronto   Sydney   Auckland

PUBLISHED BY DOUBLEDAY
a division of Bantam Doubleday Dell Publishing Group, Inc.
666 Fifth Avenue, New York, New York 10103

DOUBLEDAY and the portrayal of an anchor
with a dolphin are trademarks of Doubleday,
a division of Bantam Doubleday Dell
Publishing Group, Inc.

Library of Congress Cataloging-in-Publication Data

Shore, Dinah, 1920–
    The Dinah Shore American kitchen: homestyle cooking with flair /
Dinah Shore. — 1st ed.
        p.   cm.
    1. Cookery.   I. Title.
TX714.S55   1990
641.5—dc20   89-49468
                                                                   CIP

ISBN 0-385-24683-8

Copyright © 1990 by Dinah Shore

Food photography by: Teri Sandison, Los Angeles
Food styling by: Jean E. Carey/Kitchen Consultants and Fred Walker
Prop styling by: Mindy Hahn
Selected props furnished by Tesoro

Book Design by Antler & Baldwin, Inc.

Contents

Introduction

True to the title, this book is full of home cooking—however, it's not exclusively "down home" cooking. We're such a wonderful, delicious mix of cultures and backgrounds in this country that the cooking refers to all kinds of home cooking, whatever the original home our parents and grandparents came from—Italy, France, Mexico, Portugal, the Philippines, ad infinitum. Of course, I favor the dishes my palate first knew, but my curiosity and excitement were aroused early on when I first learned that pasta wasn't just macaroni and yellow cheese (though I always have and always will adore this pre–Hamburger Helper keeper), that fish wasn't just fried, that groats was as interesting as grits. You'll find a full variety of cuisines here.

A few problems arose in getting it together. For instance, as a frugal—well, careful—person, who worries about the starving children in Armenia or the Third World countries and the underprivileged here, the hardest part of writing this cookbook was the testing, tasting, and wasting. When you're doing four- and five- and six-course meals daily, some of which are unrelated, you don't have a perfectly balanced menu.

For instance, on the evening of this writing I have three definitely incredible pastas I want to try. So, those innocents who will be tripping through the door before dinner in anticipation of delicately balanced dining will be waddling out in a semistupor and probably won't answer my phone calls for a week. You don't exactly lose friends, but since most of mine want to stay slim and desirable, close friendships are put on hold. Of course, there are next-door neighbors who'll drop in on a couple of hours' notice. But after a few heavy tasting sessions, they get a little shy too. This is where you really have to turn on the charm. So, to go back to my original thought, no matter how sensationally sensual those dinners are, you can't possibly handle all the leftovers. If you open my refrigerator door in a hurry, your clothes and your toes are in jeopardy. It's packed pretty tight in there with tomorrow's supplies and today's irresistibles. I assure you, the lesser marvels are down the disposal.

I think you have the idea now, dear cook and diner. I really had to taste and test everything that went into this book—and I have the accountings from three post-testing "fat farms" in the area to prove it. If I liked a recipe, you have it here, exactly as it had to be done, down to the last one-fourth teaspoon of whatever it was (insofar as I can remember) I am truly "a pinch of this and a few drops of that" cook until the flavor is just the way I think it should be. That may not work for all of you, so I tried to be pretty exact. Have fun with this ... I did. It was possibly the only excuse I'll ever have for eating all those things I love— in quantity.

The Dinah Shore
AMERICAN KITCHEN

Openers

To me this is the best part of the cocktail hour (whatever that is). If somebody drops by and can or cannot stay for dinner, with a little forewarning you can whip up something tantalizing enough to make that hour more memorable than the rest of the evening. Try the various pizzas. If you're having dinner at home, the pizzas can be a first course or a great greeter. Also, try the Chopped Tomato Salad (page 29). It's a joy served on bruschetta (crisp French or Italian bread with a smidgen of olive oil and a cut clove of garlic lightly rubbed on the surface) as a first course.

❖ Pizza

These pizzas are my biggest hits to date. People have flown miles—well, they've driven around the block anyway—to taste them. I usually just make one for a sitting or dinner group, but sometimes when I'm feeling insecure, I'll make two or three different pizzas together just to hear the raves. The crust is easy. I usually make it well ahead of time and keep it in the refrigerator. It keeps for about one week. When I'm ready to roll it out, I gently pull it so thin that I have reams of dough left for two or three other pizzas.

I have two pizza bricks. (They're available at practically any cooking supply shop.) One is a 13-inch round and the other is an 11-×-14-inch rectangular one. They cook the pizzas quickly and totally, with the crispest, most delicate crust possible.

❧ Pizza Crusts

Take your pick of these two. I like both of them. Either one will come out thin and crisp with no second rising necessary.

CRUST NO. 1

1 envelope active dry yeast
¾ cup warm water (110°–115°)
½ teaspoon sugar
1⅔ cups unbleached flour, slightly warmed

⅛ teaspoon salt
1 tablespoon fresh virgin olive oil
Olive oil for brushing on pizza brick or pan

In a small bowl, combine the yeast, water, and sugar and allow to proof until bubbly and doubled in size. Place the flour, salt, olive oil, and "proofed" yeast mixture in a food processor bowl fitted with a metal blade. Process just until the dough forms a soft ball on top of the blade. Remove from the bowl and place on a lightly floured board. Knead for a minute or two. Place the dough in a lightly buttered bowl. Cover and let rise until doubled or tripled in bulk. This should take about 45 minutes to an hour.

Cut the dough in half. Roll out one half on a lightly floured board. Brush a 13-inch round or an 11-×-14-inch pizza brick with a very light coating of olive oil. Place the dough on the brick and shape and pull the dough until it comes to the outer edges of the brick. If, in doing so, you make a few holes in the center, not to worry—you can patch them with extra dough. Make a small lip on the outer edge of the dough so the filling will not run over. Repeat the rolling and shaping with the second piece of dough.

Makes two very thin 13-inch round pizzas
or two 11-×-14-inch pizzas

CRUST NO. 2

1½ cups warm water (110°–115°)
1 envelope active dry yeast
1 teaspoon sugar
4 cups flour
⅛ teaspoon salt

2 tablespoons margarine, melted, or fresh virgin olive oil
Olive oil for brushing on pizza brick or pan

In a small bowl, combine ½ cup of the warm water, the yeast, and the sugar. Allow to proof until bubbly and doubled in size. Place the flour and salt in the bowl of a food processor fitted with a metal blade.

Add the margarine or oil and the remaining 1 cup of warm water. Process until mixed (30 seconds or so, no more). Slowly add the yeast mixture through the feed tube. Process until the dough forms a ball around the blade, about 10 to 15 seconds. If it's too thick, add a little more water, or if too thin, add a little more flour.

Remove from the bowl and place on a lightly floured board. Knead for a minute or two. Place the dough in a lightly buttered bowl. Cover and let the dough rise until doubled or tripled in bulk, about 40 to 50 minutes.

Cut the dough in quarters. Roll out one quarter on a lightly floured board. Brush a 13-inch round or an 11-×-14-inch pizza brick with a very light coating of olive oil. Place the dough on the brick and shape and pull the dough until it comes to the outer edges of the brick. If, in doing so, you make a few holes in the center, not to worry—you can patch them with extra dough. Make a small lip on the outer edge of the dough so the filling will not run over. Repeat the rolling and shaping with the other pieces of dough.

Makes four 13-inch round pizzas or four 11-×-14-inch pizzas

✤ *Three Cheese Three Herb Pizza*

This has a very special flavor. I first tasted it in San Francisco and came home and tried to duplicate it. I rather like the Simon and Garfunkel touch—"Parsley, Sage, Rosemary, and Thyme." It's just that parsley would have made it four herbs, but try it. It has a nice ring to it.

CRUST

1½ cups warm water (110°–115°)
1 envelope active dry yeast
1 teaspoon sugar
4 cups flour

⅛ teaspoon salt
2 tablespoons margarine, melted, or freshest olive oil
Olive oil for brushing on pizza brick or pan

In a small bowl, combine ½ cup of the warm water, the yeast, and the sugar. Let it proof until it becomes quite bubbly. Place the flour and salt in the bowl of a food processor fitted with a metal blade. Add the margarine or oil and the remaining 1 cup of warm water, and process for 30 seconds or so—no more. Slowly add the yeast mixture through the feed tube. Process until the dough forms a ball around the blade, about 10 or 15 seconds. If the dough is too thick, add a little more water, if too thin, add a little more flour.

Place the dough in a lightly greased bowl, cover, and let rise until doubled or tripled in bulk, about 40 to 50 minutes.

Cut the dough into 4 equal pieces. Roll one piece out on a lightly floured board (save the remaining three for other pizzas), toss, and pull and stretch as much as you can without tearing the dough. (Even if you do tear it, don't worry about it. It patches easily. The idea is to get it as thin and as delicate as you can.) Lightly brush a pizza brick or pan with olive oil before placing the dough on the surface.

TOPPING

½ cup grated asiago cheese
½ cup grated Monterey Jack or provolone cheese
1 teaspoon chopped fresh sage
1½ teaspoons chopped fresh thyme

3 teaspoons chopped fresh rosemary
Freshly ground black pepper
½ cup freshly grated Parmesan cheese

Mix together the asiago and Jack or provolone cheese. Cover the pizza dough with the cheese. Sprinkle the chopped herbs over all and then add a generous grinding of black pepper. Top with the Parmesan cheese.

Bake in a preheated 450° oven for 20 minutes, until the cheeses are bubbly and the crust is lightly browned and crisp.

Makes enough topping for one 13-inch round pizza or one 11- × -14-inch pizza

Variations:

TOMATO AND THREE CHEESE PIZZA

½ recipe for pizza crust for Three Cheese Three Herb Pizza
2 ripe medium tomatoes, thinly sliced
Salt and pepper

⅔ cup grated Monterey Jack cheese
⅔ cup grated Gorgonzola cheese
⅓ cup freshly grated Parmesan cheese

Roll out the dough as directed in the preceding master recipe. Place the sliced tomatoes on the dough. Salt and pepper the tomatoes. Sprinkle the grated cheeses over the tomatoes.

Bake in a preheated 450° oven for 20 minutes, or until the cheeses are bubbly and the crust is lightly browned and crisp.

Makes enough topping for one 13-inch round pizza or one 11- × - 14-inch pizza

Note: You can substitute thinly sliced Italian sausage, sliced mushrooms, or anchovies for the tomatoes.

❀ *Pizza Brie*

¹/₂ recipe for Pizza Crust No. 1
   (page 6)
¹/₄ pound Brie cheese, thinly
   sliced, or enough Brie to
   cover the top of the pizza
   crust
¹/₂ cup slivered almonds

Cover the prepared pizza dough with Brie and sprinkle generously with almonds. Bake in a preheated 400° oven for 20 minutes, or until the cheese is bubbly and the crust is lightly browned and crisp.

Cut into squares or wedges and serve hot, with a green salad. (Be sure you pass seconds.) Or serve by itself as an hors d'oeuvre or first course.

Makes one 13-inch round pizza or one 11- × -14-inch pizza

❀ *Arugula Pizza*

¹/₂ recipe for Pizza Crust No. 1
   (page 6)
¹/₂ cup grated Monterey Jack
   cheese
¹/₂ cup grated mozzarella
   cheese

³/₄ cup arugula leaves, left
   whole

1 tablespoon capers, drained
1¹/₂ tablespoons finely minced
   onion (optional)

Sprinkle the pizza dough with the cheeses. Place in a preheated 400° oven for 15 minutes. Remove from the oven and lay arugula leaves over the cheese. Return to the oven and continue baking for another 5 minutes, or until the cheeses are bubbly and the crust is lightly browned and crisp.

Sprinkle the capers and onion over the hot arugula pizza. Cut into wedges or squares and serve immediately.

Makes one 13-inch round pizza or one 11- × -14-inch pizza

❋ *Chicken Pizza with Fresh Tomato-Basil Sauce*

½ recipe for Pizza Crust No. 1 or ¼ recipe No. 2 (page 6)
1 to 1½ cups Fresh Tomato-Basil Sauce (see below)

1 whole cooked chicken breast, marinated (see below)

YOUR CHOICE OF TOPPINGS

½ green pepper, seeded and thinly sliced
½ sweet red pepper, seeded and thinly sliced
½ yellow pepper, seeded and thinly sliced
¼ pound mushrooms, thinly sliced
3 tablespoons finely chopped fresh basil

½ cup finely grated mozzarella cheese

½ cup finely grated Parmesan or Romano cheese
Red pepper flakes
Olive oil, for brushing on filled pizza
One 4-ounce can of sliced ripe olives or Greek olives, sliced (optional)

1 tablespoon capers, drained (optional)

Brush the pizza dough with Fresh Tomato-Basil Sauce and top with any or all of the ingredients listed above. Dot lightly with more sauce if you like. Sprinkle generously with the cheeses and red pepper flakes. Brush very lightly with olive oil.

Bake in a preheated 450° oven for approximately 14 minutes. Remove from the oven and arrange the cooked chicken on top. Sprinkle with olives and capers if you like. Return to the oven, reduce heat to 400°, and bake for another 5 minutes, or until the cheese is bubbly and the crust is brown and crisp.

FRESH TOMATO-BASIL SAUCE

1 to 2 tablespoons olive oil
1 yellow onion, finely chopped
1 stalk celery, finely chopped
½ green pepper, seeded and
  finely chopped
½ carrot, finely chopped
2 cloves garlic, finely chopped
One 28-ounce can of crushed
  Italian tomatoes or whole
  Italian tomatoes, broken up

4 fresh basil leaves, finely
  chopped
2 tablespoons finely chopped
  parsley
Salt and pepper
Red pepper flakes (optional)

In a large skillet, heat the oil and sauté the onions until just soft. Add the celery, green pepper, carrot, and garlic, and cook until the vegetables are just tender. Add the tomatoes and cook over low heat until the flavors are blended, about 30 minutes, or more if you have time. During the last 15 minutes of cooking, add the fresh basil and parsley. Add salt and pepper to taste and check for seasonings, adding more salt if necessary. Add the pepper flakes if desired. Strain or blend in a food processor.

Makes approximately 3 cups

COOKED CHICKEN

Juice of ½ lemon
1 teaspoon olive oil
Pinch of ground cumin
Pinch of dried oregano
Salt and pepper
Pinch of red pepper flakes, or
  to taste

1 whole chicken breast, cut
  into thin strips about 2
  inches long
Cornstarch
¼ cup vegetable or peanut oil

Combine the lemon juice, oil, herbs, and seasonings. Add chicken strips and marinate 2 hours or longer.

Remove from marinade and dip in cornstarch and set aside.

Heat the oil in a wok or saucepan over high heat until very hot (375°). Fry the chicken strips quickly. Drain on paper towels.

Makes one 13-inch round pizza or one 11- × -14-inch pizza

❄ *Pepperoni and Italian Sausage Pizza*

*½ recipe for Pizza Crust No. 1
or ¼ recipe No. 2 (page 6)*

*¾ to 1 cup Fresh Tomato-Basil
Sauce (page 11)*

YOUR CHOICE OF TOPPINGS

*½ green pepper, seeded and
thinly sliced*

*½ sweet red pepper, seeded and
thinly sliced*

*½ yellow pepper, seeded and
thinly sliced*

*¼ pound mushrooms, thinly
sliced*

*3 tablespoons finely chopped
fresh basil*

*1 tablespoon finely chopped
fresh oregano*

*½ cup grated mozzarella
cheese*

½ cup grated Parmesan cheese

Red pepper flakes (optional)

*Olive oil, for brushing on filled
pizza*

*One 8-ounce package of
pepperoni, sliced, or ½
pound Italian sausage,
thinly sliced, cooked and
drained of excess fat*

*One 4-ounce can of sliced ripe
olives or Greek olives, sliced*

*1 tablespoon capers, drained
(optional)*

Brush the pizza dough with the tomato-basil sauce and top with any or all of the toppings listed above. Dot lightly with more tomato sauce if you like. Sprinkle generously with mozzarella and Parmesan cheese and red pepper flakes. Brush very lightly with olive oil. Add layers of pepperoni, Italian sausage, and olives and bake in a preheated 450° oven for 20 minutes, or until the cheeses are bubbly and the pizza crust is brown and crisp. Sprinkle capers over the top if you like.

Makes one 13-inch round pizza or one 11-×-14-inch pizza

❧ Smoked Salmon Pizza

Wolfgang Puck serves incredible pizza combinations for starters at his famous Spago's restaurant. This is something like ad-libbing a tune you've just heard and loved: "It goes something like this." Mine came out great every time I tried it. Yours will too.

½ *recipe for Pizza Crust No. 1*
 or ¼ recipe No. 2 (page 6)
½ *cup grated Monterey Jack*
 cheese
½ *cup grated mozzarella*
 cheese

½ *pound smoked salmon,*
 thinly sliced

1 *tablespoon capers*
1½ *tablespoons finely minced*
 onion

Sprinkle the pizza dough lightly with the cheeses. Bake in a preheated 400° oven for 15 minutes. Remove from the oven and lay the salmon over the cheese. Return to the oven and continue baking for another 5 minutes, or until the cheeses are bubbly and the crust is lightly browned and crisp.

Sprinkle the cold capers and onions over the hot salmon pizza. Cut into wedges or squares and serve immediately.

Makes one 13-inch round pizza or one 11-×-14-inch pizza

❧ Fresh Tomato Pizza

This Fresh Tomato Pizza and the Pepperoni and Italian Sausage Pizza (page 12) are particularly popular with the kids. I guess it reminds them of the ones they get from the take-out place.

½ *recipe for Pizza Crust No. 1*
 (page 6)
2 *to 3 medium-size ripe*
 tomatoes, thinly sliced
Salt and pepper to taste

⅔ *cup grated Monterey Jack or*
 mozzarella cheese
⅔ *cup grated Gorgonzola or*
 provolone cheese
⅓ *cup grated Parmesan cheese*

Place the sliced tomatoes on the pizza dough. Salt and pepper the tomatoes. Sprinkle the grated cheeses over the top. Bake in a preheated 450° oven for 20 minutes, or until the cheeses are bubbly and the crust is lightly browned and crisp. Serve immediately.

Makes one 13-inch pizza or one 11-×-14-inch pizza

❃ *Phyllo Pillows*

Phyllo dough is not as difficult to work with as you might think. It comes in convenient packages in the frozen-food section of your supermarket. Just follow the directions on the box for handling the dough and make almost any kind of filling—spinach, ricotta, sausage, et cetera.

Filling (see below)
6 sheets of phyllo dough
  (sheets are approximately
  14 × 18 inches)

3 tablespoons margarine or
  butter, or more if needed

Have the melted margarine or butter and a brush handy before you start to work with the dough. Remove the dough carefully from the box and place it on a kitchen towel. Remove one sheet and cover the remaining sheets with a damp—not wet—cloth until ready to use.

Brush one sheet of dough with margarine or butter. Lay another one over it and brush again, making sure you cover the whole surface. Continue adding sheets of phyllo and brushing each one with margarine or butter until you have used all 6 sheets. Cut into 2-×-6-inch strips and then into 3 equal sections across. Place a scant ½ teaspoon of filling on one end of each strip of phyllo dough and roll up, tucking in the ends, until you have little pillows. If they look dry, brush margarine or butter over the pastry before baking.

Bake in a preheated 350° oven for 15 to 20 minutes, or until golden brown, and serve warm.

FILLING

4 thin slices mozzarella cheese,
  cut into ½-inch cubes
3 slices feta cheese, crumbled
½ teaspoon finely chopped
  fresh mint

1 tablespoon sour cream
Dash of grated nutmeg
Freshly ground black pepper
Salt, if needed, but the feta
  cheese is pretty salty

Mix all the ingredients. Set aside.

Makes 21 pillows

Variations: Stuff with spinach and feta cheese or with any tasty leftover mixed with a melting-type cheese.

❧ Little Piroshki

I learned to make this in large form many, many years ago from George's mother and sisters in Montana. I decided one day to give it a try as a first course or an hors d'oeuvre before dinner. They found me in the kitchen hours later, buried under a mound of dumplings and dough (I'd decided to do the Lasagna on page 206 the same day) still crimping "little boats." My guests loved them and forgave me for serving dinner at 9:30 with a tee-off the next morning at 7:00 A.M.

FILLING

Scant 2 tablespoons vegetable oil, butter, or margarine
1 large onion, chopped
1 large clove garlic, finely chopped
1 zucchini, chopped
2 tablespoons chopped fresh dill
2 tablespoons chopped fresh parsley

½ bunch fresh spinach, washed and chopped
¼ pound ground meat (preferably lamb, or beef liver and beef mixed)
Salt and pepper
½ cup kasha, cooked according to package directions
Sour cream
Dill sprig, for garnish

Heat the oil in a skillet and sauté the onion, garlic, zucchini, dill, parsley, and spinach, until the onion is soft, about 2 or 3 minutes. Brown the ground meat until it loses its pink color, and season with salt and pepper. Combine the vegetables and kasha and mix well. Taste for seasoning.

DOUGH

1 envelope active dry yeast
2 cups warm milk (110°–115°)
2 teaspoons sugar
2 tablespoons butter or margarine, melted

1 tablespoon vegetable oil
½ teaspoon salt
1 egg, lightly beaten
2 cups sifted flour (more if you need it)

In a small bowl, combine the yeast, ½ cup of the warm milk, and 1 teaspoon sugar and allow to proof until quite bubbly.

In a large bowl, mix together the remaining 1½ cups milk, the melted butter or margarine, oil, salt, egg, and remaining 1 teaspoon sugar. Add the proofed yeast and then combine with the flour. Place the dough on a floured board (it will be sticky) and knead for 3 or 4 minutes. Transfer to an oiled bowl, cover with foil and a towel, and leave in a warm place until the dough doubles in bulk, about 40 to 50 minutes.

Place the dough on a floured board and roll out with a floured rolling pin to about ½ inch thick. Using a 2-inch biscuit cutter, cut the dough into rounds. Stretch each "biscuit" a little and place a spoonful of the filling mixture in each one. Pull up the edges and seal tightly to hold the filling. When all your little boats (ducks) are in a row, cover loosely with foil and leave in a warm place to rise, about 20 to 30 minutes, before frying or baking.

Fry in deep hot oil (375°) a few at a time until golden and puffed, keeping the fried piroshki warm until the rest are cooked; or place on a greased baking sheet and bake in the center of a preheated 400° oven until brown and crisp.

Serve with sour cream and garnish with a sprig of dill.

Makes 35 to 40 piroshki

✽ *Spring Rolls*

You can make your own egg-roll wrappers. They're easy, but it's even easier to buy them in the frozen-food section.

FILLING

3 teaspoons peanut oil
4 water chestnuts, finely chopped
2 small stalks celery, finely chopped (no leaves)
2 scallions, finely chopped (the white and a bit of the green part)
2 tablespoons finely chopped bean sprouts (optional)
¼ pound lump crab meat (you may use pork, beef, or any other meat or shellfish), cleaned, finely chopped, or shredded
2 tablespoons soy sauce
Freshly ground white pepper to taste
Peanut oil for frying
Hot mustard

Heat the oil in a skillet and sauté the vegetables over medium heat for 2 or 3 minutes. They should still be crisp. Add the crab, 1 tablespoon soy sauce, and white pepper, and sauté 2 or 3 minutes longer. Remove from the heat.

Place a small amount of filling in the center of a crepe. Fold over and tuck in the ends of the crepe, roll up, and seal it. If the flap does not seal well, brush with a little beaten egg yolk.

Heat ¼ inch of oil in a skillet. Fry the rolls until they are golden on each side, turning carefully. Drain on paper towels and serve with remaining soy sauce and hot mustard.

FLOUR CREPES
1 cup flour
½ cup boiling water
Peanut oil

Sift the flour and add the water. Stir to make a dough, when the dough is cool, wrap it in foil or waxed paper and chill for 1 hour.

When ready to cook, divide the dough into 8 balls. Place a piece of waxed paper on a smooth surface and brush it with oil. Pat a piece of dough into a flattened ball and place it on the paper, brush the top of the dough with oil and cover with another sheet of waxed paper. Flatten another ball of dough and place it on top of the first one, brush with oil, and top with another sheet of waxed paper. Roll out to make 2 crepes about 3 or 4 inches in diameter. Repeat until all the dough is used. Chilling the rolled out crepes for a few minutes will make them easier to remove from the paper.

Makes about 15 or 16 rolls

✽ Pot Stickers

I've had these in Hong Kong, San Francisco, Singapore, and New York City. Little did I know I could have them in Beverly Hills or Malibu with not much trouble and so much joy.

½ pound lean pork
¼ pound Chinese celery cabbage (about 4 stalks)
½ teaspoon salt
1 scallion, minced (white part only)
1 tablespoon light soy sauce
¼ teaspoon black pepper
½ teaspoon sugar

1½ teaspoons sesame oil
Chinese won ton skins (if frozen, thaw while you make the filling)
1 tablespoon peanut oil, for frying
¼ to ½ cup water
Hot chili oil
White or red wine vinegar

Cut the pork into chunks and place it in a food processor. Pulse off and on to chop or mince coarsely or have your butcher grind the pork coarsely. Chop the cabbage very fine. I used a food processor. Cut the cabbage coarsely before putting it in the processor, and place one leaf on top of the other to make it easier. Be careful not to let the cabbage get soupy. You should end up with ¾ cup. Sprinkle with ¼ teaspoon salt, place in a strainer, and let stand a few minutes to get out the excess moisture.

Mix the pork and cabbage well; they should hold together. Add the scallion, soy sauce, the remaining ¼ teaspoon salt, the pepper, sugar, and sesame oil. Mix well. Make into little portions of 1 tablespoon each.

Keep won ton skins covered with a damp (not wet) towel. Lightly oil a large plate and have a small bowl of water handy. Place 1 tablespoon of pork mixture in the center of a won ton skin. Pull the four corners of the won ton up, pinch them together to make a little triangle, and seal in the filling. If you need to, dampen the edges and corners to help hold them together. Set on the plate, pinched side up. Continue until you have used all the filling. Cover with a damp cloth and chill until ready to use.

Place a 9- or 10-inch skillet over medium-high heat, add ½ tablespoon peanut oil (just enough to cover the bottom of the pan), and remove the skillet from the heat. Arrange the dumplings in a row but *not* touching, pinched side down in the skillet. Return to the heat and fry until the bottoms are golden. Check with a spatula without shaking or tilting the skillet. Sprinkle ¼ to ½ cup water over the tops of the dumplings with your fingers, bring to a boil, cover, and reduce the heat to medium-low. Steam until the water has evaporated, about 10 minutes. (Try not to peek.)

Uncover and add the remaining ½ tablespoon peanut oil around the edges of the skillet. Now tip the pan to coat the bottom. Fry, uncovered, until the dumplings are crisp and brown on the bottom, about 2 or 3 minutes. Don't let them burn.

Serve with a little hot chili oil mixed with white or red wine vinegar.

Makes about 16 dumplings

❈ *Gloria's Shrimp Cocktail*

Gloria is Gloria Estrada from Zacatecas, Mexico—my friend and cook. She's no bigger than a minute but she loves to eat and loves to cook. One beautiful Sunday afternoon at the beach we all got into a discussion about shrimp cocktails, the dull, old, usual variety as opposed to something new and special. Gloria volunteered a very special Zacatecas shrimp cocktail. We served it in a tall stemmed beer glass—an oversized red wine goblet will do. Have a large bowl and a ladle for seconds close by—you'll need it.

*2 pounds medium uncooked
    shrimp, shelled and deveined
    (reserve shells for the broth)*

BROTH

*Reserved shrimp shells
6 cups water
6 large cloves garlic, unpeeled
1 lime, quartered*

*1 lemon, quartered
1 tomato, quartered
1 teaspoon salt*

Place the shrimp shells in the water. Add the remaining broth ingredients. Bring to a boil and boil for 30 minutes. Drain in a colander placed over a bowl, reserving the broth. Bring the broth to a boil. Place the shrimps in the broth for 2 to 3 minutes or until just pink. Remove the shrimps and place them in a bowl in the refrigerator to cool. Boil the broth for another 15 to 20 minutes, or until reduced to 3½ cups, then place it in the refrigerator to cool.

COCKTAIL SAUCE

*1 large firm tomato, peeled
    and coarsely chopped
2 scallions, coarsely chopped
2 tablespoons coarsely chopped
    onion
2 tablespoons coarsely chopped
    cilantro (coriander)*

*½ cucumber, coarsely chopped
½ avocado, coarsely chopped
9 tablespoons ketchup
6 tablespoons lemon juice
Tabasco sauce to taste*

Put 6 whole shrimp in each of 6 large wine goblets. Place 1 heaping tablespoon tomato; 1 scant teaspoon each scallions, onions, and cilantro; 1 tablespoon cucumber; 1 tablespoon avocado; 1½ tablespoons ketchup; 1 tablespoon lemon juice; and 3 or 4 drops of Tabasco in each goblet. Pour ¾ cup of reserved cold broth into each goblet. Mix gently and serve with Twice Toasted Bread (see below) or crackers.

Serves 6

TWICE TOASTED BREAD

*6 slices very thin white, wheat,
    or rye bread*

Butter, softened

Preheat oven to 200°.
Butter one side of the bread slices or both sides if desired. Cut into squares, triangles, rectangles, etc. Bake for 2 to 4 hours, or until the bread is golden brown. Store in a covered container. These toasted slices will keep for weeks. Before serving, toast again until crisp in a 250° oven.

❧ *Shrimp Balls*

12 medium uncooked shrimp,
  shelled and deveined
1 tablespoon olive oil
1 tablespoon margarine
2 scallions, finely chopped (use
  green part also)
¼ cup finely chopped green
  pepper
3 sprigs cilantro (coriander),
  chopped medium-fine
Generous 1 tablespoon light
  soy sauce
⅛ teaspoon sesame oil

Salt and pepper
⅛ teaspoon ground ginger
⅛ teaspoon ground cumin
⅛ teaspoon Chinese hot oil
Dash of rice wine vinegar
1 egg, separated
¾ cup chicken broth
1 slice fresh bread, lightly
  toasted
⅓ cup water chestnuts, cut into
  quarters
Peanut oil for frying

Sauté the shrimp in the olive oil and margarine until just pink. Remove the shrimp and set aside to cool; then chop fine.

Sauté the scallions and green pepper in the same skillet. Add the cilantro, light soy sauce, sesame oil, salt and pepper to taste, ginger, cumin, Chinese hot oil, rice wine vinegar, and beaten egg yolk. Mix until well blended. Add the shrimp and set the mixture aside.

Beat the egg white and blend into the chicken broth. Pour the chicken broth mixture over the bread and mash with a fork.

Scoop up a small spoonful of the shrimp mixture and roll it around a water chestnut. Then roll in the bread mixture to coat very lightly. Repeat this process until you have used up all the shrimp. Place the shrimp balls in the refrigerator for 1 hour or so.

Use a deep saucepan or wok for frying. Add the peanut oil. Heat until very hot. Drop a small piece of scallion or bread in the hot oil. When it begins to bubble and brown, the oil is hot enough for frying. Drop 4 or 5 shrimp balls at a time into the hot oil so as not to cool off the oil; fry the balls until golden brown. Keep warm until ready to serve, but don't let them sit too long. They're best when fresh and crunchy.

Makes about 20 to 25 balls, depending on size

❖ Shrimp in a Cloud

8 fresh uncooked jumbo
   shrimp, shelled and deveined
Cornstarch for coating shrimp
2 large eggs
4 tablespoons water-chestnut
   flour or cornstarch
1 tablespoon cold water

1 tablespoon rice wine
½ teaspoon salt
Vegetable oil for deep-drying
1½ cups 4-inch lengths of rice
   vermicelli
2 cups fresh spinach leaves,
   washed and trimmed

DIP

1 teaspoon Chinese red vinegar
2 tablespoons thin soy sauce
4 drops of sesame oil

½ teaspoon shredded fresh
   gingerroot

Lightly coat the shrimp with cornstarch and set aside to air-dry. Combine the eggs, water-chestnut flour or cornstarch, cold water, rice wine, and salt to make a batter. Set aside.

Heat about 3 inches of vegetable oil to about 350° in a wok and add the vermicelli. It should suddenly puff up into a mass of white noodles. Quickly toss to make sure all the noodles are fried. Remove them immediately from the heat to avoid browning them. Drain, and arrange on a warm platter.

Remove all food particles from the oil in the wok and add another inch of fresh oil. Reheat the oil to 350°. Coat a shrimp thoroughly with batter and, holding it by the tail, slide it into the hot oil. Deep-fry 2 shrimp at a time in the wok until all are done. Drain the shrimp and arrange them, tails up, on the bed of fluffy vermicelli, and arrange the spinach leaves on the outer edge.

Combine all the ingredients for the dip, and serve it on the side.

Serves 8

❋ *Crunchy Almond Shrimp*

Served with steamed rice topped with scallions and a fresh fruit salad, this makes a delicious main course.

1 pound uncooked medium
   shrimp, shelled and deveined
1 egg plus 1 egg white
¼ cup milk
⅓ cup flour
1 clove garlic, crushed

½ teaspoon salt
½ teaspoon white pepper
1 cup crushed blanched
   almonds
1 cup peanut oil
Fresh lime wedges

Split the shrimp butterfly fashion. Prepare a batter by beating the eggs, milk, flour, garlic, salt, and pepper together. Place the almonds on a plate.

Dip each shrimp into the batter and then in the almonds to coat evenly. Set them in a single layer on a sheet of waxed paper.

Heat the oil in a deep frying pan to about 375°. Roll each shrimp again in the nuts and place in the hot oil. Fry until golden. Drain on absorbent paper toweling.

Serve hot with wedges of lime.

Serves 3 or 4

❋ *Spicy Deviled Crab Meat*

This is delicious—depending, of course, on whether or not that beautiful, light crab meat is available.

1 tablespoon finely chopped
   sweet red or green pepper
2 scallions, finely chopped
1 shallot, finely chopped
¼ jalapeño pepper, seeded and
   finely chopped
½ teaspoon Dijon mustard

¾ ounce Cognac
¼ teaspoon capers, drained
2 tablespoons mayonnaise
1 cup lump crab meat, picked
   over to get out any bits of
   shell

Combine the first 8 ingredients in a bowl and blend well. Then add the crab meat, carefully, so as not to break it up too much.

Serve with toasted French bread rounds or your favorite cracker.

Serves 8 to 10

✿ *Peppery Stuffed Crab*

The angostura bitters gives this a special tang. Or maybe it's the lobster tail—or maybe it's the appreciation of real crab meat, which seems to be in short supply out here these days. Whatever it is, this is terrific. If you want to serve this in your favorite casserole as an hors d'oeuvre instead of in separate portions, it works just as well. Serve with crisp toast points if you want it to go around and stretch a little further.

3 slices soft bread, torn into
   small pieces (crusts and all)
1 cup milk
3 dashes of angostura bitters
1½ tablespoons finely minced
   lean bacon
1 tablespoon finely chopped
   shallots
1 small clove garlic, crushed
2 teaspoons strained lime juice
Salt and pepper to taste

4 dashes of Tabasco sauce
1 lobster tail, cooked and cut
   into chunks
½ pound lump crab meat,
   cleaned and picked over for
   bits of shell
6 ceramic shells
Oil to brush the shells
½ cup fine bread crumbs
1 tablespoon butter or
   margarine

Mix the bread with the milk and bitters. Sauté the bacon pieces in a skillet, add the shallot and garlic, and continue to cook until the bacon is crisp (not burned). Pour off the extra fat. Add the bacon, shallot, and garlic to the milk mixture. Stir in the lime juice, salt and pepper, Tabasco, lobster, and crab meat. Taste for seasoning. It should be a little spicy.

Brush the ceramic shells with a little oil and place an equal amount of mixture in each shell. Cover with bread crumbs, dot with butter or margarine, and bake in a preheated 375° oven until heated through and brown on top.

Serves 6

✽ *Stuffed Deviled Crabs*

I love crab cakes, Stuffed Deviled Crabs, Canelloni with Lump Crab Meat (page 208), etc., etc. Crab meat is easy to season and adapts to many types of flavors in many cuisines. The chilpolte sauce is found in the gourmet section of your market or in specialty stores. It's an unusual sauce made of sweet and hot peppers that gives the crab meat a special pungent flavor.

1 pound fresh crab meat
4 tablespoons lime juice
2 teaspoons finely chopped onion
1 teaspoon freshly ground black pepper
2 dashes of Tabasco sauce
1 teaspoon chilpolte sauce or salsa chilpolte
Salt
2 tablespoons butter or margarine, plus extra for topping
2 tablespoons chopped onion
2 tablespoons chopped green pepper

1 small tomato, peeled and chopped
½ clove garlic, crushed and minced
1 tablespoon chopped fresh parsley
Generous pinch of dry mustard
Pinch of ground mace
Pinch of chopped fresh basil
2 tablespoons light rum
2 tablespoons fine bread crumbs
Cracker crumbs
Freshly grated Parmesan cheese

In a bowl, mix the crab, lime juice, finely chopped onion, the black pepper, Tabasco, chilpolte sauce, and salt to taste. Let this stand in the refrigerator for a couple of hours before using.

In a skillet, melt the 2 tablespoons butter or margarine, add the 2 tablespoons onion, the green pepper, tomato, garlic, and parsley. Sauté until the vegetables are tender. Then add the mustard, mace, basil, rum, and bread crumbs. Cook over low heat for about 2 minutes.

Stir in the crab mixture and heat, stirring well, for about 5 minutes. Remove from the heat and place into individual ramekins. Sprinkle each portion with an equal amount of cracker crumbs mixed with Parmesan cheese, dot with butter, and bake in a preheated 350° oven until the tops are browned, about 5 minutes.

Serves 4 to 6, depending on the size
of your shells or ramekins or generosity

✽ Cold Scallops Dressed with Garlic-Chive Sauce

½ cup good mayonnaise
1 tablespoon lemon juice
Dash of white pepper
1 tablespoon butter
1 pound sea scallops, cut in
    half, with any juices that
    surround them

¼ cup finely sliced garlic
    chives (substitute regular
    chives if you don't have
    garlic chives, but they do
    add a distinctive flavor)
1 small white onion, sliced
    paper thin

Mix together the mayonnaise, lemon juice, and white pepper. Set aside.

In a small skillet, melt the butter over medium heat and add the scallops and their juices. Gently stir or shake the pan. Then turn each scallop over, and cook just until thoroughly heated through and opaque. Remove the scallops with a slotted spoon to a glass or enamel bowl. Continue to cook the remaining juices until reduced to almost a jellylike consistency. Immediately whisk in the sauce you have set aside. It is such a small amount that it can get thick very easily, so take care. Add the garlic chives and onion. Taste for salt. It may not need any at all. Refrigerate until ready to serve.

These are very attractive served in scallop shells with a lime or lemon wedge and a sprig of parsley.

Serves 6 to 8

❋ Leek and Tomato Quiche with Egg Beaters

If any of your friends have a cholesterol problem, this is a healthy quiche. They can gorge on it without fear—sort of.

1½ tablespoons olive oil
1 cup sliced leeks
1 large tomato, peeled and
    sliced (or enough to cover
    the bottom of the pie shell)
1 precooked Pie or Tart Crust
    (page 272)
6 ounces Egg Beaters
1⅔ cups milk
1 tablespoon finely chopped
    fresh dill, or 1 teaspoon
    dried

1 teaspoon finely chopped fresh
    oregano or ⅓ teaspoon dried
    oregano
1 cup grated cheese (Monterey
    Jack, Cheddar, ricotta, or
    Gorgonzola or a mixture of
    any of these)

In a medium skillet, heat the oil and sauté the leeks until tender. Place the sliced tomatoes in the bottom of the pie shell. Arrange the leeks over the tomatoes.

Combine the Egg Beaters, milk, dill, and oregano. Pour over the vegetables and top with the grated cheese. Bake in a preheated 400° oven for 5 minutes. Reduce the heat to 325° and bake for 40 to 45 minutes more, or until firm when a knife inserted in the center comes out clean.

Cool slightly before serving.

Serves 8 as an hors d'oeuvre, 6 as a first course

❋ Onion Quiche with Egg Beaters

1 precooked Pie or Tart Crust
    (page 272)
1 tablespoon vegetable oil
1 large green pepper, seeded
    and cut into julienne strips
1 medium onion or ½ large
    Texas sweet onion, sliced
    into rings
Salt and pepper

1¾ cups milk
One 8-ounce carton Egg Beaters
    2 tablespoons finely chopped
    fresh dill or 2 teaspoons
    dried
1 teaspoon finely chopped fresh
    oregano or ⅓ teaspoon dried
1 cup grated Monterey Jack or
    Cheddar cheese

Heat the oil in a large skillet. Sauté the green pepper and onions with salt and pepper to taste until the vegetables are just tender. Place in the bottom of the pie shell.

Combine the milk, Egg Beaters, dill, and oregano. Pour over the vegetables and top with the grated cheese. Bake in a preheated 400° oven for 5 minutes. Reduce the heat to 325°, and bake 40 to 50 minutes longer, or until firm and a knife inserted in the center comes out clean.

Cool slightly before serving.

Serves 6 to 8

❉ *Cheddar Cheese Turnovers*

DOUGH

2 cups flour
4 tablespoons butter, 1 cut into
  bits, 3 softened

¼ teaspoon salt
6 to 8 tablespoons water

FILLING

¼ pound Cheddar cheese,
  grated
¼ cup grated Swiss cheese
4 ounces (½ small can) Ortega
  green chilies
3 tablespoons mayonnaise, or
  more if necessary
1 teaspoon Worcestershire
  sauce

Dash of Tabasco sauce
1 egg, lightly beaten
⅛ teaspoon salt
Pepper to taste
1 egg, lightly beaten with 1
  tablespoon heavy cream for
  egg wash

In a bowl, combine the flour, 1 tablespoon butter cut into bits, and salt until the mixture resembles a coarse meal. Add enough water to form a dough. Form the dough into a ball, dust it with flour, and chill it, wrapped in plastic wrap, for 30 minutes. Then roll the dough into a 10-inch square on a floured surface, dot it with the 3 tablespoons of softened butter, and roll it up jelly-roll fashion. Wrap the roll tightly in a tea towel and chill it for another 30 minutes. When chilled, without unrolling the dough, roll it into a 16- × -8-inch rectangle on the floured surface. With the short side facing you, fold the dough in thirds starting from a short side. Give it a quarter turn, and roll it into a 10-inch square. Roll up the dough jelly-roll fashion again, wrap it tightly in the tea towel, and chill it for 1 hour more. Without unrolling the dough, roll it into a rough round ⅙ inch thick and, with a 3-inch cookie cutter, cut it into rounds.

In a small bowl, combine the filling ingredients. Put 1 teaspoon of the filling on half of each round and fold the rounds over the filling. Press the edges of the rounds together with a fork and chill the turnovers for 20 minutes. Brush with the egg wash, and bake them on a baking sheet in a preheated 375° oven for 25 to 30 minutes, or until they are golden. Transfer the turnovers to a rack and let them cool.

Makes about 24 turnovers

✽ *Sho's Cheese Olives*

Sho is short for Shoshone, who is really Susan Meredith. How she arrived at this name is her and Don's secret, but maybe it's because she looks like a Shoshone princess even in the kitchen. She loves to cook and loves to eat, and she helped me test recipes during golf tournament time at Rancho Mirage. Don and I play golf and she's very much into tennis, so she had a little time on her hands while we were competing with the field and ourselves.

The Merediths and the Millers live in Santa Fe and are great friends. Mary Miller's husband, Roger, plays a neat guitar, sings a great song, and is funny. It seems to me they entertain everybody in the area from time to time. Susan gave me this recipe and mentioned that Mary makes it, too, but uses a sharp Cheddar instead of the soft mild cheese and adds ½ teaspoon paprika. It makes a difference. Try them both—you'll like. I do!

1 cup soft cheese (such as Brie
    or Boursin)
4 tablespoons butter, softened
1 teaspoon Worcestershire
    sauce

1 cup flour
24 green olives stuffed with
    pimiento

Mix together the cheese, butter, and Worcestershire. Add the flour and mix to form a ball. Flatten the dough.

Drain the olives. Wrap a small amount of dough around each olive and roll between your hands to form a ball. Freeze the olive balls.

When ready to serve, preheat the oven to 400° and bake on an ungreased baking sheet for 12 to 15 minutes, until golden.

Makes 24 olives

❀ Savory Cheese Spread

I soften my cheese with a tablespoon or so of buttermilk or sweet milk, but you don't really have to.

One 8-ounce package cream
    cheese, softened
2 teaspoons finely minced
    onion

2 tablespoons Dijon mustard
2 tablespoons minced fresh
    parsley
1 small clove garlic, crushed

Combine all the ingredients thoroughly. Serve this as a dip with fresh vegetables.

Makes about 1 cup

❀ Chopped Tomato Salad with Bruschetta

2 cloves garlic, halved
2 tomatoes, peeled, seeded, and
    chopped
1 sweet onion, finely chopped
¼ cup good, soft variety
    mozzarella cheese, coarsely
    cubed
2 sweet pimientos, finely
    chopped
3 flat anchovies, rinsed and
    chopped

¼ cup finely chopped fresh
    basil
1 tablespoon chopped fresh
    parsley
1 tablespoon balsamic vinegar
Salt and pepper
French or Italian bread, sliced
    ¾ to 1 inch thick
3 tablespoons very fresh olive
    oil
Basil sprigs, for garnish

Rub the surface of a mixing bowl with a cut clove of garlic. Combine the tomatoes, onion, cheese, pimientos, anchovies, basil, parsley, vinegar, and salt and pepper. Mix well. Taste for seasoning.

Slowly toast the bread in a 200° oven, or toast it once, let it cool, and toast again. While the bread is still warm, rub it with the remaining cut garlic clove and drizzle with the olive oil. Spoon the vegetable mixture onto the warm bread and place on a cold plate. Garnish each plate with a sprig of basil. Serve immediately with a knife and fork and a large napkin.

Serves 4 as a first course, 6 as an hors d'oeuvre

❧ *Apples with Cheese on Sourdough*

I've heard all kinds of statements about the people you can't trust for a variety of strange reasons. I think it started with some literate heavy imbiber of the juice of the grape or the hops who stated he'd never trust a man who didn't drink. These "I don't trust people who" began to tumble out faster than water through a large drain pipe at high tide. There's something to it—for instance, I've never been attracted to a man who has no digestive problems and doesn't enjoy eating.

We supposedly spend three important times of our day eating a meal. Why not make it a delicious, sensual experience? So here goes one of my exaggerated contributions to the "I don't trust a person who": I don't trust a person who has an uninteresting pantry, refrigerator, and freezer. If you're on a diet, have a good supply of the right things in there so you can fix a light snack—at least have choices. For instance, two friends I hadn't seen for ages called suddenly and wanted to drop by to say hello. Nobody drops in without a little something to munch on if the conversation lags, or even if it doesn't. The call came just as I'd dropped my luggage after a week or so out of the city. I pulled walnuts and a couple of slices of sourdough bread out of the freezer, grabbed an apple, mozzarella, and a tiny piece of Brie out of the refrigerator, and the sweet onion too. We liked it.

*4 large slices sourdough or
   French bread, thinly sliced
Butter or margarine
1 large or 2 medium apples,
   cored and thinly sliced
¼ sweet onion, thinly sliced*

*½ cup coarsely chopped
   walnuts
1 cup freshly grated
   mozzarella cheese
¼ pound Brie cheese, thinly
   sliced lengthwise*

Cut the bread into strips about 2 inches wide. Butter lightly. Cover with a layer of apples, then onion, and sprinkle nuts over all. Cover with mozzarella and a thin strip of Brie. Place on the upper rack of the oven and bake at 450° until the cheese is melted and the bread is crisp.

Serves 4 or 5

❧ *Chilaquiles*

I know this is listed under appetizers, but I first had it for breakfast, and sometimes I wake up in the middle of the night craving Chilaquiles (and I can't even spell or say it). One morning during the Nabisco Dinah Shore Tournament at Mission Hills, when Don and Sue Meredith were my houseguests, Mack Rankin, a great golfing friend of mine, came over early before we all teed off for the morning's round. Gloria thought we'd had too much fun the night before to eat just the usual fruit, toast, and coffee—we needed something to kick us all into high gear. She made Chilaquiles—I don't know about the high gear, but there was a certain zest and Chilaquiles in my game that hadn't been there before. I'd like to have some right now.

1/4 cup peanut oil
4 corn tortillas, quartered
4 tablespoons Red Tomatillo
  Sauce (below)

2 tablespoons finely chopped
  sweet onion
2 tablespoons freshly grated
  Parmesan cheese

Heat the peanut oil in a large skillet. Sauté the corn tortillas until crisp. Drain well on paper towels. Set aside and keep warm. Place the tortillas on a warm plate and pour a scant tablespoon of the tomatillo sauce over them. Sprinkle the onions over the sauce and then the Parmesan cheese. Serve very hot. It's going to wake you up anyway.

Serves 4

❁ Red Tomatillo Sauce

4 dried arboles chilies
2 California chilies
1 pound fresh tomatillos

1/2 cup water
1/2 clove garlic
3/4 teaspoon salt

Place the chilies in a foil-lined skillet to brown. (This protects your skillet and keeps everything from sticking.) Turn the chilies often to brown on all sides. When the chilies are brown, remove them from the skillet and wrap them in plastic wrap. Let them sit for a while, then peel them. Place the peeled chilies in a blender. Remove the outer skins from the tomatillos, place them in the same foil-lined skillet, and cook over low heat for 10 or 15 minutes, or until done. They'll be tender and soft. Add the tomatillos to the blender, then the water, garlic, and salt. Blend until well mixed. Taste for seasoning. Because the chilies and tomatillos vary in size, you may need a little more salt.

I'd suggest tasting it on a tortilla chip or cracker instead of a teaspoon. It'll make you weep with joy if you're not careful.

Makes approximately 3 cups

✳ *Nopales Strips*

If cactus is not available, you may substitute zucchini. I ran short of cactus one day and used a combination of the two. It worked.

4 small nopales *(cactus leaves)*
1 egg
½ cup milk
Dash of salt
1½ cups fresh bread crumbs

1 teaspoon finely minced garlic
¼ cup finely minced fresh
  cilantro (coriander) leaves
2 tablespoons chili powder
Oil for deep-frying

Clean and remove the spines from the cactus leaves. Cut the leaves into ¾-inch-wide strips.

Combine the egg, milk, and salt, mixing well. In a separate bowl, mix together the bread crumbs, garlic, cilantro, and chili powder.

Dip the cactus strips in the egg mixture and then in the bread crumbs, coating each one well with the crumb mixture. In a skillet, heat the oil to 350° and deep-fry the cactus for 1 to 2 minutes, until just golden brown. Drain on paper towels.

Serves 4

✳ *Mushrooms Provençale*

2 pounds mushrooms
Scant ¼ cup olive oil
½ cup chopped fresh parsley
½ cup bread crumbs
1 tablespoon finely chopped
  fresh rosemary or 1 teaspoon
  dried, crushed

2 cloves garlic, chopped
Salt and pepper
8 romaine lettuce leaves
½ cup finely chopped sweet
  onion for garnish
Lemon juice, for garnish

Wipe the mushrooms clean with a damp paper towel. Peel the stems and twist them off. Chop the stems medium-fine. Slice the caps into bite-size pieces.

Heat the oil in a skillet, add the mushrooms, and sauté until soft and lightly browned. Add the parsley, bread crumbs, rosemary, garlic, and salt and pepper to taste. Toss until heated through.

Serve on 8 romaine lettuce leaves, taken from the heart. Sprinkle with sweet onion and lemon juice.

Serves 8

✽ Mushroom Chicken Livers

A few people I know have strong feelings about some foods. Johnny won't eat liver... Lee won't eat mushrooms... Ali wouldn't be caught dead eating eggplant. I combined the three maligned foods in this dish and my most appreciative diners are the converts mentioned above—I forget to tell them the ingredients before they start eating. I've used this as a main course with the Risotto (page 236).

¼ *cup chopped onion*
2 *tablespoons olive oil, or just enough to cover the bottom of the pan*
1 *clove garlic, chopped*
½ *eggplant, peeled and cut into chunks (salt and let stand in a colander set over a bowl for a few minutes to drain)*
½ *cup chopped mushrooms (stems and all)*

2 *tablespoons pimiento strips, cut into chunks*
6 *fresh chicken livers, coarsely chopped*
½ *teaspoon curry powder*
Salt and pepper
2 *tablespoons good sherry*
6 *or 7 pitted large black olives, coarsely chopped*

Sauté the onions in the olive oil, then add the garlic. Add the eggplant and sauté until it starts to soften, then add the mushrooms and pimiento. Stir in the chicken livers and cook until they lose their pink color. Add the curry powder, salt and pepper, and sherry. Taste for seasoning. Add the olives and heat through. Serve at once.

Serves 6 as an appetizer, serves 4 as a main course with the Risotto

❧ Sautéed Mushrooms

8 medium mushrooms
1 tablespoon olive oil
¼ green pepper, seeded and
    chopped
2 scallions, chopped (white
    part only)
Salt
White pepper

Dash of light soy sauce
½ teaspoon sesame oil
Dash of Tabasco sauce
1 teaspoon instant flour (optional)
1 teaspoon plain nonfat yogurt
Thin slices of toasted French bread
Scallion tips, for garnish

Wipe the mushrooms with a damp paper towel. Remove the stems and slice the mushrooms medium thick.

Heat the olive oil in a skillet and sauté the green pepper and scallions. Add the mushrooms and sauté lightly. Sprinkle with salt, white pepper, soy sauce, sesame oil, and Tabasco sauce.

If the sauce appears too thin, tip the pan and remove a few teaspoons of sauce. Mix with instant flour, return to the pan, and blend well. Add the yogurt and carefully blend (using a wooden spoon) into the mushroom mixture. Serve with thin slices of toasted French bread. Garnish with scallion tips.

Serves 6

❧ Roman Spiced Artichokes

Three 1-pound artichokes
2½ lemons
1 teaspoon coriander seeds
1 teaspoon peppercorns

3 large eggs, hard-boiled, finely
    grated (use only the whites if
    you prefer)
1 tablespoon capers, drained

DRESSING

1 small onion, sliced
6 parsley sprigs
¾ tablespoon minced fresh
    basil or ¾ teaspoon dried
3 tablespoons white wine
    vinegar
1 teaspoon balsamic vinegar

1 teaspoon Dijon mustard
1 clove garlic, sliced
½ teaspoon sugar
Salt to taste
⅓ cup olive oil
⅓ cup vegetable oil

Break off and discard the stems and tough outer leaves of the artichokes. Cut off the top half of each artichoke with a very sharp stainless-steel knife, snip off any remaining sharp tips from the leaves with scissors, and rub the cut surfaces with the ½ lemon. Trim the bases, dropping the artichokes as they are trimmed into a bowl of cold water with the juice of 1 lemon added.

In a stainless-steel or enameled saucepan of boiling salted water, combine the drained artichokes with the juice of the remaining lemon, the coriander seeds, and the peppercorns, and simmer them for 40 minutes, or until the bottoms are tender and a leaf pulls away easily. Remove the artichokes with tongs and set upside down on a rack until they are just cool enough to handle.

Reduce the cooking liquid to about 2 cups and strain it, reserving 2 tablespoons of the liquid and 1 teaspoon of the spice mixture. Cut the artichokes in half lengthwise and, with a small spoon, remove the prickly leaves and the chokes. Cut each half into 3 wedges and arrange the wedges cut side up on a platter. Sprinkle the artichokes with the grated eggs and the capers.

In a food processor or blender, blend the reserved cooking liquid, the reserved spice mixture, the onion, parsley, basil, white wine vinegar, balsamic vinegar, mustard, garlic, sugar, and salt, scraping down the sides with a rubber spatula, until the mixture is smooth. With the motor running, add the olive oil and the vegetable oil in a smooth stream and blend the dressing until it is emulsified. Pour the dressing around the artichoke wedges. Serve extra dressing in a small bowl or pitcher for dipping. Have a dish or bowl on the side to catch the leftovers from the artichoke leaves.

Serves 3 as a first course, 6 as an hors d'oeuvre

❦ Eggplant, Peppers, and Cucumber Spread

1 medium eggplant
1 tablespoon olive oil
Scant ¼ teaspoon minced garlic
1 tablespoon finely chopped red onion
2 tablespoons finely chopped cucumber
2 tablespoons finely chopped sweet red pepper

2 tablespoons finely chopped yellow or green pepper
1 tablespoon minced Italian parsley
Salt and pepper
Lemon juice
Pita bread, toasted, cut into small wedges

Roast the eggplant over a flame or in the oven, turning it often, until very soft, about 15 minutes. Be careful not to break the skin. Place on a baking sheet and set aside to cool.

When the eggplant is cool, remove the stem, skin, and seeds. Chop the pulp, place it in a strainer, and drain for about 15 minutes. Place the drained eggplant in a bowl, add the olive oil, then the garlic, and mix well. Add the red onion, cucumber, red pepper, yellow or green pepper, and the parsley, stirring to blend. Season to taste with salt, pepper, and lemon juice.

Serve on toasted pita bread wedges.

Makes 1¾ cups

❈ *Kalamata Tapenade*

This is a hurry-up "They're on the way with four extra people" sort of thing. It's easy, fast, and really, really good—and it keeps for days.

6 anchovies plus 2 teaspoons
  of their oil
1⅓ cups Kalamata (Greek)
  olives, pitted and lightly
  crushed

2 tablespoons capers, drained
2 tablespoons olive oil
1 egg, hard-boiled, grated, for
  garnish
French bread, lightly toasted

Rinse the anchovies and place them, with 2 teaspoons of their oil, in a food processor along with the olives, capers, and olive oil. Process to desired consistency; it should not be too soupy. Place in a serving bowl and garnish with the grated hard-boiled egg.

Serve with thin slices of lightly toasted French bread.

Makes about 1½ cups

❈ *Niçoise Olive and Red Pepper Tapenade*

One 7½-ounce jar Niçoise
  olives
½ cup bottled roasted red
  peppers, drained (half a
  7-ounce jar)
1 tablespoon capers, drained

Crush the olives lightly with the flat side of a large knife, discard the pits, and puree the olives in a food processor, stopping the motor and scraping down the sides with a spatula several times.

Rinse the peppers in a sieve and pat them dry with a paper towel. Add the peppers and the capers to the olive puree and process until the mixture is well combined.

Serve the tapenade as a spread for toasted French bread slices, or as a filling for cherry tomatoes, or serve on zucchini sliced lengthwise.

Makes about 1 cup

❧ Salmon Dip

½ cup plain low-fat yogurt
¼ cup diced celery
2 tablespoons minced shallots
2 tablespoons minced pimiento
2 tablespoons minced fresh
   dillweed
1 teaspoon grated lemon peel

½ pound cooked salmon,
   chilled and flaked (you may
   substitute tuna if you prefer
   or if you don't have salmon)
Few drops of hot pepper sauce
Few drops of Worcestershire
   sauce

Mix together the yogurt, celery, shallots, pimiento, dillweed, and lemon peel. Gently stir in the salmon. Season to taste with hot pepper sauce and Worcestershire sauce.

Serve with rye toast points or crisp vegetable sticks.

Makes about 2 cups

❧ Stuffed Dates

One 3-ounce package
   Neufchâtel cheese
2 tablespoons chopped walnuts

1½ tablespoons chutney
24 whole pitted dates

Mix together the cheese, walnuts, and chutney. Fill each date with about 1 teaspoon of mixture and chill.

Makes 24 dates

❉ *South American Black Bean Dip*

Have you figured out yet that I love grains, legumes, and beans in almost any form? Pinto beans, red beans, white beans, mixed beans, black-eyed peas, lentils—they're all through this book. Here's a recipe you can share with special people (or even some not so special), there's enough to go around and it's another one of those keepers you can reheat and use for days.

1 pound dried black beans
6 cups water
1 tablespoon salt
1 pound lean ground pork
2 teaspoons dried oregano
2 tablespoons butter
1 cup chopped onions
5 medium radishes, sliced
1 to 4 hot green chilies (serrano or jalapeño), peeled, seeded, and minced

6 tablespoons lemon juice
1 cup canned green chili salsa
½ pound Monterey Jack cheese, shredded
¼ cup chopped fresh cilantro (coriander), for garnish
Tortilla chips

Soak the beans in water overnight. The next day drain the beans and place them in a large saucepan. Add the 6 cups water and the salt. Bring to a boil, cover, and simmer for 2 hours, or until the beans are tender. Remove the beans with a slotted spoon and set aside.

Bring the bean stock to a boil. Add the pork and oregano and bring to a boil again. Drain the pork and reserve.

Melt the butter in a large saucepan over medium heat. Add the onions, radishes, and chilies, and sauté until tender. Add the beans, pork, and lemon juice. Lower heat, cover, and simmer for 10 to 15 minutes, until tender. Add the salsa and cheese and simmer until the cheese melts. Taste and add salt if needed. Pour into a serving dish, sprinkle with cilantro, and surround with tortilla chips. Serve warm.

Serves 10 to 12

✽ Green Tomatillo Sauce

2 pounds tomatillos
4 or 5 fresh serrano chilies
1 clove garlic

2 teaspoons salt
5 to 6 sprigs cilantro
   (coriander)

Cover the tomatillos with water and bring to a boil. Reduce the heat to medium and cook for 15 minutes, or until the tomatillos are soft. Drain, and place the tomatillos and chilies in a blender with the garlic, salt, and cilantro. Puree until smooth.
Serve with crisp tortillas.

Makes about 1 quart

✽ Hot Artichoke Dip

Esther and Walter Schoenfeld are great friends of mine who live at Mission Hills in the Palm Springs area in the winter and in beautiful Seattle the rest of the time. I play golf with Walter, and Esther plies the tennis courts with skill. We dine together a lot and celebrate anything at the drop of a reason. Recently we celebrated Walter's father's 107th birthday—isn't that comforting. It means with those great genes they'll be around for years to come, as I plan to, so we can keep playing golf and dining. One evening Esther served this lovely artichoke-jalapeño casserole dip as an hors d'oeuvre for some British houseguests of theirs and lucky me.

One 8-ounce can artichoke
   hearts, packed in water, plus
   one 4-ounce can, drained
   and chopped
1 cup mayonnaise
1 cup freshly shredded
   Parmesan cheese

¼ cup blanched almonds,
   chopped
Dash of garlic salt
Juice of ½ lemon
One 4-ounce can diced green
   chilies
Butter or margarine

Combine all the ingredients in a mixing bowl, reserving some of the Parmesan cheese for topping. Mix well. Place the mixture in a buttered casserole and top with the reserved Parmesan cheese.
Bake in a 375° oven for 20 to 25 minutes.
This can be assembled ahead of time and refrigerated, but bring to room temperature before baking. Serve with crisp tortilla chips, crisply toasted pita bread triangles, or whatever you like.

Serves 8 to 10

Soups

I hardly ever met a soup I didn't like—I lean toward the hot ones like the Black Bean Soup (page 44) or the Fresh Tomato Soup (page 54), but when I find a cold one that's really tasty, such as the Cucumber Soup with Fresh Herbs (page 58) or the Cold Tomato-Vegetable (page 59), I make enough to serve for days.

❧ Country-Style Split Pea Soup

¾ cup sweet onion, chopped
2 small cloves garlic, minced
1 tablespoon olive oil
1 cup dried green peas
2 cups chicken broth
2 cups water
1 bay leaf
Dash of black pepper

1 carrot, peeled and thinly
  sliced into rounds
1 stalk celery, thinly sliced
1 medium potato, peeled and
  coarsely diced
2 medium-hot sausages or hot
  dogs, sliced crosswise into
  rounds and crisply fried, for
  garnish

Sauté the onion and garlic in the oil in a large saucepan until tender. Add the peas, broth, water, bay leaf, and pepper. Heat to boiling, then reduce the heat and simmer, covered, stirring occasionally, until the peas are tender, about 30 minutes. Add the carrots, celery, and potato, cover, and simmer until the vegetables are just tender, about 10 to 15 minutes. Serve with medium-hot sausage or hot dogs, sliced and crisply fried, for garnish.

Serves 4

✽ Five Bean Soup

At Christmastime some good friends, who help support a marvelous cause, the Special Olympics for Children, sent me a pint bottle of dried mixed beans—red, pinto, black-eyed peas, and navy. The instructions were very simple. "Wash the beans in a sieve and cull over thoroughly, but do not soak them." This was followed by the directions for cooking the soup. I varied it somewhat and put together my own combination of dried beans. I do believe soaking the beans makes a more consistent texture.

1 handful dried navy beans
1 handful dried black-eyed peas
1 handful dried kidney beans
1 handful dried lima beans
1 handful dried pinto beans
4 cups water
1 cup chicken broth
½ pound Tennessee ham, chopped, or 1 ham hock
1 stalk celery, chopped
½ green pepper, seeded and chopped
1 medium-large sweet onion, chopped
2 cloves garlic, chopped

1 tablespoon ground cumin
1 generous tablespoon chili powder
3 sprigs fresh marjoram, chopped
3 sprigs fresh basil, chopped, or any of your favorite herbs that happen to be handy at the time
Salt and freshly ground black pepper
1 cup fresh okra, cut crosswise into rounds
Pinch of red pepper flakes (optional)
2 cups cooked rice

Place all the beans in a sieve, wash thoroughly, and cull any that are imperfect. Place the beans in a large heavy saucepan and add the water and chicken broth and soak for 3 hours or overnight. Add the ham or ham hock, the celery, green pepper, onion, and seasonings. Cook slowly until the beans are soft. Turn off the heat and allow the soup to rest.

About 1 hour before serving, heat again, add the okra, and cook for 15 minutes, or until tender. Taste for seasoning. I like it spicy, so I add red pepper flakes.

When my beans were soft, they had absorbed quite a bit of the liquid; you may want to add a little more chicken broth. If using a ham hock, remove it from the soup and chop the meat from the bone. Return the chopped meat to the soup.

Ladle into hot, deep soup bowls and add a scoop of hot cooked rice to each bowl. It is *good!*

Serves 6

❖ Barley Soup the Easy Way

¼ cup raw barley	1 tablespoon olive oil
2 cups water	2 carrots, peeled and cut into
½ teaspoon salt	1-inch lengths
1 clove garlic	3 small potatoes, finely
1 medium onion, quartered	chopped
1 pound mushrooms	1 tablespoon lemon juice
¼ cup whole parsley leaves	1 cup milk
3 cups chicken broth	Salt and freshly ground black
4 tablespoons margarine or	pepper
butter	½ cup sour cream

Simmer the barley in the water with ½ teaspoon salt, uncovered, for about 25 minutes. Drain and reserve.

Mince the garlic in a food processor (it's easier). Remove and set aside. Then chop the onion, half the mushrooms, and the parsley separately. Rinse the processor out with some of the chicken broth and reserve the broth.

Melt 2 tablespoons of the margarine or butter with the oil in a large saucepan over medium heat. Add the chopped onion and garlic and stir to coat with the margarine or butter and oil. Cook over low heat for 10 minutes, stirring occasionally. Add the chopped parsley; then add the carrots and chopped mushrooms to the pot and stir in all the chicken broth. Add the potatoes. Simmer covered for 25 minutes, until the vegetables are soft. Strain the mixture through a large sieve and return the liquid to the pot. Place the vegetables in the food processor and process until smooth. Pour 1 cup of the liquid from the pot through the feed tube and process for 30 seconds longer.

Stir the vegetables into the remaining liquid in the saucepan and add the barley, lemon juice, and milk. Season with salt and pepper to taste and simmer until heated through, about 10 minutes.

Meanwhile, slice the remaining ½ pound of mushrooms and sauté them in the remaining 2 tablespoons of margarine or butter over medium heat until softened, about 1 minute. Remove the soup from heat. Whisk in the sour cream and stir in the sautéed mushrooms.

Serves 6

❈ Black Bean Soup

1 cup dried black beans,
  soaked overnight in water to
  cover
1 quart lightly salted water
Ham bone or a chunk of
  smoked pork or country ham
4 bay leaves
4 whole cloves
¼ teaspoon celery seed
2 stalks celery, finely chopped,
  leaves and all
1 large red onion, chopped

1 large clove garlic, chopped
1 tablespoon olive oil
¼ teaspoon dry mustard
1 teaspoon chili powder or 1
  dried red chili pepper
2 dashes of Tabasco sauce
Sherry or Madeira wine
Thin lemon slices, for garnish
1 egg, hard-boiled, grated, for
  garnish
Chopped fresh parsley, for
  garnish

Drain the beans and put them in a soup pot with the salted water, the ham bone, bay leaves, cloves, celery seed, and celery. Sauté the onion and garlic in the olive oil until tender. Add to the pot along with the mustard, chili powder or chili pepper, and Tabasco. Bring to a boil and simmer for 2 hours, or until the beans are quite tender, but not falling apart. Remove the ham bone and bay leaves.

Reserve ½ cup of soup and place the remainder in a food processor and puree. Place a teaspoon or two of reserved soup in each heated bowl along with a teaspoon of sherry or Madeira. Add the pureed soup and garnish with thin slices of lemon, hard-boiled egg, and chopped parsley.

Serves 6

❈ Tomato-Lentil Soup

June is our winter in southern California for some reason. Most times it feels colder than January because it's not expected. This soup is great to have when you come in on a cold, drizzly day or after a hard day on the golf course—it'll cure your cold or blues.

2 tablespoons olive oil
1 tablespoon margarine
¼ cup finely chopped onion
¼ cup finely chopped celery
¼ cup finely chopped carrots
2 cloves garlic, finely chopped

¾ cup Tennessee, Virginia, or
  plain ham, or 1 or 2 beef
  wieners, cut into chunks
2 cups chopped tomatoes (if
  using canned tomatoes, juice
  and all)

*2 cups dried lentils, washed
and drained
4 cups beef or chicken broth
4 cups water
Salt and pepper to taste*

*Freshly grated Parmesan
cheese, for garnish
Strips of ham or small chunks
of a good beef wiener crisply
fried, for garnish*

Heat the oil and margarine in a large heavy pot and sauté the onions until translucent. Add the celery, carrots, and garlic and sauté for 2 or 3 minutes. Add the ham or wieners and sauté to blend. Stir in the tomatoes, reduce the heat, and simmer for about 30 minutes. Add the lentils, broth, and water, a little salt (you can always add more later) and pepper. Bring to a boil, reduce the heat, and cook until the lentils begin to soften, about 45 minutes to an hour. Don't let the soup get too thick.

Serve in warmed bowls garnished with Parmesan cheese and strips of crisply fried meat. You can do all of this early in the day—it reheats and reheats for several meals.

Serves 6

❋ Chili–Pinto Bean Soup

Slowly cooked—mellow and satisfying. This is a spicy whole meal for most people; however, I never found anything wrong with adding a nice green salad, a soft cheese, and a crusty bread.

*1 cup chopped onion
1 cup chopped green pepper
1 cup chopped celery
3 tablespoons vegetable oil
3½ cups chicken broth
2 cups tomato sauce
1 tablespoon white vinegar
1 tablespoon honey
1 tablespoon fresh lemon juice
1 teaspoon Tabasco sauce or to
taste*

*1 tablespoon crushed fresh
garlic (about 1 clove)
½ teaspoon white pepper
1 tablespoon salt
1 bay leaf
2 cups cooked pinto beans
1 large or 2 small fresh
tomatoes, coarsely chopped,
for garnish
½ sweet onion, coarsely
chopped, for garnish*

Sauté the onion, green pepper, and celery in the oil until transparent. Add the chicken broth, tomato sauce, vinegar, honey, lemon juice, Tabasco, garlic, pepper, salt, and bay leaf. Bring to a boil and add the pinto beans. Simmer for 2 hours. Taste for seasoning and remove the bay leaf. Top with chopped tomatoes and onions as a garnish.

Serves 6

✤ *Winter Wonder Soup*

1 small onion, chopped
2 tablespoons butter or
   margarine
1 cup chicken broth
2 medium turnips, cut into
   large chunks
2 medium potatoes, cut into
   large chunks

¾ to 1 cup low-fat milk
Salt and white pepper
Pinch of ground ginger
Pimiento strips, for garnish
Chopped fresh parsley, for
   garnish

Sauté the onion in the butter until transparent. Add well-seasoned chicken broth (your own if possible), then add the turnips and potatoes and bring to a boil. Cook the turnips and potatoes for about 20 minutes, or until just done.

Place the mixture in a blender or food processor, add the milk, salt and white pepper, and ginger, and blend until smooth or to the desired consistency. Remove from the blender and reheat carefully, do not let the soup brown. Taste for seasoning. It may need a little more salt and white pepper, it shouldn't be too bland. Garnish with pimiento strips and chopped parsley. Serve very hot.

Serves 4 to 6

If you can afford it weightwise, cream, half and half, or even whole milk would be heavenly.

✤ *All-Year-Round Vegetable Soup*

Corn, limas, okra, celery, onion, tomato, potato vegetable soup. There you have the whole recipe and practically my favorite soup in the whole world. The recipe that follows if for the winter version. Don't be afraid to substitute fresh vegetables in the summer.

1 tablespoon vegetable oil
1 onion, finely chopped
2 stalks celery, finely chopped
One 28-ounce can Italian
  plum tomatoes
2 potatoes, peeled and cut into
  1-inch cubes
5 ounces frozen corn

5 ounces frozen okra
5 ounces frozen lima beans
4 cups chicken broth or water
Salt and pepper
Fresh spinach leaves (optional)
Red pepper flakes (optional)
Small pasta (optional)
Freshly grated Parmesan cheese

Heat the oil in a large heavy saucepan and sauté the onion until soft. Add the celery, then the tomatoes, potatoes, corn, okra, lima beans, and chicken broth or water. Bring to a boil and season generously with salt and pepper. Reduce heat and simmer for 1½ hours, or until the vegetables are cooked and the flavors are blended. You can add spinach leaves at the last moment, red pepper flakes (if you like), even a handful or two of a small pasta, but if you do that, call it minestrone. Serve hot, with Parmesan cheese on the side.

Serves 6

❧ *Asparagus Soup*

A low-calorie, creamy asparagus soup.

1 tablespoon margarine
1 tablespoon flour
1 cup good, well-seasoned
  chicken broth
1 pound asparagus, peeled,
  ends cut off and reserved

½ cup low-fat milk
Salt and white pepper
½ teaspoon dried chervil

Melt the margarine in a heavy saucepan. Add the flour and mix until well blended. Pour in the chicken broth. Add the peeled ends of the asparagus and cook slowly until soft. Add the milk and continue to cook for 5–10 minutes. Add the salt, pepper, and chervil. Taste for seasoning, it should have a strong, good asparagus flavor.

Cut the remaining asparagus into 2½- to 3-inch-long pieces, tips and all. In a separate saucepan, boil salted and peppered water and cook the asparagus until almost done. Remove with a slotted spoon and set aside.

Pour the soup mixture into a blender or processor and puree. Taste for seasoning. Return to the saucepan, add the cooked asparagus spears, and heat slowly over low heat until ready to serve in hot soup bowls.

Serves 4

❧ *Shrimp-Scallop Soup-Stew for Company*

My gourmet friend—and yours—Carl Sontheimer, who started us all on the road to Cuisinart ease, now has a new venture—Soul Food from the Sea. This is the first dish I cooked with his exquisite sea scallops, a few shrimp and a pinch of saffron, etc., sent to me over the holidays (New Year's Day football-watching time to be exact). This dish came before the black-eyed peas and cornbread that are mandatory on New Year's Day for good luck the rest of the year. There were so many seconds served of this soup-stew that there almost wasn't room for the Lucky Peas.

1½ pounds raw medium shrimp	2 small stalks celery, sliced
9 or 10 large raw prawns or shrimp	2 carrots, sliced
1½ pounds large fresh sea scallops	2 bay leaves
Salt and white pepper	4 or 5 sprigs parsley, coarsely chopped
Juice of ½ lemon	1 teaspoon black peppercorns
2 large leeks, sliced medium-thin halfway through green part	1 teaspoon salt
5 tablespoons butter or margarine	2 cups dry white wine
6 to 7 cups water	6 large or 8 medium mushrooms, sliced
1 pound firm white fish filets, such as halibut or sea bass, cut into chunks	4 teaspoons flour
2 large stalks celery, sliced or chopped	Lemon juice, to taste
	⅛ teaspoon cayenne pepper
	⅛ teaspoon saffron threads or generous pinch
	Chopped chives or parsley, for garnish (optional)
	Crisp French sourdough bread or toast

Clean, shell and devein the shrimp and prawns, leaving the tail on the prawns, and reserve the shells. Clean the scallops and cut in half or in quarters, depending on their size. Salt and pepper the shrimp, prawns, and scallops. Squeeze lemon juice over shrimp and prawns and set aside. Set scallops aside.

In a large stockpot, sauté the leeks in 2 tablespoons butter or margarine until soft. Add the water, white fish, shrimp shells, celery, carrot, bay leaves, parsley, and peppercorns. Bring to a boil and skim the froth from the top. Add 1 teaspoon salt and the white wine. Simmer for an hour or more. Strain through a fairly fine sieve into a large stockpot. Press with a spoon to extract all liquid possible and discard bulk. Bring the broth to a boil. Add shrimps and prawns and cook about 1 minute, until barely pink—no more. Remove the shrimp and place in a bowl. Add scallops to broth and cook 30 seconds, *no more*. Remove scallops and place in bowl with shrimp. Cover lightly with foil to keep warm. Let the broth keep simmering to reduce and thicken a little.

Melt 3 tablespoons of butter or margarine in a saucepan, add the sliced mushrooms, and sauté lightly; then add the flour and stir, forming a roux. Cook slowly for about 5 minutes. Slowly add the reduced broth, whisking and beating to avoid lumps. Take about 6 imperfect shrimp and overcooked pieces of scallops and place in blender or food processor. Add ½ cup of the broth and lightly puree. Add mixture to the soup along with lemon juice to taste, cayenne pepper, saffron, and salt to taste. All of this can be done ahead of time. Before serving, reheat the soup over low heat until hot. Add the shrimp and scallops and cook until just warmed through. Don't overcook. Sprinkle with a little chopped chives or parsley if you like. Serve in hot soup bowls with 1 large prawn decorating each portion. Serve with crisped French sourdough bread or toast.

Serves 8

❖ *Cream of Corn Chowder*

1 medium onion, finely
   chopped
1 tablespoon olive oil
1 stalk celery, chopped
¼ green pepper, seeded and
   chopped
1 medium potato, peeled and
   cut into medium-size cubes
1½ cups water
1 large tomato, peeled and
   chopped

1 serrano chili, seeded and
   chopped
4 cups raw fresh corn, cut off
   the cob
2 cups milk
1 teaspoon flour
Salt to taste
4 strips bacon, cooked,
   drained, and cut into small
   pieces

Sauté the onion in the olive oil. Add the celery and green pepper and sauté lightly. Add the potato and water and bring to a boil. Stir in the tomato and serrano chili, return to the boil, reduce heat, and cook for about 10 minutes, or until the potatoes are soft. Add the corn and cook for 15 minutes more. Add the milk and simmer for about 15 minutes over low heat. If the soup seems too thin, dissolve the flour in an equal amount of water, add a little of the corn mixture, and mix back into the soup, stirring constantly. Add salt and taste. Remove from the heat, and add half the bacon.

Place in batches in a food processor and process lightly; leave a little texture to the soup. Serve in hot bowls garnished with the remaining bacon.

Serves 4

✿ *Katie's Chowder*

Katie is Katie Korshak, age seventeen, the granddaughter and best friend of a dear friend of mine. I was having a tasting-testing party for eight or ten people one night and Katie volunteered to do her chowder. I politely agreed. It was the hit of the evening. That pretty child knows a thing or twelve about cooking.

BROTH

¼ cup olive oil
1 tablespoon butter
1 shallot, coarsely chopped
1 clove garlic, coarsely chopped
Heaping 4 cups coarsely chopped onions
2 cups water
3 cups sliced raw potatoes
Three 8-ounce bottles clam juice
⅛ teaspoon dried thyme
⅛ teaspoon fennel seeds

½ teaspoon salt
⅛ teaspoon white pepper
1½ cups whole milk

16 raw clams in their shells
3 large filets orange roughy, or any firm fleshed white fish such as halibut or rock cod, cut into 2-inch chunks
½ pound uncooked medium shrimp, shelled and deveined
Salsa (see below)

Heat the olive oil and butter in a deep soup pot. Add the shallot, garlic, and onions. Sauté until all ingredients are transparent. Add the water, potatoes, clam juice, and all the remaining seasonings including salt and pepper. Bring to a boil, lower the heat, and simmer for 20 minutes, or until the potatoes are tender. Remove ½ cup of sliced potatoes from the soup pot and set them aside.

Place the chowder in a blender and puree by adding milk gradually until it is smooth. Return the chowder to the soup pot. Add the clams, cover, and cook over low heat for approximately 4 minutes, or until the clam shells just barely start to open. Discard any clams that don't open. Add the orange roughy and shrimp. Cover and cook over low heat until the fish flakes and the shrimp are pink.

When you are ready to serve the chowder, place 1 or 2 of the sliced potatoes you have set aside in the bottom of each warmed serving bowl. Ladle chowder into each bowl, dividing the fish evenly. Garnish each serving with a small portion of salsa and 2 small leaves of fresh basil. Serve immediately.

SALSA

1 teaspoon butter
1 very large, ripe beefsteak
 tomato, coarsely chopped
1 leek, coarsely chopped (white
 part only)
1 teaspoon finely chopped
 oregano

1 teaspoon finely chopped fresh
 thyme
Dash of Tabasco sauce
16 small leaves of fresh basil,
 for garnish

Heat the butter in a skillet and sauté all the ingredients except the fresh basil for 1 minute over high heat. Garnish with fresh basil leaves.

Serves 8

❧ Emerald Soup

This is pretty as well as nutritious, and, of course, that old standby, delicious.

2 tablespoons margarine or
 butter
1 tablespoon olive oil
1 bunch broccoli, stems peeled
 and flowerets and stems
 chopped (reserve 4 to 8
 whole tiny flowerets for
 garnish)
1/2 green pepper, seeded and
 finely chopped
1/2 onion, finely chopped
2 medium potatoes, diced
1 clove garlic, minced
1 1/2 cups chicken broth
Dash of Tabasco sauce
1 tablespoon Worcestershire
 sauce

1 teaspoon dry mustard
1/8 teaspoon grated nutmeg
Salt and pepper to taste
1 tablespoon finely chopped
 fresh oregano or 1/2 teaspoon
 dried
4 small spinach leaves, finely
 chopped
1 tablespoon finely chopped
 fresh basil or 1/2 teaspoon
 dried
1 1/2 cups low-fat milk
4 small whole spinach leaves,
 for garnish

Heat the margarine or butter and the oil in a large saucepan. Sauté the broccoli stems, green pepper, and onion until the onion is just soft. Then add the potatoes, broccoli flowerets, garlic, and chicken broth. Add the Tabasco, Worcestershire, dry mustard, nutmeg, salt and pepper, and oregano. Cook over moderate heat for about 20 minutes, or until the vegetables are soft. Add the chopped spinach and the basil and cook for 2 minutes more.

Remove the vegetables from the broth, reserving the broth. Place the vegetables in a blender or food processor. Add 4 tablespoons of the broth, or more if needed. Puree the vegetables until smooth and then add the milk gradually, ½ cup at a time.

Return the soup to the saucepan. Add the reserved broth and stir well with a wire whisk. Adjust the seasonings—it should be a little spicy. The soup should be thin but very tasty.

Serve in hot bowls, garnished with the reserved broccoli flowerets set on a small spinach leaf.

Serves 4

�֍ *Cauliflower Soup*

A low-calorie soup that doesn't taste like you're weight-watching, with a variation you'll enjoy.

½ onion, diced
1 clove garlic, minced
1 tablespoon olive oil
2 tablespoons margarine
1 head cauliflower, cut up
  (reserve 8 small cauliflower
  flowerets for garnish)
2 potatoes, diced
1½ cups chicken broth
Dash of Tabasco sauce
1 tablespoon Worcestershire
  sauce

1 tablespoon dry mustard
¼ teaspoon dried oregano
1 tablespoon chopped fresh
  basil or ½ teaspoon dried
Dash of grated nutmeg
Cayenne pepper to taste
Salt and white pepper
1½ cups low-fat milk
Pimiento strips, for garnish
Paprika (optional)

In a large saucepan, sauté the onion and garlic in the margarine and olive oil until translucent, but not brown. Add the cauliflower, potatoes, and chicken broth. Add the Tabasco, Worcestershire, mustard, and other seasonings. Cook until the vegetables are just soft.

Remove the vegetables with a slotted spoon and place them in a blender or food processor. Reserve the broth. Add 4 tablespoons of reserved broth (more if needed) to the vegetables and puree until smooth. Gradually add the milk, ½ cup at a time.

Pour the pureed vegetable mixture into the reserved broth in a saucepan. Taste for seasoning and reheat. The soup should be thin. Garnish with reserved cauliflower flowerets and pimiento strips or lightly sprinkle flowerets with paprika.

For a variation of this and the preceding soup, use one half cauliflower and one half broccoli and take your choice of garnishes.

Serves 4

❧*Mushroom Soup*

A pure, deeply flavored mushroom soup—without cream.

½ *sweet onion, chopped*
3 *tablespoons butter*
1 *tablespoon vegetable oil*
1 *small clove garlic, chopped*
1 *cup chopped mushrooms*
1 *tablespoon chopped fresh*
  parsley
1 *tablespoon chopped fresh*
  tarragon or ½ *teaspoon dried*

4 *cups chicken broth (if*
  necessary add water to
  augment the broth)
1 *tablespoon dark soy sauce*
White pepper to taste
4 *tablespoons good dry sherry*
1 *cup mushrooms, sliced*

Sauté the onion in 2 tablespoons of the butter and oil until translucent, then add the garlic and sauté until soft. Add the chopped mushrooms and continue to sauté until soft. Add the parsley, tarragon, broth, soy sauce, and white pepper to taste. Cook for 5 minutes until very well blended. Add the sherry and bring to a boil. Reduce the heat and simmer for about 10 minutes, until the soup thickens slightly. Sauté the sliced mushrooms in the remaining butter and add them to the soup. Let the soup cook slowly, about 15 minutes, or until ready to serve. Taste frequently for seasoning. It's nice in heated shallow soup bowls rather than the soup cup type.

Serves 4

❊ *Fresh Tomato Soup*

I don't know how large the tomatoes grow in your part of the country, but out here they sometimes get enormous—about five inches in diameter and bright, juicy red all the way through. I happened to have some vine-ripened beauties on the day I tried this recipe. Other times they weren't quite as large, so I used twelve Roma or Italian tomatoes. They really should be as ripe and juicy as you can find. I urge you to try this soup, either pureed, as I have done it here, or in the rough.

P.S. I'm not really that particular, I love this soup so much I've used the 28-ounce can of Roma tomatoes when fresh tomato season was over.

3 tablespoons good fresh olive oil

1 large sweet Texas onion or 2 medium onions, finely chopped

2 cloves garlic, chopped (not too fine if you want to pick them out later)

2 stalks celery, finely chopped

2 carrots, peeled and finely chopped

5 beautiful very large ripe summer tomatoes or 12 Roma or Italian tomatoes, peeled and cut into chunks

2 tablespoons tomato paste

2 cups chicken broth and 2 cups beef broth (not consommé), or 4 cups chicken broth

1 teaspoon sugar

Salt and pepper to taste

2 tablespoons finely chopped fresh basil or 2 teaspoons dried

2 tablespoons finely chopped fresh parsley or 2 teaspoons dried

1 tablespoon chopped fresh thyme or 1 teaspoon dried

Low-fat milk (optional)

Crisp fried croutons, for garnish

Heat the oil in a large saucepan over moderate heat. Sauté the onion, garlic, celery, and carrots for about 10 minutes, until just soft. Add the tomatoes mixed with the tomato paste. Add the broth and cook for 5–10 minutes until the flavors are well blended. Add the sugar, salt and pepper, basil, parsley, and thyme. Simmer over low heat as long as you can. This can be done in the morning, set aside, and reheated.

Before serving, puree the soup in a blender or food processor until smooth. Return to the saucepan and heat. Add a little milk if you want the cream of tomato soup you remember. Taste for seasoning. Add salt and pepper if needed. Garnish with crisp fried croutons—you owe it to yourself. (Look how healthy and thinning the soup is.)

Serves 6

✤ *Chinese Noodle Soup*

There was a restaurant in Hollywood that had a soup like this on the menu—early on in my life out here. While the rest of us were ordering shrimp and egg roll and barbecued pork, Jack Benny ordered lo mein— Chinese Noodle Soup. If the great Jack Benny did it, it had to be good. This is as close as I could get . . . see what you think.

4 dried black Chinese mushrooms, 1 to 1½ inches in diameter
½ cup warm water
½ cup cooked chicken, sliced ⅛ inch thick
½ cup cooked roast pork, sliced ⅛ inch thick
½ cup cooked ham, sliced ⅛ inch thick

¼ cup thinly sliced canned bamboo shoots
½ cup loosely packed watercress leaves
2 quarts water
½ pound fresh Chinese egg noodles or substitute narrow Italian egg noodles, such as tagliarini
4 cups fresh or canned chicken stock
1 teaspoon salt

Prepare ahead: In a small bowl, cover the mushrooms with the warm water and let them soak for 30 minutes. With a cleaver or sharp knife, cut away and discard the tough stems of the mushrooms, and cut the caps in halves. Cut the chicken, pork, and ham into 1-inch squares. If it is impossible to cut into squares, cut into thin strips. (No big chunks please, as you must make them as uniform in shape as you can.) Put the meat, bamboo shoots, and watercress in separate small bowls, cover, and place in the refrigerator until you are ready to use them.

When you are ready to prepare the soup, bring the 2 quarts of water to a boil over high heat in a heavy 3- or 4-quart saucepan. Drop in the noodles and boil them vigorously, uncovered, for 2 minutes, or until they are almost but not quite done, stirring occasionally. Drain the noodles and run cold water over them to stop their cooking.

Now bring the stock to a boil in the same saucepan, add the mushrooms, bamboo shoots, watercress, salt, and noodles, and reduce the heat to low. Simmer, uncovered, for about 2 minutes.

To serve, lift the noodles and vegetables out of the simmering soup with a bamboo strainer or slotted spoon, and transfer them to a large tureen or serving bowl or to individual soup bowls. Arrange the chicken, pork, and ham on top of them. Pour the soup stock down one side of the tureen or bowl so as not to disturb the arrangement. Serve at once. It's beautiful—it's delicious—just be sure it's hot.

Serves 4 to 6

❧ *Almond Soup*

This is a party winner. Crunchy, full of flavor, and not too caloric.

2 cups blanched almonds
4 to 5 cups chicken broth
1½ tablespoons very lean ham,
  chopped
Generous pinch of ground
  cloves (scant ⅛ teaspoon)
¼ teaspoon ground mace
¼ teaspoon grated nutmeg
Salt

Cayenne pepper to taste
Bouquet garni (bay leaf; 1
  stalk celery, tops and all;
  sprig thyme; sprig basil—if
  fresh herbs are not available,
  use 2 pinches each dried
  herbs)
1 tablespoon good sherry

Finely mince 1½ cups of the almonds. Then, using a mortar and pestle, pound them into a smooth paste. If you do not have a mortar and pestle, do it in a food processor. Coarsely chop the remaining ½ cup of the almonds and set aside.

Pour 4 cups of chicken broth into a large saucepan. Add the ham and all the seasonings including the bouquet garni. Simmer slowly for 20 minutes; strain through a fine sieve. Add the pounded almonds and simmer 20 minutes more. Stir in the ½ cup reserved almonds, bring to a full boil briefly, adding more broth, if necessary, so the soup won't be too thick. (It is a first course, after all.) Add the sherry, return to a full boil, and serve in very hot bowls with crisp toast points.

Serves 4

❋ Cold Cucumber Soup

I confess I've never been nutty about cold soup, iced tea, or iced coffee. I like most things hot—this is the exception. It was a really hot day—we don't get too many out here in Los Angeles, no matter what you've heard to the contrary, but this one happened to be a scorcher. I had other things to cook and this uncooked jewel was a big hit, and easy!

4½ cups peeled, seeded, and chopped cucumbers (about 6 medium cucumbers)
1 cup water
1½ cups plain nonfat yogurt
1 clove garlic
4 fresh mint leaves
Generous dash of grated nutmeg
¼ to ½ teaspoon Tabasco sauce

1½ tablespoons honey
1½ to 2 teaspoons salt
1½ teaspoons fresh or ½ teaspoon dried dillweed
Chopped scallions or snipped chives and 1 perfect mint leaf for each serving, for garnish

Place all the ingredients except the garnish in a food processor or blender. Blend until fairly smooth (little chunks are nice). Taste constantly to check seasoning. Chill as long as you can, at least 2 hours. Garnish with scallions or chives and mint.

Serves 4 to 6

�֍ *Cucumber Soup with Fresh Herbs*

3 large crisp cucumbers
¼ cup red wine vinegar
1 tablespoon sugar
1 teaspoon salt
2 tablespoons sweet butter or
margarine
¼ cup dry white vermouth or
dry white wine

Salt and pepper
¾ cup buttermilk
¾ cup plain low-fat yogurt
¾ cup chopped fresh dill
¼ cup chopped fresh parsley

Peel and chop 2 of the cucumbers coarsely and soak them with the vinegar, sugar, and salt. Let stand for 30 minutes.

Peel and slice the remaining cucumber and sauté in the butter in a heavy skillet until just transparent and a little soft. Remove from the skillet and set aside. Deglaze the skillet with the vermouth or wine and reduce to a few spoonsful. Pour the deglazing liquid over the sliced cucumber and season with salt and pepper.

Drain the chopped cucumbers and process briefly in a food processor (they should remain coarse) fitted with a steel blade, then add the buttermilk and yogurt and process until smooth. Add the fresh dill and parsley, reserving some for garnish. Combine the sliced cucumber and cucumber mixture in a large bowl and chill. Taste for seasoning.

Garnish with the reserved herbs and serve in chilled bowls with a slice of cucumber on top.

Serves 6

CLOCKWISE FROM TOP: Mixed Seafood Provençale
p. 166 Sweet Pepper Sauté p. 188 French-style
Bread with Greek Olives p. 255 Braised Fennel in
White Wine p. 186

CLOCKWISE FROM TOP: Little Piroshki p. 15 Hot Artichoke Dip p. 39 Green Tomatillo Sauce p. 39 Pizza Brie p. 9 Smoked Salmon Pizza p. 13 Three Cheese Three Herb Pizza p. 7 Cold Scallops Dressed with Garlic-Chive Sauce p. 25 Peppery Stuffed Crab p. 23 Mushroom Chicken Livers p. 33 Chilaquiles p. 30

CLOCKWISE FROM TOP: Steamed Rock Cod or Bass with Soy Dipping Sauce p. 156   Pot Stickers p. 17   Chinese Roast Pork p. 104   Shrimp in a Cloud p. 21   Chinese Chicken Salad by Dan Lee p. 78

✾ Cold Tomato-Vegetable Soup

2 eggs, hard-boiled
2 tablespoons good fresh
   Italian olive oil
1 clove garlic, minced or
   crushed
1 sweet onion, finely chopped
1½ teaspoons Worcestershire
   sauce
Couple of dashes of Tabasco
   sauce
Salt and freshly ground black
   pepper to taste
1 teaspoon dry mustard

5 large fresh tomatoes or 4
   cups chopped canned
   tomatoes and their juice
1 small cucumber, finely
   chopped
1 sweet green pepper, seeded
   and finely chopped
Thin strips of green pepper
Thin strips of pimiento
Thin slices of lime or lemon,
   for garnish
Hot fried croutons, for garnish

Carefully remove the yolks from the hard-boiled eggs, keeping the whites as intact as possible. Set the whites aside. Mash the yolks and olive oil into a smooth paste in the bottom of a salad bowl. Add the garlic, onion, Worcestershire, Tabasco, salt and pepper, and mustard.

If using fresh tomatoes, peel them. Push the tomatoes through a coarse sieve and work the tomato pulp into the ingredients in the bowl, mashing until well blended. Add the chopped cucumber and green pepper. Chill as long as you can, 2 or 3 hours at least.

Cut the egg whites into strips and lay them in the bottom of chilled glass or crystal bowls. A few strips of green pepper and pimiento would be pretty. Gently pour in the soup and float lemon or lime slices on top. The soup should be really cold. Serve with hot fried croutons on top.

Serves 4

Salads and Dressings

We're big salad folk out here in California, but I guess that's true all over the country. It's a refresher, it's healthy, it has all the vitamins you're supposed to have in the course of a meal—or maybe in the course of a day. It can be a whole meal as in the case of my Whole Meal Salad fix (page 62). I say fix because I *have* to have it at least once a week.

There's this earth-shaking controversy about whether the salad comes first or after the entrée. It's your choice. In the case of the Chopped Tomato Salad with Bruschetta (page 29), open with it. It puts the whole meal in a lovely frame of mind. In the case of the Arugula and Spinach Salad with White Wine–Honey Vinaigrette (page 71), after the meal and before the dessert, with a little soft cheese and crusty bread, it clears the palate for that luscious dessert. The Beet and Onion Salad (page 67) and the Cucumber Salad (page 74) are great served as a complement to the entrée. If you're serving buffet, consider the White and Red Bean Salad with Fresh Herbs and Mustard Dressing (page 68) and the Black-Eyed Peas Like Mother Never Made (page 80).

✽ Warm Potato and Sausage Salad

Picnic fare. Winter, in front of the fireplace; summer, outside with iced tea, grilled hot dogs, hamburgers, steaks, chicken—whatever you please.

3 medium boiling potatoes, white rose or the red ones if they're in season
1 clove garlic
Salt
2 Polish sausages

1 scallion, sliced (white part and some green)
French, Italian, or mayonnaise dressing (my favorite is Basic French Dressing, page 81)
Red pepper flakes (optional)

Boil the potatoes with their skins on, adding a garlic clove and salt to the water. Cook for about 20 minutes, or until just done; don't let them get too mushy. Cook the Polish sausages: They can be baked slowly in the oven, or an easier way is to place them in a skillet with water halfway up the sides of the sausages. Bring to a boil and when the water cooks away, add a little oil to the skillet and cook slowly, turning the sausages often until they are brown and crisp. Remove and let cool. This can be done ahead of time. Slice the sausages crosswise into ½-inch pieces. Fry until the sausage slices are browned.

Peel the potatoes while they are hot and cut into 1-inch pieces, slices, or sticks. Turn the hot sausages, potatoes, and scallion into a warmed bowl. Pour French, Italian, or mayonnaise dressing over all, turning gently to coat thoroughly without breaking up the potatoes too much. I add a smidgen of red pepper flakes before tossing. Serve at room temperature.

Serves 4

❋ *A Whole Meal Salad—*
A Real Mexican Treat

As I mentioned in the introduction to this chapter, this is one of my favorite combinations. I have it at least once a week. We cook the beans early in the week, have them with tortillas, and finish them off with this salad and salsa. We make that fresh once a week too—it keeps beautifully.

As you may note, some of the vegetables are optional because the salad works just as well with just a variety of lettuces and greens—a whole plateful.

*Salad greens: lettuces
(romaine, iceberg, red leaf,
Bibb), Belgian endive,
spinach leaves, Chinese
cabbage, or very young
cabbage
String beans (optional)
Broccoli flowerets (optional)
Cauliflower flowerets
(optional)
Carrot sticks (optional)*

*Salt and pepper
Green and red pepper strips
Celery, chopped (optional)
Small tomato wedges
Onions or scallions, sliced
Italian or Basic French
Dressing (page 81)
Hot cooked Pinto Beans (see
below)
Red Tomato Salsa (page 83)*

Wash the greens thoroughly and tear into bite-size pieces. Place in a large salad bowl and chill. Blanche the string beans, broccoli, cauliflower, and carrot sticks in boiling salted and peppered water, drain, let cool and add to the greens along with the pepper strips, celery, tomatoes, and onions or scallions. Just before serving, mix well with your favorite French or Italian dressing. Place the salad on individual plates, put ½ cup drained hot pinto beans on each portion, and top with 2 tablespoons fresh Red Tomato Salsa.

Serves 6 to 8

PINTO BEANS
2 pounds dried pinto beans
2 teaspoons salt
1 clove garlic (optional)

Wash and pick over the pinto beans, cover with cold water, and soak for 2 to 3 hours or overnight. Drain, place in a saucepan, add water to cover, the salt, and garlic. Bring to a boil, reduce the heat, cover, and simmer 2½ to 3 hours, or until the beans are soft, not mushy. Do not remove the lid except to check after 2½ hours to see if the beans are done or if you need a little more (½ cup) boiling water. When tender, let them sit in the liquid until cool. Refrigerate with their liquid. They will keep for a week to 10 days.

Makes 6 to 8 cups

❋ Mushroom and Endive Salad

2 heads Belgian endive
1 cup watercress
8 medium mushrooms, thinly
* sliced*

1 tablespoon finely chopped
* walnuts*
Basic French Dressing (page
* 81)*

Mix the endive, watercress, mushrooms, and walnuts together. Chill. Pour the dressing over all and mix lightly.

Serves 4

❋ *Vegetable Salad*

This one can be done ahead, refrigerated, and then brought to room temperature before serving.

½ cup broccoli stems, peeled, chopped into bite-size pieces
Salt and pepper
1 chayote squash, chopped into bite-size pieces
3 large carrots, thinly sliced
2 medium potatoes, cut into small cubes

2 zucchini, cut into ¼-inch-thick slices
½ cup cooked Pinto Beans (see Whole Meal Salad, page 62)
Basic French Dressing (page 81)

Cook the broccoli in boiling salted and peppered water until just tender. Remove with a slotted spoon, add the squash, and cook until just tender. Repeat with the remaining vegetables, cooking them one at a time.

Place all the vegetables and cooked pinto beans in a salad bowl. Pour the French dressing over all and mix well to coat. Serve at room temperature.

Serves 4 to 6

❋ *Coleslaw with Boiled Dressing*

Remember how special coleslaw was at those summer barbecues? I've tested and tasted dozens and still haven't found that one that was like the one from the good old days. Well, this is pretty close and, on second thought, I think I like this better than those "good old days." (After all, now is here and the "good old days" are there.)

½ cup cider vinegar
⅓ cup water
2 tablespoons sugar
2 tablespoons flour
2 teaspoons dry mustard
2 teaspoons salt

½ cup heavy cream
2 tablespoons butter
4 eggs, lightly beaten
2 pounds firm white cabbage
1 cup grated carrots

In a 2- to 3-quart saucepan, combine the vinegar, water, sugar, flour, mustard, and salt, and beat vigorously with a wire whisk until the mixture is smooth. Place over moderate heat and, whisking constantly, add the cream and butter and cook until the butter melts and the sauce comes to a simmer. Stir 2 or 3 tablespoons of the simmering liquid into the beaten eggs and when they are well incorporated, pour the mixture back into the sauce, whisking it constantly. Reduce the heat to low and continue to whisk until the sauce thickens heavily. With a rubber spatula, scrape the contents of the saucepan into a deep bowl and cool to room temperature.

Wash the head of cabbage under cold running water, remove the tough outer leaves, and cut the cabbage into quarters. To shred the cabbage, cut out the core and slice the quarters into ⅛-inch-wide strips.

Add the shredded cabbage and the carrots to the sauce, toss together gently but thoroughly, and taste for seasoning.

Cover with foil or plastic wrap and refrigerate for 2 or 3 hours before serving.

Serves 8 to 10

❋ *Russian Coleslaw*

Brenda Hall—Mrs. David Hall—lives in Franklin, Tennessee. She claims she can't cook a lick but she served us this coleslaw along with the Squash Casserole (page 192) and a few other great dishes, proving she can!

1 head cabbage, finely chopped	*1 cup sugar*
1 medium onion, finely chopped	*1 cup vegetable oil*
1 cucumber, peeled and finely chopped	*1 teaspoon celery seed*
	1 teaspoon salt
1 cup white vinegar	*1 teaspoon black pepper*

Place the cabbage, onion, and cucumber in a large mixing bowl. Combine the vinegar, sugar, oil, celery seed, salt, and pepper in a saucepan and bring to a boil. Set aside and cool. Pour over the vegetables and mix well. Chill before serving. This is better if you have time to let it sit overnight.

Serves 6

❋ *Coleslaw with Peanuts*

This is simply wonderful—the peanuts give it something special, even for this coleslaw connoisseur.

1¼ *pounds cabbage*
¼ *cup chopped scallions*
   (white part only)
2 *tablespoons sugar*
1½ *teaspoons seasoned salt*

⅓ *cup unsalted peanuts*
⅓ *cup chopped celery*
2 *tablespoons red wine vinegar*
1 *cup Italian-style salad*
   dressing

Remove the outer leaves of the cabbage. Core and cut into quarters, then shred.

Place the cabbage, scallions, sugar, salt, peanuts, and celery in a large bowl. Toss thoroughly. Add the vinegar and Italian dressing and mix only enough to season evenly. Do not overmix. Serve as soon as possible.

Serves 6

❋ *Fruit Salad with a Different Dressing*

This is definitely a party salad. It's piquant and full of surprises. The dressing alone is so good we almost tasted it out of existence before serving it for a dinner party.

6 *cups cut-up fresh fruit:*
   melons, berries, pineapple,
   strawberries, kiwis, Queen
   Anne cherries (unpitted with
   stems left on), bananas,
   apples, grapes, oranges—
   whatever is in season

Lettuce leaves to line the bowl
Mint sprigs, for garnish

DRESSING
½ *cup vegetable oil*
2 *tablespoons rice wine*
   vinegar
2 *tablespoons lemon juice*
Scant 3 tablespoons grated
   fresh gingerroot

1 *teaspoon grated orange or*
   lemon peel
2 *tablespoons honey*
Pinch of red pepper flakes
Salt to taste

Wash, peel, core, cut up, and otherwise prepare the fruit. Wash, dry, and chill the lettuce leaves. (I wrap lettuce in a clean kitchen towel after washing and drying and keep it in the refrigerator until ready to use.)

Whisk together the dressing ingredients in a jar with a tight-fitting lid. Refrigerate.

Just before serving, carefully toss the fruit with the dressing, reserving some dressing to serve on the side.

Place the salad on lettuce-lined plates garnished with mint sprigs.

Serves 4 to 6

✤ *Beet and Onion Salad*

Nothing lasts forever—this comes close however. Make a large amount, it keeps for weeks and just seems to get better. Besides, it's so beautiful to look at—I always wanted a dress that color.

1 pound fresh, firm, small beets
¼ cup red wine vinegar
1 teaspoon salt
¾ teaspoon sugar

2 small sweet onions, cut into
slices ¼ inch thick, separated
into rings, and cut again if
necessary

Cut the tops from the beets, leaving about 1 inch of stem on each. Scrub the beets under cold running water then drop them into lightly salted boiling water to cover them completely. Turn the heat to low, partially cover the pan, and simmer for about 30 minutes, or until the beets are tender. The beets should be kept constantly covered with water; add boiling water if necessary.

Drain the beets in a colander, and when they are cool slip off their skins. Cut the beets lengthwise into slices ¼ inch thick and then into strips about ¼ inch wide, or slice them into rounds ¼ inch thick.

Combine the vinegar, salt, and sugar in a deep bowl and stir until the sugar dissolves. Drop in the beets and the onions and turn them with a spoon until they are coated with the vinegar mixture. Let the salad marinate at room temperature for about 30 minutes, turning the beets and the onions every 10 minutes or so. Serve at room temperature.

Serves 4

❊ Salmon Salad

When broiling salmon steaks, I always do two more than I need so that I can make this salad. The same is true for swordfish. It's a nice change from tuna salad and can be used as an hors d'oeuvre for un-expected guests.

1 pound cooked salmon
   (leftover broiled salmon
   steaks, for example), broken
   with a fork into bite-size
   pieces
3 teaspoons soy sauce
1 teaspoon sesame oil
1 tablespoon mayonnaise

2 eggs, hard-boiled, chopped
¼ green pepper, seeded and
   chopped
1 stalk celery, chopped
1 carrot, chopped
3 tablespoons grated onion
Tabasco sauce to taste

Combine all the ingredients gently in a bowl and mix well, but try not to mush up the salmon.

Serves 4 to 6

❊ White and Red Bean Salad with Fresh Herbs and Mustard Dressing

I'm not much of one for planning ahead—for instance, I always forget to soak the beans the night before. It's so much easier if you do it that way. Wash the beans, pick out the discolored ones, soak overnight, and drain. The next morning, put in fresh water to cover, add your salt, and let them boil for about an hour until tender, then proceed with the recipe, or try Gloria's way (see Pinto Beans in Whole Meal Salad recipe, page 63). She never takes the lid off the pan, except to check if they're soft, until they're ready to serve. They're perfect. However, if you forget the night before, try soaking the quick-cooking way in this recipe. It's almost as good.

1 quart water
¼ pound dried navy beans
¼ pound dried pinto beans
2 teaspoons salt
1 tablespoon tarragon vinegar
2 teaspoons mustard
2 drops of Tabasco sauce
¼ teaspoon freshly ground
   black pepper
⅓ cup olive oil
2 tablespoons finely chopped
   fresh basil
2 tablespoons finely chopped
   fresh chives

2 tablespoons finely chopped
   fresh parsley
1 teaspoon finely chopped fresh
   dill
3 small mint leaves, finely
   chopped
½ teaspoon finely chopped
   garlic
2 medium-size fresh tomatoes,
   peeled, seeded, and coarsely
   chopped

In a heavy 2- to 3-quart saucepan, bring the water to a boil over high heat. Drop in the dried beans and boil them uncovered for about 2 minutes. Turn off the heat and let the beans soak uncovered for 1 hour. Then add ½ teaspoon of the salt and bring to a boil again. Reduce the heat to low, partially cover the pan, and simmer for about 1 hour, or until the beans are tender but still intact. Drain the beans and set them aside in a bowl to cool to room temperature.

In a small bowl, combine the vinegar, mustard, Tabasco, the remaining 1½ teaspoons of salt, and the pepper and, with a wire whisk, stir them to a smooth paste. Whisking the mixture constantly, add the oil in a slow stream and continue to beat until the dressing is thick and creamy.

Place the herbs and garlic in a large serving bowl and mix them well. Add the cooled beans and the tomatoes, pour the dressing over them, and stir gently until the beans and tomatoes are thoroughly coated with the herbs and dressing.

Cover tightly with plastic wrap and marinate in the refrigerator for at least 4 hours. Just before serving, taste for seasoning and stir the salad briefly.

Serves 4 as a main dish, 6 to 8 as a side dish

❋ *Molded Chicken Salad*

A few years ago—quite a few—my friend Barbara Sinatra and I would have these great luncheons after tennis. Sometimes the lunches were better than the tennis, especially when it was Barbara's turn, and she'd serve "that" molded chicken salad. It was made by her housekeeper, a lady named Versa. Though I asked and then begged, Versa never could seem to remember the recipe, but it was such a memorable experience it stayed with me all this time. I've tried to re-create it, and I think this comes close. Incidentally, I'm sure Versa put one-fourth or one-half cup of pure, heavy cream in with the mayonnaise. I saved us that.

2 small skinless and boneless chicken breasts
Chicken broth or water for poaching
Salt and pepper to taste
Juice from ¹/₂ lemon
¹/₄ cup fresh dill coarsely chopped or 2 tablespoons dried (optional)
2 envelopes unflavored gelatin
2 cups water
2 cups chicken broth
¹/₄ sweet red pepper, seeded and thinly sliced
¹/₄ green pepper, seeded and thinly sliced
¹/₄ yellow pepper, seeded and thinly sliced
1 cup mayonnaise
2 tablespoons Dijon mustard

1 tablespoon Worcestershire sauce
¹/₄ teaspoon Tabasco sauce
¹/₄ teaspoon sesame oil
2 eggs, hard-boiled, coarsely chopped
¹/₂ cup coarsely chopped toasted almonds
1 carrot, peeled and coarsely chopped
2 tablespoons finely chopped or grated sweet onion
¹/₄ cup peeled and cubed broccoli stems
1 small orange, peeled, sectioned, seeded, and each section cut into 3 pieces
¹/₄ cup finely chopped fresh dill
Dressing (see below)

Poach the chicken in chicken broth or water to which you have added salt and pepper, lemon juice, and the dill, until just done, about 30 minutes or so. Remove the chicken from the poaching liquid, cool, and cut into small pieces.

Dissolve the gelatin in boiling water and chicken broth. Let cool. Lightly oil a 10-inch ring mold. Pour a couple of scoops of cooled gelatin into the bottom of the mold and chill. Lay the red, green, and yellow pepper strips over the chilled gelatin in a decorative pattern.

Mix the mayonnaise, Dijon mustard, Worcestershire, Tabasco, and sesame oil into the remaining cooled gelatin. Then fold in the chicken, eggs, almonds, carrot, onion, broccoli, orange, and chopped dill. Mix carefully and thoroughly, but don't mush up your ingredients. Pour into the mold and chill until firm and beautiful.

Unmold by gently loosening the sides with the blade of a thin sharp knife. Set the mold in hot water for several seconds, then reverse it onto a serving platter. Fill the center with a small bowl of dressing.

Serves 8

DRESSING

½ cup mayonnaise
2 teaspoons Dijon mustard
⅛ teaspoon Tabasco sauce

¼ teaspoon Worcestershire
  sauce
1 tablespoon whipping cream

Place all ingredients in a small bowl and mix well.

Makes ½ cup

✽ Arugula and Spinach Salad with White Wine–Honey Vinaigrette

3 bunches arugula
½ bunch spinach
White Wine–Honey Vinaigrette
  (see next page)
1 sweet red pepper, roasted in
  a skillet

3 cloves garlic, halved
1 tablespoon olive oil
2 small tomatoes, cut into
  small chunks

Wash the arugula and spinach well. Remove the stems from the arugula and trim the spinach. Drain well, wrap in paper towels or a dish towel, and place in the refrigerator to crisp until ready to use.

Pour the White Wine–Honey Vinaigrette over the arugula and spinach, reserving 2 tablespoons of dressing, and toss lightly with your fingers to coat well.

Arrange on individual plates. Peel the roasted pepper and slice it into ¼-inch julienne strips. Sear the garlic in the olive oil until crisp. Remove the garlic and reserve it. Place the red pepper and tomatoes in the reserved 2 tablespoons of dressing and stir lightly to season. Sprinkle the peppers and tomatoes over the arugula and spinach and scatter the roasted garlic on top.

Serves 4

WHITE WINE–HONEY VINAIGRETTE

3 tablespoons honey
½ cup olive oil
2 tablespoons soy sauce
6 tablespoons white wine
1 teaspoon chopped fresh
  rosemary

½ teaspoon white pepper
2 teaspoons grated fresh
  gingerroot
2 teaspoons minced garlic
½ teaspoon salt
4 teaspoons lemon juice

Combine all the ingredients except the lemon juice in a large mixing bowl. Whisk well. Slowly add the lemon juice and whisk lightly until well blended.

Makes approximately 1½ cups

❧ *Green Salad with Pears and Pecans*

6 to 8 cups loosely packed
  salad greens (a mixture of
  romaine, butter lettuce, dark
  leaves from iceberg, etc.)
1 fresh pear, peeled and very
  coarsely chopped

¼ cup halved or broken pecans
  or walnuts
2 tablespoons Roquefort cheese
Basic French Dressing (page
  81)

Wash the salad greens thoroughly and chill. When ready to serve, add the chopped pear and the pecans or walnuts to the salad greens. Add the Roquefort to the Basic French Dressing and mix well. Pour over the salad and toss gently

Serves 4

❧ *Orange and Almond Salad*

ORANGE DRESSING

2 tablespoons safflower or pure
  olive oil
¼ cup tarragon vinegar
½ cup orange juice
1 tablespoon chopped fresh
  parsley

⅛ teaspoon black pepper
⅛ teaspoon salt
Pinch of dry mustard
Honey (add if necessary,
  depending on the sweetness
  of the orange juice)

SALAD

12 cups mixed greens
1½ cups orange segments (peel the orange and cut out the segments with a paring knife between the membranes)

½ cup slivered almonds (toast the almonds in a 400° oven for 10 minutes)

Make the Orange Dressing by mixing all the ingredients together. Taste for seasoning and chill well.

Before serving, gently toss the greens, orange segments, and almonds with the dressing. Reserve some orange segments and almonds for garnishing the top of the salad. Serve in a well-chilled bowl.

Serves 4 to 6

❋ *Salad Sonora*

This is spicy, textured, and served with toasted pita bread.

1 cup dried lentils
1 medium onion, chopped
2 cloves garlic, minced
1½ teaspoons chili powder
½ teaspoon ground cumin
2 cups water
1 cup fresh or frozen cooked corn kernels
½ cup Red Tomato Salsa (page 83)
One 4-ounce can chopped green chilies

½ cup chopped green pepper
½ cup sliced ripe olives
½ cup chopped fresh cilantro (coriander)
2 to 3 tablespoons lemon or lime juice or cider vinegar
½ teaspoon cayenne pepper
1 teaspoon salt
Toasted pita bread, cut into triangles

Wash and pick over the lentils. Place in a medium saucepan with the onion, garlic, chili powder, cumin, and water. Heat to boiling, cover, reduce heat, and simmer for 20 minutes, until the lentils are just barely tender. Don't let them get mushy. Drain if necessary.

Add the corn, salsa, green chilies, green pepper, olives, cilantro, and lemon or lime juice or vinegar. Season with cayenne pepper and salt. Cover and chill several hours or overnight to blend the flavors.

Serve with the toasted pita bread triangles.

Serves 4 to 6

❊ *Cucumber Salad*

*2 cucumbers, peeled, sliced
lengthwise down the center,
seeds scooped out with a
spoon and sliced crosswise
to form little half circles*
*¼ cup Japanese rice wine
vinegar*

Salt and white pepper
*2 tablespoons fresh dillweed or
1 tablespoon dried*
*1 medium tomato, cut into
wedges (optional)*
*2 tablespoons sour cream or
plain low-fat yogurt*

Drain the cucumbers on paper towels.

Place all the ingredients in a medium-size bowl and mix well. Chill before serving.

Serves 4

❊ *Orange and Cucumber Salad*

An unusual combination—but cooling on a hot day, and crisp and delicious.

*1 cucumber, peeled and sliced
into thin rounds*
*1 orange, peeled (remove the
white membrane) and sliced
into thin rounds. Cut the
rounds in half and remove
the seeds*

*5 or 6 small radishes, sliced
into thin rounds*
*3 or 4 fresh mint leaves, finely
chopped*
Italian or French dressing*

Place the cucumber, orange, radishes, and mint leaves in a bowl. Pour the dressing over all. Mix well.

*I like a simple dressing, 3 tablespoons oil to 3 tablespoons vinegar or lemon juice, ½ teaspoon salt, ½ teaspoon white pepper, and a crushed garlic clove.

Place all the ingredients in a jar with a tight lid and mix thoroughly.

Serves 4

✻ Macedonian Salad

We call this Macedonian Salad because it's Greek, and it does have eggplant, yogurt, tomatoes, cucumbers, and all those wonderful goodies.

MARINADE

2 cloves garlic, crushed
2 tablespoons dry red wine
Juice of 1 lemon
¼ cup olive oil
¼ cup safflower oil

½ cup wine vinegar
½ teaspoon salt or to taste
Black pepper
3 tablespoons chopped fresh basil

SALAD

2 small eggplants
2 medium tomatoes, peeled and cut into small chunks
1 cucumber, peeled and cut into small chunks
1 green pepper, seeded and cut into small chunks
1 sweet red pepper, seeded and cut into small chunks

2 scallions, chopped, (white and some of green part)
3 tablespoons chopped fresh parsley
Lettuce leaves
Yogurt for topping

Combine all the marinade ingredients and mix well.

Peel and slice the eggplant ½ inch thick. Lightly salt the eggplant and let it stand for 10 minutes. Rinse the eggplant and drain. Place the slices on an oiled tray and broil until brown on both sides. The slices should be tender, not mushy. Chop the warm eggplant into bite-size chunks, cover with the marinade, and let it absorb as it cools. Chill for 2 hours.

When ready to serve, add the cut up vegetables, the scallions and parsley, and toss to cover well with the marinade. Salt to taste.

Serve on lettuce leaves and top with yogurt.

Serves 6 to 8

❧ *Malaysian Chicken Salad with Peanuts*

Did I tell you this was home cooking international-style? Now you'll understand—I couldn't leave this one out.

2 tablespoons vegetable oil
2 whole chicken breasts, boned, skinned, and cut into thin slices
1 sweet red pepper, seeded and cut into julienne strips
1 carrot, cut into julienne strips

1 head iceberg lettuce, finely shredded
Fresh cilantro (coriander) chopped, for garnish
¾ cup dry roasted peanuts, for garnish

DRESSING
1 cup vegetable oil
⅓ cup white vinegar
2 tablespoons soy sauce
2 tablespoons chunky peanut butter

4 medium cloves garlic, minced (about 2 teaspoons)
1 teaspoon crushed dried red chilies

Heat the oil in a large skillet or wok. Add the chicken and stir-fry over high heat for 4 or 5 minutes, or until done. Remove with a slotted spoon. Add the red pepper and carrot to any remaining oil and stir-fry for 4 or 5 minutes, or until tender-crisp. Return the chicken to the skillet and keep warm.

Mound the shredded lettuce onto a serving platter. Mound the chicken and vegetables on the lettuce and garnish with cilantro and peanuts.

Make the dressing: Combine all ingredients in a jar, shake well and refrigerate for approximately 2 hours. Before serving, pour half the dressing over the salad. Pass the remaining dressing for individual use.

Serves 6

❧ *Chicken Salad with Potatoes*

A great luncheon or buffet dish! It's delicious and fun to make the mayonnaise described below, but you can use your favorite store-bought mayonnaise instead. Just add a little sour cream if you want it thinner.

The directions say to tear the chicken into pieces, since it absorbs the other flavors better than when cut into chunks. I also find the white new potatoes better for this than the large baking variety—the latter are inclined to crumble more easily when cooked.

1½ pounds thin-skinned potatoes, peeled and cut lengthwise into 2-inch sticks
3 tablespoons dry white wine
3 tablespoons tarragon vinegar
1½ cups Mayonnaise (see below)
½ cup snipped fresh chives
½ cup chicken broth
Salt and white pepper to taste
Lemon juice to taste
4 cups well-seasoned cooked chicken, torn into large pieces

½ green pepper, seeded and cut into strips
½ sweet red pepper, seeded and cut into strips
¼ cup minced onion
3 slices smoked cooked ham, cut into julienne strips, for garnish
2 mushrooms, diced, for garnish
Sliced tomatoes or small cherry tomatoes, for garnish

Place the potatoes in a bowl of cold water as they are cut, and let them stand for 30 minutes. Drain the potatoes and cook in boiling salted water until just tender. Drain them, transfer to a bowl, and while they are still hot, toss with the white wine and tarragon vinegar. Let the potatoes cool and chill them, covered.

Combine the mayonnaise with the snipped chives, chicken broth, salt, white pepper, and lemon juice to taste.

Place the chicken in a large bowl and add the potatoes and the green and red pepper. Fold in 1 cup of the mayonnaise mixture and the minced onion. Mound the salad in a shallow salad bowl and garnish it with ham and diced mushroom. Serve with tomato garnish and the remaining mayonnaise mixture.

Serves 8

MAYONNAISE
2 egg yolks
½ teaspoon salt
1 teaspoon sugar
1 teaspoon Dijon mustard

4 tablespoons lemon juice or vinegar
1¼ cups vegetable oil

Place all the ingredients except the oil in the container of a food processor fitted with a steel or plastic blade. Process for a few seconds.

Turn off the machine and scrape down the sides. With the machine running, add the oil through the tube in a thin stream. Blend until thick.

Makes 1½ cups

✣ *Chinese Chicken Salad by Dan Lee*

Since our last cookbook—called The Dinah Shore Cookbook *(what else?)—I've tasted fifteen Chinese chicken salads. They're all nice, but this one is the best. Yes, I borrowed it from Dan Lee via* The Dinah Shore Cookbook, *but then I've been told there is no such thing as an original recipe unless, possibly, it was that time Eve steamed the apple for Adam.*

1 cup cornstarch
1 teaspoon salt
1 frying chicken (3–4 pounds),
  left whole
4 cups oil for deep frying
1 cup rice noodles (Maifun),
  fried and broken up
1 cup shredded iceberg lettuce
½ bunch cilantro, coarsely
  chopped

3 scallions, tops included, cut
  into 4 pieces and sliced
  lengthwise

Sauce
1 tablespoon white sesame
  seeds
1½ tablespoons almonds or
  cashews (or mixture of
  both), chopped

Mix cornstarch with salt and pat on chicken to coat completely.

Cook chicken in bamboo steamer or vegetable steamer 45–50 minutes. Refrigerate until ready to make salad.

Split chicken in half and deep-fry in hot (375°) oil until skin is crisp and golden. Drain on paper towels. Debone chicken by shredding meat by hand (*do not cut*) into strips. Go along the grain and not crosswise.

In large bowl mix together shredded chicken, rice noodles, lettuce, cilantro, and scallions. Pour sauce over all and mix gently but thoroughly, making sure sauce coats all ingredients well. Sprinkle sesame seeds and nuts over salad.

SAUCE

1 heaping tablespoon dry
  mustard mixed with 1
  tablespoon water to make a
  paste

⅓–½ cup peanut oil
¼ teaspoon sesame seed oil
½ teaspoon salt
2 teaspoons dark soy sauce

Mix all ingredients in small bowl.

Serves 4 as main course; serves 8 as salad

❖ Cold Carrot Salad

This is a surprise! It's not just your everyday carrot sticks nor is it the one you see on all buffets with raisins—it's not as sweet. I served it as an hors d'oeuvre first. It was a hit. I served it later as a salad and once again on that ever-popular (with everyone but me) buffet.

2 pounds carrots, peeled and cut into uniform sticks 2½ to 3 inches long
Salt and pepper
1 tablespoon olive oil
1 tablespoon butter or margarine
2 cloves garlic, halved and crushed with the back of a knife (you want to be able to remove the garlic before serving)
White pepper to taste

Pinch of sugar
4 tablespoons red wine vinegar
4 tablespoons good fresh olive oil
2 tablespoons finely chopped fresh parsley
2 tablespoons finely chopped scallions (white and some of green part)
Dash of paprika
Dash of ground cumin
Fresh mint leaves, for garnish

Drop the carrot sticks into boiling salted and peppered water. Cook for 1 minute, until just al dente. Drain well and rinse under cold water.

In a large skillet heat the 1 tablespoon olive oil and the butter or margarine. When the butter is foamy, add the carrots, garlic, salt, white pepper, and sugar, and gently sauté for a couple of minutes over low heat.

Place in a serving bowl and pour the vinegar and 4 tablespoons olive oil over all. Add the parsley, scallions, paprika, and cumin. Gently stir and mix well. Chill in the refrigerator for at least 2 hours (overnight is even better). Taste for seasoning, you may need more salt and pepper. Serve garnished with fresh mint leaves, if you have them.

Serves 6 to 8 as a side dish, 8 to 10 as an hors d'oeuvre

❀*Black-Eyed Peas Like Mother Never Made*

2 zucchini, sliced ¾ inch thick
1¼ cups well-seasoned cooked
   black-eyed peas
½ cup Basic French Dressing
   (page 81)
Bibb or romaine lettuce leaves
   to line the platter

2 tablespoons chopped
   pimiento
2 tablespoons finely chopped
   onion

Cook the zucchini until just tender, about 3 minutes. Rinse the peas in cool water and drain well. Drizzle a little French dressing over the zucchini and peas.

Line a salad platter with the lettuce leaves and arrange the zucchini slices, overlapping, on the lettuce. Spoon the peas over the zucchini and sprinkle with the pimiento and onion.

Pour the remaining dressing over the salad and serve.

❀*A Yogurt Dip for Fresh Vegetables*

Another fling at dieting. Use all the cold vegetables you want, such as, mushrooms, carrots, green, red, and yellow peppers, celery, jicama, broccoli, cauliflower, whatever.

4 tablespoons plain nonfat
   yogurt
Juice of ⅓ lemon
Salt and pepper to taste

2 teaspoons finely chopped
   fresh dill or ½ teaspoon
   crushed dried
½ teaspoon capers, drained

Mix all the ingredients together in a small bowl. Chill before serving.

Makes approximately ¼ cup

❀ Basic French Dressing

If you read through this book you'll find I repeatedly urge you to use fresh, fresh olive oil. For some reason, this particular dressing is much better with light vegetable or peanut oil.

1¾ cups corn oil or your
  favorite light vegetable or
  peanut oil
¾ cup white wine vinegar or
  champagne vinegar
Scant 2 teaspoons salt or to
  taste

1 teaspoon pepper
1¾ teaspoons sugar
2 to 3 teaspoons Dijon
  mustard or to taste
3 cloves garlic, 1 crushed, 2
  halved

Put all the ingredients in a jar with a tight-fitting lid and shake well. Keeps in the refrigerator for weeks.

Suggestion: When using as a dressing for a simple green salad, place 1 tablespoon Basic French Dressing with 2 tablespoons rice wine vinegar in the bottom of the salad bowl. Mix lightly with the greens (your fingers are the best utensils). Make sure your greens are washed, dried, and chilled according to the directions on page 71 in the Arugula and Spinach Salad. Then add the additional dressing you need. Turn gently but thoroughly to make sure every leaf is covered, but don't drown the salad in dressing.

Makes 2½ cups

❀ Honey-Lime Dressing

6 tablespoons vegetable oil
3 tablespoons lime juice
1 tablespoon rice wine vinegar
2 tablespoons honey
1 tablespoon minced fresh
  mint leaves or 1 teaspoon
  dried

1 tablespoon minced fresh
  chives
1 teaspoon salt
1 teaspoon white pepper
1 clove garlic, peeled and
  halved

Combine all the ingredients in a jar with a tight-fitting lid. Shake to mix well. Refrigerate.

Makes ¾ cup

❋ Tangy Greek Dressing

This is a little heavier than Basic French Dressing, but it's delicious with heavier salads: for instance, vegetables as well as dark greens, cooked or uncooked cauliflower or broccoli flowerets, radishes, cooked string beans, and other leftover vegetables.

1½ cups low-fat cottage cheese
¼ cup mayonnaise
¼ cup plus 2 tablespoons
  buttermilk
1½ cups plus 2 tablespoons
  tomato puree
¼ cup tomato juice
½ cup soy sauce

2¼ teaspoons chopped fresh
  oregano or ¾ teaspoon dried
2¼ teaspoons chopped fresh
  tarragon or ¾ teaspoon
  dried
¼ teaspoon crushed garlic
¼ teaspoon Tabasco sauce

Place all of the ingredients in a blender and mix until smooth.

Makes 1 quart

❋ Boiled Salad Dressing

3 tablespoons sugar
1 tablespoon flour
1 teaspoon dry mustard
1 teaspoon salt
½ cup white vinegar

½ cup water
1 tablespoon butter or
  margarine
2 eggs, lightly beaten

Mix the sugar, flour, mustard, and salt together in a stainless-steel saucepan. With a wire whisk, stir in the vinegar, water, and butter or margarine and cook over medium heat, whisking constantly, until the mixture comes to a boil and starts to thicken. Remove from the heat. Stir 2 tablespoons of the mixture into the beaten eggs, then pour the eggs into the saucepan and whisk until smooth. Cook over low heat for 30 seconds.

Transfer the dressing to a bowl and cool. Serve warm or cold, with coleslaw, fish, chicken, or turkey salad.

Makes 1 cup

❋ Red Tomato Salsa

This is a perker-upper in small quantities for small dishes and is great with salads, scrambled eggs, tortillas, tamales, pinto beans, and soups.

3 firm tomatoes, peeled and coarsely chopped
3 to 4 serrano chilies, finely chopped
½ bunch cilantro (coriander) (leaves only), finely chopped

2 or 3 scallions, finely chopped (both green and white part)
Salt to taste

Mix all the ingredients together in a small bowl and chill. Serve with tortilla chips.

Makes about 1 cup

Meats

I keep hearing people say they don't eat much meat anymore and I'm tempted to use the old comeback, "They don't eat it any less." I found as I began to test and taste and retest for this chapter that I wasn't running out of customers—and the sight and smell of the tender "heavies" coming out of the kitchen started a Pavlovian-like response: instant salivating. For instance, the pot roast cooked in parchment paper (page 89), the leg of lamb cooked in a similar fashion (page 99), the not-so-old-fashioned Layered Meat Loaf (page 111), Middle Eastern Lamb Stew with Prunes (page 97), and that Roast Loin of Veal à la Craig (page 109) shortened the "happy hour" to a fast fifteen minutes or as soon as we could get it all together.

The lighter dishes, such as the Braised Pork with Mixed Fruit (page 105), A Cowboy's Pie (page 88), Diced Pork with Walnuts (page 102), and the Asian or Chinese-style Beef and Broccoli (page 94) made me dare to hope that maybe—just maybe—we'll start eating these dishes with relish and stop apologizing. It's not exactly Dark Age Dining, you know.

Flank steak is a lean cut of meat that stretches to accommodate extra guests and blends itself beautifully around seasonings, particularly in the form of stuffings. I couldn't decide which of these I liked better, so you have them both. They're quite different.

✴ Shirley's Stuffed Flank Steak

Shirley is Shirley Secretary or Shirley Schroer, no relation, mentioned from time to time in here. She is an experienced cook—loves it and is very good at it, obviously. I believe if she had her way she'd begin and end any meal with luscious desserts and perhaps serve a couple in between courses. She's great at those in-betweens; however, this flank steak is delicious—an inexpensive lean cut of meat with a lovely aromatic filling.

Flour, well seasoned with salt
  and pepper
One 2-pound flank steak
2 tablespoons butter or
  margarine
1/2 medium onion, finely
  chopped
1 clove garlic, finely chopped
1/2 cup coarsely chopped
  mushrooms
3 tablespoons finely chopped
  celery
1/8 teaspoon grated fresh
  gingerroot
1/4 cup finely chopped fresh
  parsley
1 cup bread crumbs
1/8 teaspoon paprika

1/4 teaspoon dry mustard
2 teaspoons finely chopped fresh
  basil or 1/2 teaspoon dried
  1 teaspoon finely chopped fresh
  oregano or 1/4 teaspoon dried
1/2 teaspoon salt
Freshly ground black pepper to
  taste
1 egg
1/4 cup pine nuts (pignolia),
  coarsely chopped or left whole
  if you prefer
1 tablespoon olive oil combined
  with 1 tablespoon margarine
  or butter
3/4 cup red wine
1/2 cup or more chicken broth
2 teaspoons instant flour

Pound the seasoned flour into the steak and set aside. Preheat the oven to 350°.

In a large skillet, heat the butter or margarine. Add the onion and garlic and cook until translucent. Add the mushrooms, celery, and ginger and cook for 3 to 4 minutes. Add the parsley, bread crumbs, seasonings, egg, and pine nuts and mix well. Spread the mixture on the floured steak, roll lengthwise to encase the filling, and tie with string at 1-inch intervals.

Brown the meat on both sides in a mixture of olive oil and margarine or butter in an oven-proof skillet or Dutch oven. Add the wine and bake, covered, for 2 hours. Remove the cover occasionally and add a little chicken broth as the wine evaporates. Remove the meat from the skillet and place on a warm platter.

With a slotted spoon, skim any dressing that has come out of the steak from the juices. Mix the instant flour with 1 tablespoon of the chicken broth and add it to the juices in the skillet. Bring to a boil and simmer for a few minutes. Taste for seasoning.

Slice the steak about ½ to ¾ inch thick and serve with the sauce on the side.   *Serves 6 to 8*

❁ *Another Stuffed Flank Steak*

1½ pounds flank steak
4 tablespoons flour, well
   seasoned with salt and
   pepper
2 cloves garlic, 1 finely minced
   and 1 halved
4 tablespoons olive oil
½ onion, finely chopped
¼ cup raw rice
½ cup fresh bread crumbs
6 mushrooms, finely chopped
1 teaspoon dried Italian
   seasoning

2 tablespoons finely chopped
   fresh basil, or 2 teaspoons
   dried
2 tablespoons finely chopped
   fresh parsley
1 tablespoon finely chopped
   fresh oregano, or 1 teaspoon
   dried
2 tablespoons freshly grated
   Parmesan cheese
¾ cup chicken broth
Salt and pepper
2 medium tomatoes, coarsely
   chopped

Cut the flank steak in two, horizontally, leaving one side intact, so that when you open it up you have a flat piece of meat. Pound the seasoned flour into the flank steak and rub with the cut clove of garlic, reserving the garlic. Set aside.

Heat 2 tablespoons of the olive oil in a large Dutch oven with a cover. Sauté the minced garlic and the onion until soft. Add the rice and coat with the oil. Add the bread crumbs, mushrooms, seasonings, Parmesan cheese, ¼ cup of the chicken broth, and salt and pepper to taste. Mix well.

Spread the mixture over the opened flank steak, roll it up jelly roll fashion, and tie with string at 1-inch intervals.

Heat the remaining 2 tablespoons of olive oil in the Dutch oven and brown the meat on all sides. Add the tomatoes, the reserved cut garlic cloves and the remaining ½ cup chicken broth. Bake, covered, in a preheated 350° oven for 1½ hours, basting occasionally with the sauce, or until tender. Cook uncovered to brown during the last half hour, if necessary.

Serves 4 to 6

❋ Steak Dinah

I listened to the news and laid off steaks for a while, but soon went back, not with a vengeance but lightly. This is one of my trips into the light fantastic. It's a little different from the great Steak Diane recipe created by some love-struck maître d' or chef, and easy. Be sure to turn your head away when you ignite the brandy. It might melt your mascara—if you wear it.

Two 1-pound boneless sirloin
   steaks, 1½ to 2 inches thick
Black peppercorns, crushed
4 tablespoons clarified butter
   (see page 122)
1 tablespoon olive oil
Salt

1 tablespoon chopped shallots
½ cup chicken broth
1 teaspoon Dijon mustard
½ teaspoon lemon juice
Juices from steaks
¼ cup brandy
½ cup half and half

Trim any excess fat and tissue from the steaks. Press the crushed peppercorns evenly into the surface of the meat and let the steaks sit at room temperature until you are ready to cook them. Heat 2 tablespoons of the clarified butter and the olive oil over high heat in a skillet large enough to hold both steaks. When the meat is brown and beautiful on one side (about 5 to 7 minutes, depending on whether you like your steak rare or medium), turn with tongs, salt the steaks generously, and reduce the heat. Cook for about 5 to 7 minutes on the other side and remove the steaks to a warm platter. Slice about ½ inch thick, reserving the juices. Cover and keep warm.

To the same skillet, add the remaining 2 tablespoons of clarified butter and the shallot and sauté until soft. Add the chicken broth, bring to a boil, lower the heat, and simmer until reduced by one half. Add the mustard, lemon juice, reserved steak juices, then the brandy. Flame the brandy, then stir in the half and half. Pour the hot sauce over the steaks or slip the steaks back into the sauce for an instant. Then return the steaks to the warm platter with the sauce.

Serves 4

❋ A Cowboy's Pie

If shepherds can have a pie made out of lamb, why can't cowboys have a hearty, spicy one made out of beef? (Of course, lean and very healthy beef.)

1 medium onion, finely
   chopped
1 large clove garlic, finely
   minced
Vegetable oil
2 pounds lean ground chuck
3 tomatoes, coarsely chopped
2 carrots, peeled, blanched, and
   thinly sliced
1/2 cup sliced mushrooms
1 bay leaf

1 teaspoon fresh marjoram or
   1/2 teaspoon dried
1 generous tablespoon chopped
   fresh dill
2 teaspoons chili powder
1 teaspoon salt
Pinch of cayenne pepper
1 teaspoon Worcestershire
   sauce
2 cups Mashed Potatoes (see
   below)

In a large skillet sauté the onion and garlic in the oil until soft. Add the chuck and brown lightly. Add the tomatoes, carrots, mushrooms, seasonings, and Worcestershire sauce. Cook about 10 minutes, or until the flavors are well blended. Remove the bay leaf. Place the meat mixture in an oven-proof casserole and cover with the mashed potatoes. Bake in a preheated 350° oven for 10 minutes, or until the potatoes are a light golden brown. Serve very hot.

MASHED POTATOES

Mash potatoes with salt, white pepper, margarine, and enough warm milk to make them smooth but still stiff. If they're too loose, beat 1 egg into them.

Serves 6

Variation: Boil carrots and mash them with the potatoes for a golden topping.

❀ *Juicy Tender Pot Roast*

I've always avoided the use of parchment paper for cooking. It sounded a little biblical. But it's not that rare and is found alongside the foil, waxed paper, and plastic wrap in the grocery store. This recipe works better for some reason with the parchment-wrap treatment than with aluminum foil. And it is all the title implies—just meltingly delicious. The roast is fork-tender, falling away from the bone, as a good pot roast should. Serve with a simple green vegetable or a generous green salad and crusty bread.

I've told this story before, but this roast is a great house seller. When I was selling my home, I asked the agent to make the date at 5:00 P.M. when everybody is the most hungry. The aroma of the roast and fresh bread wafting through the house from the kitchen made the sale faster than his spiel.

One 4½- to 5-pound chuck
  roast, bone in
½ lemon
1 clove garlic, halved
2 teaspoons salt
1 teaspoon black pepper
1½ teaspoons minced garlic
1 teaspoon dried oregano
1 teaspoon dried basil
2 tablespoons fresh dill or 2
  teaspoons dried
1 teaspoon dried marjoram
1 tablespoon chopped fresh
  parsley
½ cup chopped onion
1 teaspoon Dijon mustard

½ cup red wine
½ cup tomato juice cocktail
  (V-8)
2 tablespoons ketchup
12 potatoes (thin-skinned or
  new potatoes, if they're
  available), peeled and
  quartered
1½ cups water
Butter or margarine
Additional chopped parsley
  (optional)
1 tablespoon instant or regular
  flour
½ to 1 cup chicken or beef
  broth or water

Rinse the roast and pat it dry. Pierce the meat all over with a large fork. Rub it with lemon, the cut garlic clove, 1 teaspoon of salt, and ½ teaspoon of pepper.

Mix together the remaining salt and pepper, the minced garlic, seasonings, onion, mustard, wine, tomato juice cocktail, and ketchup.

Place the roast on large pieces of parchment paper or 3 or 4 sheets of waxed paper. Rub the marinade over the roast, coating it thoroughly. Pour the remainder over the top and let the roast stand for at least an hour. The longer it stands the better it is. Wrap the roast tightly with the parchment paper, catching all the marinade. Place in a baking pan, cover the pan with foil, and bake in a preheated 325° oven for about 2½ hours.

About an hour before the roast is done, place the potatoes around the roast and add the water to the pan. Replace the foil. The potatoes will steam with the meat. Open the parchment wrap the last 30 minutes of cooking and remove the foil to brown the roast. Don't take the wrappings off yet. When the potatoes are done, take the wrap off carefully, over the roasting pan, being careful not to waste any of the precious juices for the sauce. The meat will fall into bite-size pieces.

Remove the roast and potatoes to a serving dish. Brush the potatoes lightly with butter or margarine and sprinkle with a little parsley if you like.

Ladle ¾ cup of the gravy into a cup and add the flour to make a thin paste. Return it to the roasting pan and heat until the gravy thickens, then add enough broth or water to make a gravy of the desired consistency. Taste for seasoning. Serve hot—you'll get applause!

Serves 4 to 6

❉ *Barbecued Pot Roast*

One 4½- to 5-pound chuck
   roast with bone
2 garlic cloves, halved

Salt and freshly ground black
   pepper to taste

MARINADE

1 teaspoon dry mustard
1 teaspoon salt
Freshly ground black pepper
1 tablespoon ketchup
2 tablespoons tomato sauce
¼ cup red wine
1 tablespoon vegetable oil
Generous ¼ teaspoon each of
   dried tarragon, chervil,
   oregano, and paprika

Generous ¼ teaspoon minced
   garlic
1 red chili pepper, seeded and
   minced
1 tablespoon minced onion
1 tablespoon brown sugar
1 tablespoon chili powder
½ teaspoon Tabasco Sauce
1 tablespoon Worcestershire
   sauce

Rinse the roast and pat dry. With a large fork, pierce the meat all over and rub it generously with the garlic cloves and salt and pepper. Place the roast on large pieces of parchment paper or 3 or 4 sheets of waxed paper.

Mix together all the ingredients for the marinade and pour it over the roast and into every crevice, coating it thoroughly. Let the roast stand a while before cooking if you have time. Wrap it completely with parchment paper, catching all the marinade. Place it in a baking pan, cover with foil, and bake in a preheated oven at 325° for about 2½ to 3 hours. Open the wrap during the last half hour of cooking to brown the meat, but don't take off the wrappings yet. Remove the paper carefully over the roasting pan, trying not to lose any of those great juices and sauce. The meat will fall into bite-size portions. Taste for seasoning.

Serve with crisp sourdough rolls that have been warmed or toasted. (Hollow out the extra bread before heating so you'll have plenty of room for your barbecue and sauce.) Serve with extra sauce on the side.

Serves 6 to 8

❧*A Party Pot Roast*

½ cup small mushrooms
2 teaspoons butter
¾ pound uncooked ham
3 cloves garlic, minced or
  pressed
One 5- or 6-pound pot roast of
  beef
Salt and pepper to taste
Flour, seasoned with salt,
  pepper, and paprika
¼ cup vegetable oil

1 medium-size onion, chopped
One 28-ounce can whole
  Italian tomatoes with their
  juice, chopped
1 bay leaf
¼ teaspoon dried thyme
½ to 1 cup white wine
½ cup chicken broth or water,
  as needed
One 5-ounce jar pimiento-
  stuffed olives

Sauté the mushrooms in the butter for about 5 minutes and set aside. Cut the ham into strips 1 inch long and ½ inch wide. Rub with the garlic.

Make 1-inch pockets in the pot roast by inserting and twisting a sharp pointed knife. Salt and pepper the pockets and insert the ham strips. Rub the roast well with salt and pepper and roll in the seasoned flour.

In a heavy roasting pan, brown the meat on all sides in hot oil. Add the onion, tomatoes, bay leaf, thyme, white wine, and more salt and pepper, if needed. Taste for seasoning. Cover and simmer until the meat is tender, about 2½ to 3 hours. If your liquid has cooked away, add an extra ½ cup white wine mixed with ½ cup chicken broth or water. During the last 5 minutes of cooking add the sautéed mushrooms and the olives to heat through.

Serve with boiled potatoes sprinkled with butter and parsley or with rice—a simple starch that will appreciate being a sopper for this tasty sauce. Add one crisp green vegetable to the meal and enjoy.

Serves 8 to 10

❧*Beef Teriyaki*

MARINADE
½ cup sake (rice wine)
½ cup soy sauce

½ cup chicken broth
½ teaspoon sesame oil

GLAZE

¼ *cup of Marinade*
2 *teaspoons sugar*

1 *teaspoon cornstarch mixed*
   with 1 tablespoon water

One 1-pound boneless steak,
   sliced about ⅛ inch thick

Warm the sake in a small saucepan and light with a match. Let it burn until the flame goes out. Add the soy sauce and then the chicken broth and sesame oil. When blended, remove from the heat and cool.

Remove all but ¼ cup of marinade from the saucepan. Add the sugar and cook over medium-high heat until the sauce comes to a boil. Add the cornstarch mixture and cook, stirring, over medium-high heat until the cornstarch is dissolved.

Place the beef in the marinade for approximately 45 minutes or more. Transfer to a preheated charcoal broiler or your oven broiler. Broil 2 inches from the heat for approximately 1 minute. Baste with the marinade. Brush the slices lightly with the glaze. Remove from the broiler and serve immediately.

Serves 4

❖ *Summer Steaks*

I'm not a big charcoal-broiler fan. It seems to scorch things and it drys them out—maybe I just never got the hang of it, but this recipe is great. It's a perfect summer outdoor grill dish, as is the Beef Teriyaki in the preceding recipe.

6 *small boneless sirloin steaks,*
   ½ inch thick
2 *unpeeled oranges, the more*
   tart the better, cut into
   wedges. (Try small tart
   grapefruit, peel and all, if
   you have them.)

2 *small cloves garlic, minced*
Salt to taste
Olive oil
Freshly ground black pepper to
   taste
Butter or margarine (optional)

Place the steaks between sheets of waxed paper and pound them thinner with the flat side of a mallet or cleaver. Rub the steaks with the rind, squeezing some juice over them. Lightly rub the steaks with the garlic and salt. Place them in a mixing bowl in layers, squeezing orange juice over each layer.

Marinate as long as you can, at least 2 hours.

Have your grill, charcoal broiler, or oven broiler extremely hot. Brush the steaks lightly with the olive oil. Sear on one side and then the other, but don't cook too long. Salt and pepper immediately (if you feel thin, put a small dollop of butter on each steak) and serve on very hot plates.

Serves 6

❖ *Beef and Broccoli*

1 tablespoon oyster sauce
2 teaspoons rice wine or sherry
1 teaspoon sugar
2 teaspoons cornstarch
½ pound boneless beef (I used sirloin), trimmed of fat and gristle and cut into thin strips
3 tablespoons peanut oil
2 slices fresh gingerroot

½ teaspoon salt
1 bunch broccoli, cut into flowerets, leaving a little of the stem on
¼ cup water
2 teaspoons dry sherry
1 teaspoon cornstarch mixed with 2 tablespoons water
2 teaspoons sesame oil

Mix together the oyster sauce, rice wine or sherry, ½ teaspoon of the sugar, and the cornstarch. Place the beef in a bowl and pour the mixture over it. Chill in the refrigerator until ready to use.

Heat a wok very hot, add 2 tablespoons of the peanut oil, and swirl it around. Add the ginger and salt, reduce the heat, add the broccoli, and stir-fry for 1 minute to coat with oil. Don't let it burn. When the broccoli is bright green and getting tender, add the water, turn the heat to high, cover, and cook for 1 or 2 minutes longer, or until the broccoli is tender but still crunchy. When the liquid has evaporated, remove the broccoli to a plate.

Heat the wok again. Add the remaining tablespoon of peanut oil, then the beef, and cook until separated and brown. To crisp, flatten it against the sides of the wok. Don't stir too much; stirring makes it a little watery.

In a small bowl combine the sherry, the remaining ½ teaspoon sugar, and the cornstarch mixed with water. Return the broccoli to the wok and, when it is thoroughly reheated, add the sherry mixture and cook, stirring, until the sauce thickens and the broccoli is well coated. Remove to a platter and sprinkle the sesame oil over all.

Serves 4 as a side dish, 2 as your one and only

✾ *Gloria's Carne Adobado*

Gloria, my cooking friend from Mexico, threw this one together one day for lunch. I made her cook it again so I could take it down step by step for all of us. Incidentally, her favorite dish of all the ones she tasted in this book is the Fried Noodles with Mixed Meat and Vegetables (page 223), a Chinese dish.

2 pounds thin sirloin steak
1 small tart grapefruit
Salt and pepper to taste
1 teaspoon chopped garlic
2 tablespoons olive oil
Sauce (see below)
Rice (see below)
Sliced onions

Place the steaks between sheets of waxed paper and pound until about ½ inch thick. Transfer the steaks to a baking dish, squeeze the grapefruit juice over them, and rub them with the rind. Sprinkle with salt and pepper and rub with the chopped garlic. Marinate as long as you can.

Remove from the marinade and cut into 1-inch cubes. Brown the beef cubes in the olive oil and pour the sauce over all. Simmer 10 to 15 minutes, until the sauce is just slightly thickened. Serve over the rice, topped with sliced onions.

SAUCE

4 sweet dark pasillo chilies
2 California chilies
4 squares German sweet chocolate
¼ teaspoon dried oregano
12 peppercorns
One 1-inch cinnamon stick
1 whole clove
1 tablespoon sugar
1 clove garlic
2 tablespoons white vinegar
⅔ cup chicken broth

Wash the chilies well, cut off the stems, and remove the seeds. Place them in a saucepan with water to cover and cook for about 20 minutes, or until tender. Pour off all but ½ cup water. Place the chilies and ½ cup cooking water in a blender. Add the chocolate, oregano, peppercorns, cinnamon stick, clove, sugar, garlic, vinegar, and ⅓ cup of the chicken broth. Blend well and pour over the meat. Rinse the blender with the remaining ⅓ cup chicken broth and add to the sauce.

RICE

2 cups raw rice
2 tablespoons vegetable oil, or
    enough to coat bottom of the
    saucepan
Celery strips
Green, red, and yellow pepper
    strips (if you have them)

1 tablespoon chopped fresh
    parsley
4 cups hot salted water
1 chicken or beef bouillon
    cube

Brown the rice lightly in the oil. Add the celery, peppers, and parsley. Add the bouillon cube to the hot water and pour over the rice. Let the water come to a boil, cover, and cook over very low heat, approximately 20 to 30 minutes, or until the liquid is absorbed.

Serves 6

✻ Lamb with Couscous

This has a lot of the textures and tastes I love—the garbanzo beans, the okra, and the couscous (which reminds me of grits and kasha and pasta combined). It's a great Middle Eastern stew that is a complete meal with a green salad and crusty bread or crisped pita bread.

2 tablespoons olive oil
1 pound lean shoulder of
    lamb, cut into bite-size
    pieces
Dash of Tabasco sauce
1/4 teaspoon cayenne pepper
Salt and black pepper to taste
1 teaspoon ground cumin
1/2 teaspoon ground allspice
1 cup chopped onions
2 stalks celery, chopped
2 carrots, finely chopped
1/2 green pepper, seeded and
    coarsely chopped

1 medium zucchini, sliced
One 15-ounce can Italian
    plum tomatoes with their
    juice, broken into small
    pieces
5 okra, sliced (optional)
1 potato, coarsely chopped
1/2 cup canned garbanzo beans,
    drained and rinsed
2 cups water or chicken broth
1/2 cup each water and chicken
    broth, mixed
1 cup raw couscous or kasha

Heat the oil in the bottom of a large saucepan or Dutch oven. Sprinkle the meat with the Tabasco, and seasonings. Brown in the hot oil. Add the vegetables, potato, and garbanzo beans. Add the water or broth. Cook, uncovered, until the mixture comes to a boil. Taste for seasoning; you may need more. Reduce the heat and cook covered for 45 minutes to an hour, or until the meat is very tender and the vegetables are cooked through.

While the lamb is cooking, bring the mixed cup of water and chicken broth to a boil. Add the couscous, reduce the heat, and cook, covered, for 7 minutes, or cook kasha according to package directions. Keep covered until ready to use.

Place the cooked couscous or kasha in the bottom of a serving bowl and pour the lamb mixture over it. Serve.

Serves 4 to 6

❀ *Middle Eastern Lamb Stew with Prunes*

This can be done ahead in the morning and reheated. It should be served on a warm plate with Raisin-Saffron Rice (page 240). Don't worry about pitting the prunes—you can warn your guests.

2 pounds very lean lamb stew meat	One 2-inch cinnamon stick
2 tablespoons butter or margarine	1 teaspoon salt
	⅛ teaspoon black pepper
1 medium onion, chopped	1 whole red dried chili
1½ tablespoons flour	1 cup large prunes
2 cups water	2 tablespoons dry sherry
¼ teaspoon powdered saffron	2 teaspoons grated orange peel
	2 teaspoons sugar

Cut the meat into 1½-inch cubes and brown in the butter or margarine. Remove the meat with a slotted spoon, add the onion to the drippings, and cook for about 4 to 5 minutes, until tender, but not browned. Stir in the flour and cook, stirring, until well browned.

Add the meat and the water and bring to a boil, stirring until smooth. Stir in the saffron, cinnamon, salt, pepper, and dried chili. Cover, reduce the heat, and simmer for 1½ hours, adding water if the sauce becomes too thick.

Meanwhile, cover the prunes with cold water and let them stand for 1 hour. Drain and add to the stew. Stir in the sherry, orange peel, and sugar. Heat thoroughly. Remove the cinnamon stick and chili before serving.

Serves 6

✤ *Lamb Shanks*

A clunky-sounding name for a succulent, juicy, irresistible dish. Serve with steamed or boiled potatoes, or the Scalloped Potatoes (page 227), rice, noodles, anything to use with that lovely gravy.

8 lamb shanks
2 cloves garlic, finely chopped
Salt and pepper to taste
Flour for dredging
4 tablespoons olive oil
4 cups water
Bouquet garni (3 sprigs rosemary, 2 sprigs marjoram, 2 sprigs mint, 3 sprigs parsley)
A few sprigs extra parsley for the broth
1½ cups finely chopped carrots
½ cup finely chopped scallions (white part only)

1½ cups freshly squeezed orange juice; cut pulp and skin into pieces
3 tablespoons lemon juice
1½ cups chicken or lamb broth
¼ cup orange liqueur
Scant 2 tablespoons brown sugar
1 tablespoon soy sauce
1 tablespoon cornstarch
Orange wedges, for garnish
Parsley sprigs, for garnish

Trim the lamb shanks of their skin. Rub with the garlic and generously with the salt and pepper. Let them stand until ready to brown, a couple of hours if you have the time. Dredge the lamb shanks in the flour. Heat the oil in a heavy pot large enough to hold all the shanks. Brown the shanks in the oil. (Don't let them burn.) Add the water, bouquet garni, and parsley sprigs. Cover and cook over low heat for 1 hour or more, or until the meat is tender. Remove the cover from time to time to let the water cook away a little. Add the carrots and scallions during the last half hour of cooking.

When lamb shanks are done drain the liquid from the pot and use it for sauces at another time.

Mix together the orange juice, pulp and rinds, the lemon juice, broth, orange liqueur, brown sugar, and soy sauce. Add to the lamb and vegetables. Simmer over low heat for 10 to 15 minutes, or until the sauce is reduced by half and the lamb shanks are very tender. During the last 5 minutes of cooking, mix the tablespoon cornstarch with 2 tablespoons of sauce from the pot, add to the sauce, and continue cooking to thicken a bit.

Garnish the platter with the orange wedges and parsley.

Serves 8

✤ A Very Special Leg of Lamb

This is probably the best leg of lamb I've tasted. Its flavors blend all the way through the meat and it just falls off the bone—it's so tender. Cooking with heavy-duty paper is great for the "heavier" cuts of meat— for instance, the Barbecued Pot Roast (page 91) and the Juicy Tender Pot Roast (page 89).

One 4¹/₂- to 5-pound leg
  of lamb
¹/₂ lemon
Salt and freshly ground black
  pepper
¹/₂ teaspoon dry mustard
4 cloves garlic, slivered
Rosemary leaves

¹/₂ cup butter melted, plus 2
  tablespoons butter, softened
Juice of ¹/₂ lemon
¹/₄ cup white wine
¹/₂ teaspoon dried oregano
12 small potatoes, unpeeled, or
  6 medium potatoes, peeled
  and quartered

Rinse the lamb and pat dry. Rub the meat with the cut side of the lemon. Make incisions in several places in the lamb. Combine a teaspoon of salt, 1 teaspoon of pepper, and the dry mustard, and rub the mixture over the lamb and into the incisions. Insert the garlic slivers and rosemary leaves into each incision. Mix the melted butter with most of the lemon juice and the white wine and pour over the lamb. Sprinkle lightly with the pepper and oregano. Let stand until ready to cook, a couple of hours if possible.

Wrap the lamb airtight in large pieces of parchment paper or 3 or 4 sheets of waxed paper. Place in a baking pan, cover the pan with foil, and seal airtight. Bake in a preheated 325° oven for 3 hours. About 45 minutes to an hour before the meat is done, place the potatoes around the outside of the parchment. Sprinkle with the remaining lemon juice, salt, and pepper and brush with the softened butter. Add a small amount of water to the bottom of the pan to help cook the potatoes, and replace the foil.

During the last half hour of cooking, unwrap the lamb and allow it to brown. When the lamb is done, the meat will separate easily from the bone. Cut the meat into portions and serve with the potatoes and juices from the pan.

Serves 6

✽*Lamb with Kasha, Spinach, and Mushrooms*

Kasha is a special treat. It's a natural grain, easy to cook, that bites back a little—not like noodles, or rice, or potatoes. Perfect as a gravy or sauce sopper, you don't waste a teaspoonful. It's perfect, too, with this lamb—with the Juicy Tender Pot Roast (page 89) or A Party Pot Roast (page 92). If you prefer this nutty flavored grain all by itself, cook it according to the directions on the package.

1 cup kasha
2 cups boiling chicken broth
1 tablespoon olive oil
½ cup finely chopped onion
1 clove garlic, minced
1 bunch fresh spinach, cleaned, stems removed, and coarsely chopped
4 mushrooms, coarsely chopped

2 tomatoes, peeled, seeded, and diced
¼ cup toasted pine nuts (pignolia)
1 cup diced cooked lamb
1 tablespoon fresh oregano leaves
Salt and pepper
¼ pound crumbled feta cheese

Rinse the kasha, drain well, and place in a large mixing bowl. Stir in the boiling broth to cover, place a towel over the bowl, and set aside for 30 minutes. Preheat the oven to 350°.

Heat the oil in a skillet, add the onion and garlic, and sauté for a few minutes, just until the onion softens. Stir in the spinach leaves and the mushrooms. Cook, stirring, until the spinach wilts and the mushrooms begin to soften.

To the kasha, add the spinach mixture, tomatoes, pine nuts, lamb, and oregano, tossing lightly to mix well. Season to taste with salt and pepper. Turn the mixture into an oven-proof casserole and bake for 20 minutes. Sprinkle with the feta cheese and bake for 10 minutes longer, or until heated through.

Serves 6 to 8

*If you have any lamb left over from the Very Special Leg of Lamb (unlikely), use it in this recipe. If not, use a small 1-pound lamb roast seasoned with salt and pepper and browned in vegetable oil and cooked, covered, in ¼ cup chicken broth with 1 small carrot, chopped; 1 stalk celery, chopped; 1 clove garlic, chopped; and 1 small onion, chopped, for 1 to 1½ hours.

❀ Baked Lamb Pies

DOUGH

About 2¾ cups lukewarm
    water (110°–115°)
2 envelopes active dry yeast
Pinch of sugar

3 cups flour
2 teaspoons salt
¼ cup olive oil

    Pour ¼ cup of the lukewarm water into a small bowl and sprinkle with the yeast and sugar. Let the mixture rest for 2 to 3 minutes, then stir to dissolve the yeast completely. Set the bowl in a warm, draft-free place for about 5 minutes, or until the mixture doubles in volume.

    In a deep mixing bowl, combine the flour and salt; make a well in the center and into it pour the yeast mixture, olive oil, and 2 cups of lukewarm water. Gently stir the center ingredients together with a large spoon, then slowly incorporate the flour and continue to beat until the ingredients are well combined. Add up to ½ cup additional lukewarm water, beating it in, a tablespoon or so at a time, using as much as is necessary to form a dough that can be gathered into a compact ball.

    Place the dough on a lightly floured surface and knead by pressing it down, pushing it forward several times with the heel of your hand, and folding it back on itself. Repeat for about 10 minutes, or until the dough is smooth and elastic. Sprinkle from time to time with a little flour to prevent it from sticking to the board.

    Shape the dough into a ball and place it in a lightly oiled bowl. Drape loosely with a kitchen towel and set aside in a warm, draft-free place for 45 minutes to 1 hour, or until the dough doubles in bulk.

    Punch down the dough and divide it into 16 equal pieces. Roll each piece into a ball about 1½ inches in diameter, cover the balls with a towel, and let them rest for 30 minutes, during which time you can prepare the filling.

FILLING

2 large onions, finely chopped
1 tablespoon plus 2 teaspoons
    salt
1 tablespoon olive oil
½ cup pine nuts (pignolia)
2 pounds lean boneless lamb
    shoulder, coarsely ground
2 medium-size fresh, ripe
    tomatoes, peeled, seeded, and
    finely chopped

½ cup finely chopped green
    pepper
½ cup finely chopped parsley
    (preferably flat-leaf Italian)
½ cup fresh lemon juice
¼ cup red wine vinegar
1 tablespoon tomato paste
1 teaspoon cayenne pepper
1 teaspoon ground allspice
Freshly ground black pepper

Place the onions in a deep bowl and sprinkle with the 1 tablespoon salt, coating them evenly. Set aside for at least 30 minutes, then wrap the onions in a kitchen towel, squeeze them dry, and return them to the bowl.

In a small skillet or saucepan, heat 1 tablespoon of the oil until a light haze forms. Add the pine nuts, stirring constantly until they are lightly browned. Add the onions along with the lamb and all the remaining filling ingredients, including a liberal grinding of black pepper. Remove from the heat and cool. Knead the mixture vigorously with both hands, then beat with a wooden spoon until smooth and fluffy. Taste for seasoning.

ASSEMBLY

3 tablespoons olive oil for coating pans

Plain low-fat yogurt (optional)

Preheat the oven to 500°. With a pastry brush, coat 3 large baking sheets or jelly-roll pans with the 3 tablespoons oil.

On a lightly floured surface, roll each dough ball into a round about 4 inches in diameter and no more than ⅛ inch thick. To make open-faced pies, spoon about ½ cup of lamb filling onto the center of each round. Then, with a spatula or the back of a spoon, spread the filling to about ½ inch of the edge. To make closed pies, spoon about ½ cup of filling on the center of each round. Pull up the edges from 3 equally distant points to make a roughly triangular-shape pie. Pinch the dough securely together at the top.

With a metal spatula, arrange the pies on the baking sheets. Bake in the lower third of the oven for 30 minutes, or until the pastry is lightly browned. Serve hot, or at room temperature, accompanied, if you like, with yogurt.

Makes 16 pies

❈ *Diced Pork with Walnuts*

One tip about Chinese cooking: Have all your ingredients handy in an array of small dishes or bowls placed in the order in which they're used in the recipe. This is one form of cooking that can have much preparation ahead and instant results—the wok won't wait.

Chinese cooking is economical to our way of thinking because it uses small amounts of ingredients for large amounts of quality and exotic flavor.

This dish is beautiful to look at and to taste and is really simple to cook. Serve with Chinese or Japanese Rice (page 240), or with Pork Fried Rice (page 239).

*½ pound lean pork, cut into
   ½-inch dice
½ teaspoon baking soda
4 teaspoons cornstarch
1 tablespoon water
⅔ cup walnut halves
½ teaspoon salt
1 tablespoon chicken broth
Dash of white pepper*

*1 cup peanut oil for deep-
   frying
4 or 5 thin slices carrot
4 or 5 thin slices fresh
   gingerroot
2 scallions, cut into 1½-inch
   lengths (white part plus ½ of
   green part)*

Mix the diced pork with the baking soda, 2 teaspoons of the cornstarch, and the water.

Boil the walnuts until they soften, 5 to 6 minutes. Drain the walnuts and let them set until partially dry.

Mix together the salt, chicken broth, the remaining 2 teaspoons of cornstarch, and the white pepper. Set aside.

Heat a wok, add the oil, and when the oil is very hot reduce the heat slightly and deep-fry the walnuts until they turn a deeper brown, about 2 minutes. Remove the walnuts, drain, and set them aside. Reheat the oil, add the pork, and cook on moderate heat for 1½ minutes, until cooked through. Remove and drain. Discard most of the oil. Reheat the wok and stir-fry the carrot, ginger, and scallions for 1 minute, then add the pork. Pour in the chicken broth mixture and return the walnuts to the wok. Stir-fry for 1 minute longer.

Serves 4 with other Chinese dishes, 2 as a main course

❋ Roast Loin of Pork with Thyme

*One 4- to 5-pound boneless
   pork loin, securely tied
4 tablespoons coarsely chopped
   fresh thyme or 1 tablespoon
   dried
4 tablespoons butter or
   margarine and light
   vegetable oil mixed in equal
   proportions*

*1½ teaspoons salt
Freshly ground black or white
   pepper
2¾ cups milk
¼ cup warm chicken broth*

Make slits in the pork loin with a sharp knife. Insert the chopped thyme in the slits. Brown the meat on all sides in a large Dutch oven in the butter and oil. Add the salt, pepper, and milk. Bring to a boil, reduce the heat, and cover loosely. Cook for approximately 30 minutes per pound, about 2½ to 3 hours, or until the meat is tender. Baste frequently. Lift out the meat and allow it to cool for 5 minutes or so. Remove the string and slice medium-thick. Arrange the slices on a warm platter.

Your Dutch oven will have cooled a bit by now, so skim off as much of the fat as you can, leaving the rest of the goodies. Add the warm chicken broth, bring to a boil, and reduce, scraping and loosening all the particles in the Dutch oven. Taste for seasoning. Add salt and pepper if necessary. Spoon the sauce over the sliced pork and serve immediately.

Serves 8

❖ *Chinese Roast Pork*

This is the real thing—that meltingly tender first course you've had in Chinese restaurants. I really like it cooked in the oven as directed, but you can do it over charcoal if you're careful about your fire. I cook an extra pound—it keeps well and can be used in a number of delicious Chinese dishes—for instance the Pork Fried Rice (page 239).

MARINADE
4 cloves garlic, minced

3 tablespoons dark soy sauce

2 tablespoons hoisin sauce

2 tablespoons good sherry

2 tablespoons honey

½ teaspoon five-spice powder

3 pounds lean boneless pork
loin, cut into strips about
1½ inches wide by 2 inches
long, and trimmed of fat

In a baking dish, mix together the marinade ingredients. Roll the pork strips in the marinade to coat well. Cover with foil or plastic wrap and marinate in the refrigerator for 2 to 3 hours, turning the pork from time to time.

Use a roasting pan deep enough so that you can rig a rack over 2 inches of water without its touching the water. Lay the pork strips carefully on the rack, not overlapping or touching. Bake for 15 minutes in a preheated 450° oven, turning once at this temperature. Reduce the heat to 350° and roast, basting frequently with the remaining marinade, until brown and beautiful, about 45 minutes to an hour.

This will keep very well at room temperature until ready to serve for the evening and can be used in many Chinese dishes. Serve it with a dipping sauce of chili sauce, or ketchup mixed with a dab of hot mustard (dry mustard mixed with a little water to make a paste).

Serves 4 to 6

✤ *Braised Pork with Mixed Fruit*

As you may have gathered, everybody—but everybody in my house-hold—cooks. They love it, they're really good at it. For instance one day when I'd been toiling over a hot unfriendly golf course, I came home to the most beautiful aroma wafting from the kitchen. Long, tall Shirley (Shirley Hunt) had tried this braised pork with prunes, apricots, apples, and spices. Just a little something for an afternoon snack. Never mind what happened to the highly touted raw vegetables we'd sworn to chomp on between meals—it was testing time for this book and we were all kind of on a roll. Try this one and the Middle Eastern Lamb Stew with Prunes (page 97). We did that one as a sure threat to the waist, hips, et cetera one evening. You take your choice, they're both wonderful.

⅓ cup flour
1 teaspoon salt
¼ teaspoon black pepper
½ teaspoon ground ginger
½ teaspoon ground allspice
1½ pounds pork shoulder, cut into 1-inch cubes
2 to 3 tablespoons vegetable oil
1 large onion, coarsely chopped

2 cloves garlic, minced
2 cups beef broth
1 cup chicken broth
1 teaspoon minced fresh gingerroot
¾ teaspoon dried tarragon
¾ cup dried apricot halves
½ cup dried pitted prunes
1 large tart apple, peeled, cored, and sliced

In a plastic bag, combine the flour, salt, pepper, ground ginger, and allspice. Add the pork cubes in small batches and shake to coat.

In a Dutch oven or a large heavy saucepan, heat the oil over medium-high heat. Brown the pork cubes on all sides, a third at a time. As they are browned, remove with a slotted spoon to a bowl. Pour off all but 1 tablespoon of fat. Add the onion and garlic and sauté until tender, about 5 minutes. Return the pork to the Dutch oven. Add the beef broth, chicken broth, gingerroot, and tarragon. Cover and simmer for 45 minutes. Taste for seasoning. Add the apricots and prunes and simmer for 10 minutes. Add the apple slices and simmer for 10 minutes longer. Serve over hot cooked rice.

Serves 4 to 6

✽ *Veal Stew*

2 tablespoons finely chopped shallots or onion
3 tablespoons vegetable oil
2 tablespoons butter or margarine
1½ pounds boneless veal stew meat, cut into 1½-inch cubes
Flour, seasoned with salt and freshly ground pepper
2 teaspoons salt

About 6 grindings pepper
1 cup peeled and coarsely chopped fresh tomatoes with their juice
2 pounds fresh peas (unshelled weight) or one 10-ounce package frozen small peas, thawed

In a heavy casserole sauté the shallots or onion in the oil and butter over medium heat until golden. Dredge the veal in the seasoned oil and shake off the excess. Add the meat to the casserole and brown well on all sides. If all the meat won't fit into the casserole at one time, you can brown a few pieces at a time, but dip them in the flour only when you are ready to put them in the casserole or the flour coating will get soggy and the meat won't brown properly.

When all the meat is browned, return it to the casserole, add the salt, pepper, and the tomatoes with their juice. When the tomatoes begin to boil, cover and reduce the heat so the tomatoes are barely simmering. Cook until the veal is very tender when pricked with a fork, an hour to 1½ hours. If you are using fresh peas, they should be added about 15 minutes before the stew is done; thawed frozen peas go in during the last 5 minutes. Serve hot with the Italian Rice (page 235).

Serves 4 to 6

❉ Thin Veal with Rosemary

8 thin slices of veal scaloppini
¼ cup fine dry bread crumbs
1 tablespoon minced fresh
  rosemary leaves
3 tablespoons extra-virgin
  olive oil
1 onion, minced
1 clove garlic, minced
1 stalk celery, diced
1 carrot, peeled and diced
¾ cup white wine

¼ cup chicken broth or as
  needed (optional)
1 pound tomatoes, peeled,
  seeded, and coarsely chopped
2 tablespoons chopped fresh
  basil
1 teaspoon salt
Freshly ground black pepper to
  taste
Red pepper flakes to taste
1 tomato, diced, for garnish

Place the veal on a flat surface and pound thin with the flat side of a mallet between 2 sheets of waxed paper.

Rinse and pat the veal dry. Mix the bread crumbs with the rosemary and coat the veal on both sides.

Heat 2 tablespoons of the olive oil in a large nonstick skillet. Add the veal and cook for 1 minute on each side. Set aside and keep warm.

Heat the remaining 1 tablespoon olive oil in a separate skillet. Add the onion, garlic, celery, and carrot. Cook for 20 minutes, until mushy and saucelike. Stir in the wine (if the mixture seems too dry add a little chicken broth as needed to keep it moist).

Add the chopped tomatoes and 1 tablespoon of the basil. Simmer over low heat, whisking until the sauce is reduced to a smooth puree, about 10 minutes. Add salt, pepper, and red pepper flakes.

Place the veal in the hot sauce to reheat. Transfer to a serving platter, top with some of the sauce, and sprinkle with the remaining fresh basil. Garnish with the diced tomato and serve the remaining sauce on the side.

Serves 4

❦ *Veal Scallopini with Cream, Calvados, and Apples*

When you're feeling blue or great and especially slender, give your-self and a treasured friend or two a treat.

3 medium-size tart green
  apples (I like Granny Smith)
Juice of 1½ lemons
12 veal scallopini, ⅜ inch
  thick (about 3½ to 4 inches
  in diameter)
1½ teaspoons salt
1 teaspoon freshly ground
  black pepper

½ cup flour
4 tablespoons sweet butter
2 tablespoons vegetable oil
½ pound prosciutto or Virginia
  ham, minced
⅓ cup Calvados or applejack
  liqueur
1½ cups heavy cream

Peel and core the apples, then cut into ⅛-inch cubes. Place the cubes in a bowl, add the lemon juice, and mix thoroughly so the apples are well coated. Set aside.

Sprinkle the veal with 1 teaspoon of salt and the pepper. Dredge them in the flour and shake off any excess.

Heat the butter and oil in a large heavy skillet. When hot, add the proscuitto or Virginia ham, crisp, and remove it with a slotted spoon and set aside to drain. Add the veal, a few pieces at a time, and sauté over medium heat until lightly browned on both sides, approximately 2 to 3 minutes on each side. When the veal is cooked, set it aside in a warm (180°) oven.

Add the apples with the lemon juice, and the Calvados or applejack to the pan. Deglaze the pan and cook over high heat for 3 to 4 minutes, stirring frequently, to reduce the sauce. Add the cream and continue cooking until the mixture has turned a rich ivory color. Reduce the heat and cook, stirring frequently, until the cream has reduced to about half and the sauce coats a spoon, almost 10 minutes. Add the prosciutto or Virginia ham. Taste for seasoning, you may need about ½ teaspoon salt.

Arrange the veal attractively on a heated platter and spoon the apples, ham, and sauce over all.

Serves 6

❀ Roast Loin of Veal à la Craig

*I love Craig Claiborne—but then who doesn't? I also love his cook-
ing—this is the perfect Roast Loin of Veal—à la Craig. I added the
rosemary and the marjoram.*

One 3- to 4-pound loin of veal
Salt and freshly ground pepper
    to taste
2 tablespoons butter or
    margarine
½ cup carrots, sliced crosswise
    ¼ inch thick (2 medium
    carrots)
½ cup chopped celery
½ cup chopped onion
1 clove garlic

1 cup coarsely chopped fresh or
    canned tomatoes
Bouquet garni (4 or 5 sprigs
    fresh parsley, 3 sprigs fresh
    thyme or ½ teaspoon dried,
    1 sprig fresh rosemary, 2
    sprigs fresh marjoram or ½
    teaspoon dried, 1 bay leaf)
Chicken or veal stock as
    needed

Preheat the oven to 425°. Sprinkle the veal with salt and pepper and
rub with the butter or margarine. Arrange the veal in a shallow roasting
pan, fat side up. Place the pan in the oven and bake for 30 minutes,
basting occasionally with whatever pan juices there are or a little extra
butter or margarine if the meat appears dry. Turn the meat fat side down
and scatter the carrot, celery, onion, and garlic around it. Bake for 15
minutes, basting occasionally. Turn the meat fat side up and scatter the
tomato around it. Add the bouquet garni. Reduce the heat to 400° and
bake for 15 minutes. Cover the meat with foil and bake for about 30
minutes longer. The total baking time is about 1½ hours.

Remove the roast to a warm platter. Discard the bouquet garni and
pour the vegetables and pan juices into a blender and puree; if the puree
appears too thick, add a little chicken or veal stock. Serve the sauce on
the side.

Serves 6 to 8

✣ *Braised Veal with Mushrooms and Red Wine*

One 3-pound boneless breast of veal	*2 sprigs fresh tarragon*
Salt and freshly ground black pepper to taste	*1 sprig fresh rosemary*
	6 sprigs fresh parsley
Flour for dredging	*¾ cup red wine*
2 tablespoons butter	*¾ cup chicken broth*
1 tablespoon olive oil	*1 whole carrot*
2 large shallots, thinly sliced	*½ onion*
8 large mushrooms, thinly sliced	*1½ cloves garlic*
	1 tablespoon plain nonfat yogurt (optional)

Wash and pat dry the veal breast. Season generously with salt and pepper and let the veal sit for a couple of hours if you have time. Dredge in flour and shake off the excess.

In a large Dutch oven with a good-fitting lid, heat the butter and oil. Sauté the shallots for 2 to 3 minutes, or until just soft. Remove and set aside. Add the mushrooms and sauté until just soft. Remove and set aside. Place the veal in the pan and brown on both sides over high heat, turning as necessary. This should take 5 to 6 minutes. (It's pretty if it's browned but not absolutely necessary for flavor to have it dark golden. Just try to brown it enough to seal in the juices.)

Place the fresh tarragon, rosemary, and 3 sprigs of the parsley on top of the breast. Add half the red wine and half the broth to the Dutch oven. Let the liquid come to a full boil, reduce the heat, and cover tightly. Baste from time to time, adding more wine and broth as necessary. After braising for about 35 minutes, add the whole carrot, the onion, garlic and the remaining 3 sprigs of parsley. Continue cooking for 1 hour more, or until the breast is fork tender. Remove the veal breast to a warmed platter and set aside. Remove the whole carrot, the onion, garlic, and discard. To the pan in which the meat was cooked add the shallots and mushrooms, reserving some mushrooms for garnish, to the liquid remaining in the Dutch oven and warm through. Add the yogurt and blend well.

Slice the meat, transfer it to a serving platter, and layer the reserved mushrooms over the top. Serve the sauce on the side.

Serves 6

✽A Layered Meat Loaf

This is a new look for an old favorite. It's pretty sliced warm and just as pretty and delicious sliced cold the next day.

1 pound lean ground beef chuck	Salt and freshly ground pepper to taste
¼ pound ground lean pork	6 mushrooms, thinly sliced
¼ pound ground lean lamb	2 tomatoes, thinly sliced
1 egg	6 slices prosciutto ham
1 tablespoon Dijon mustard	½ cup coarsely grated mozzarella cheese
1 teaspoon chili sauce	
¼ cup bread crumbs	1 tablespoon capers, drained
1 small onion, grated	2 to 3 tablespoons margarine
½ cup chicken broth	1 teaspoon cornstarch

Delicately and lightly mix together the beef, pork, lamb, egg, mustard, chili sauce, bread crumbs, onion, broth, and salt and pepper. Place one fourth of the meat mixture in the bottom of a loaf pan. Place half the sliced mushrooms down the center of the layer and surround with half the sliced tomatoes; sprinkle with salt and pepper. Cover with another fourth of the meat mixture, cover with a third of the prosciutto, sprinkle generously with the grated mozzarella, and cover with another third of the prosciutto. Add another fourth of the meat mixture and place the remaining sliced tomatoes down the center and the remaining sliced mushrooms down the sides; cover with the remaining prosciutto. Add the last layer of the meat mixture and place the capers down the center of the layer. Dot with the margarine, cover with foil, and bake in a preheated 350° oven for 1 hour. Remove the foil during the last 15 minutes of cooking.

Remove the meat loaf from the oven and let it sit for a minute or two. Pour off some of those lovely pan juices into a bowl. Turn the meat loaf out onto a warm platter, then carefully turn it right (brown) side up.

Mix the cornstarch with 2 tablespoons of hot pan juices, add this to the remaining juice, and place in a saucepan. Bring to a boil and simmer until the sauce thickens a little. Pour over the meat loaf and serve.

Serves 6

✽ *Beef-and-Pork-Filled Corn-Husk Tamales*

What can you say about tamales that hasn't already been said over and over? These are particularly good. Gloria Estrada makes them from scratch. It takes a little time, of course, but what wonderful, worthwhile thing doesn't. The masa can be purchased at specialty shops carrying the products of Mexico. Out of fresh-corn season they might even carry the corn husks for wrapping—ours do.

6 large ears of corn in husks
¼ pound lean pork
½ pound lean beef chuck
1 teaspoon ground cumin
1 teaspoon chili powder
½ teaspoon ground coriander
½ teaspoon salt
Dash of cayenne pepper
Black pepper to taste
1 fresh serrano chili, seeded and chopped

½ medium sweet red pepper, seeded and chopped
½ medium green pepper, seeded and chopped
5 scallions, chopped (part of the green portion left on)
2 tablespoons coarsely chopped fresh cilantro (coriander)
½ cup instant masa mix
Fresh Chili Salsa (see below)

Discard the outer layer of husk from each ear of corn. Peel the remaining leaves back, leaving them attached to the bottom of the cob. Snap off the ear of corn, leaving the bottom of the cob and the husks intact. Soak the husks in cold water. Clean the silk from the corn. Slice the corn kernels off the cobs. Transfer the kernels to a food processor and coarsely grind, using off and on turns; do not puree. Remove the corn from the processor and set aside.

Place the pork and beef in the food processor and coarsely grind, using off and on turns; do not puree. Place the meat in a skillet and fry until the fat is rendered. Add the seasonings, the chili, red and green peppers, the scallions, and the cilantro and cook until tender, stirring frequently, about 10 minutes. Add the corn kernels and sauté for 2 minutes. Gradually stir the instant masa mix into the meat filling, forming a thick paste.

Drain the husks and pat dry. Spoon one sixth of the filling into the center of each husk. Fold in the ends and sides and tie with string. Prepare a gas barbecue by turning the burner to high, or have your charcoal grill very hot. Arrange the tamales on the edge of the grill. Cook until the filling is almost set, 45 to 60 minutes, turning and spraying them with water occasionally. Serve immediately with the salsa.

Serves 6

FRESH CHILI SALSA

2 cups chopped tomatoes

8 scallions, chopped

6 fresh green Anaheim chilies, roasted, peeled, seeded, and chopped

2 fresh poblano chilies, roasted, peeled, seeded, and chopped

2 fresh California chilies, roasted, peeled, seeded, and chopped*

½ cup fresh green peas

¼ cup chopped cilantro (coriander)

2 tablespoons red wine vinegar

½ teaspoon salt

½ teaspoon ground cumin

2 cloves garlic, minced

Combine all the ingredients in a bowl. Cover and refrigerate.

Makes about 4 cups

*Place the chilies under the broiler, turning occasionally, until blistered and blackened. Remove from the oven and place in a paper or plastic bag for about 5 minutes. The skins will slip off easily.

Poultry

There are more ways to cook the friendly fowl than there are fast or (slow) food joints to serve it. It's a staple part of diets all over the world, and with reason. It's economical and there are ways to stretch it for extra servings if you have to. It can be boiled, baked, steamed, fried, sautéed, or stuffed, all with great flavor and success. There are many suggestions here—simple ones from Poached Chicken Breasts on Spinach (page 124) to the complex and festive Gloria's Celebration Chicken Mole (page 132), and you're just looking at the top of it too. Meaning, you should have seen the ones I almost wept at having to leave out—I urge you to try them all.

❇ Broiled Chicken Marinated in Lemon, Pepper, and Olive Oil

Almost everybody has a great broiled or barbecued chicken recipe. Here's mine. I think what bothers me most about grilled or broiled chicken is that while the legs and outer skin are beautifully moist and flavored, the breast meat is sometimes dry and practically tasteless. This one is moist and wonderfully flavored all the way through. It's the little extra marinating time that does it.

One 2-pound broiling chicken, quartered
4 tablespoons lemon juice
1 tablespoon crushed peppercorns

3 tablespoons olive oil
2 teaspoons salt
Pinch of crushed black pepper

Preheat the broiler to its maximum setting at least 15 minutes ahead of time. Pound both sides of the chicken quarters with a mallet or the side of a meat cleaver to flatten them. Place the chicken in a deep dish, pour the lemon juice over it, then add the peppercorns and olive oil. Cover the dish and marinate the chicken for at least 2 hours, basting from time to time with the marinade.

When the grill or broiler is heated, remove the chicken from the marinade, sprinkle it with the salt, and place it, skin side down, on the grill or broiler pan. The chicken should be about 5 inches from the heat. Broil, basting with marinade, until the skin has turned light brown, then turn it over and broil skin side up. Continue to baste and, after about 10 minutes, turn the chickens again and cook briefly on each side, until the thigh is tender at the pricking of a fork. The total cooking time should be about 35 minutes. If the marinade should run out before the chicken is done, baste it with a teaspoon of olive oil from time to time. Season with a pinch of crushed pepper before serving.

Serves 4 (if 2 like white meat 2 like dark)

❦ Roast Chicken with Orange Juice and Spices

MARINADE

⅔ cup fresh orange juice
2 tablespoons olive oil
2 tablespoons fresh lemon juice
4 large cloves garlic, crushed
2 bay leaves, crushed
1 tablespoon grated orange zest

2 teaspoons sugar
¼ teaspoon ground cinnamon
⅛ teaspoon freshly ground pepper
⅛ teaspoon dried pepper flakes

2 small frying chickens, cut up
Salt to taste
8 boiling potatoes, skins on, cut into 2-inch slices

2 tablespoons olive oil
4 fresh sage leaves, finely chopped

Combine the marinade ingredients in a large shallow baking dish. Place the chicken pieces in the marinade, turning to coat them thoroughly. Cover and refrigerate for 3 hours or so.

Place a rack in the center of the oven. Preheat the oven to 350°. Line a large shallow baking pan with foil. Place a rack on top of the foil. Drain the chicken, reserving the marinade, and season well with salt. Arrange the chicken, skin side up, on the rack in the pan. Baste with the marinade.

Rub the potatoes with the olive oil and sage. Sprinkle them with salt, and place around the chicken. Roast the chicken, basting very often with the rest of the marinade, for about 1½ to 2 hours. If the chicken is not brown enough to suit your eye, remove the potatoes to a warm serving platter and put the chicken under the broiler for a few moments, until golden brown.

Serves 6

✤ Roast Chicken with Rice and Pine-Nut Stuffing

*1 cup raw long- or medium-
  grain white rice*
4 tablespoons butter, 2 melted
½ cup finely chopped onions
1 clove garlic, finely chopped
*2 teaspoons chopped fresh
  mint*
*1 teaspoon chopped green
  pepper*
*1 teaspoon finely chopped
  carrot*

*2 tablespoons pine nuts
  (pignolia)*
2 cups water
*1 tablespoon dried currants or
  raisins*
2 teaspoons salt
Freshly ground black pepper
One 3- to 3½-pound chicken
*2 tablespoons plain low-fat
  yogurt*

Place the rice in a sieve or colander and wash under hot running water until the water runs clear. Drain and set aside. In a heavy 3- to 4-quart saucepan, melt 2 tablespoons of the butter over moderate heat. When the foam begins to subside, add the onions, garlic, 1 teaspoon chopped mint, green pepper, and carrot, and, stirring frequently, cook for 5 minutes, or until the onions are soft and transparent but not brown. Add the pine nuts and cook for 3 minutes. When the pine nuts are a delicate brown, stir in the rice and continue cooking until the grains glisten with butter. Add the water, currants or raisins, 1 teaspoon of the salt, and a few grindings of pepper. Bring to a boil, reduce the heat to low, cover, and simmer for 25 to 30 minutes, until the rice has absorbed all the liquid in the pan. Remove from the heat and stir in the 2 table-spoons of melted butter with a fork.

Preheat the oven to 400°. Pat the chicken thoroughly dry inside and out with paper towels, and spoon about 1 cup of the rice mixture into the cavity. Set the remaining rice aside. Lace the opening closed with skewers or by sewing it with a large needle and heavy white thread. Fasten the neck skin to the back with a skewer and truss the bird securely.

Combine the yogurt and remaining 1 teaspoon of chopped mint with the remaining 1 teaspoon of salt and a few grindings of pepper and brush about half the mixture over the chicken. Place the chicken, breast side up, on a rack in a shallow roasting pan. Roast in the middle of the oven for 15 minutes, then reduce the heat to 350°. Baste the chicken with the remaining yogurt mixture and roast for 1 hour more. To test the chicken for doneness, pierce the thigh with the point of a small, sharp knife. The juice that runs out should be pale yellow; if it is tinged with pink, roast the chicken for another 5 to 10 minutes.

Transfer the chicken to a heated platter, remove the trussing strings, and let the chicken rest for 5 minutes or so for easier carving. Fluff the reserved rice mixture with a fork, warm it over low heat, and serve it around the chicken.

Serves 4

❧ *Luscious Roast Chicken*

This is a whole meal and one of our most dependable standbys. When I'm coming home from a trip or a long workday, we have this succulent roast chicken. It makes up for traveling, jet lag, tough taping sessions, and—almost—a bad day on the golf course. Be sure to ask company for this one. Better still—plan on chicken sandwiches, chicken salad, chicken on corn bread, et cetera.

1 large (4 to 5 pounds) roasting chicken
Salt and pepper to taste
3 stalks celery (leaves and all)
1 green pepper, seeded and cut into chunks
3 scallions, cut into large pieces (white and green parts)

1 medium-size onion, cut into chunks
4 fresh basil leaves
3 parsley sprigs, left whole
1 each green and sweet red pepper, seeded and cut into wedges
3 medium potatoes, cut into large wedges

2 tomatoes, cut into large
  wedges
1 carrot, sliced
1 zucchini, sliced
Whatever compatible
  vegetables you have on hand

4 sprigs parsley, coarsely
  chopped
2 tablespoons margarine,
  softened
Juice of 1 lemon

Season the cavity of the chicken with salt and pepper. Stuff it with the celery stalks and leaves, green pepper chunks, scallions, onion, basil leaves, and parsley sprigs.

Place the chicken in a large roasting pan and surround it with the cut-up vegetables and chopped parsley. Rub the chicken with margarine, sprinkle with salt and pepper, and squeeze lemon juice over all. Cover and bake in a preheated 400° oven for 30 minutes. Uncover and cook another 1 to 1½ hours, depending on the size of the chicken. It is done when juices from the thigh run clear.

Serves 6

❉ Chicken Breasts with Parmesan Cheese

There are products on the market now that are perfect for this dish, thin filets of chicken breast, about four to a package. If you use these "time-savers," bake them only about fifteen minutes—you don't want to overcook them.

8 boneless and skinless chicken
  breast halves
Salt and pepper to taste
¾ cup freshly grated Parmesan
  cheese
½ cup dry bread crumbs
½ cup flour
1 tablespoon finely chopped
  fresh thyme

1 tablespoon finely chopped
  fresh tarragon
1½ tablespoons clarified butter
  (see page 122)
1½ tablespoons olive oil
½ cup white wine or
  champagne
½ cup chicken broth

Season the chicken breasts well with salt and pepper. Mix together ½ cup of the Parmesan cheese, the bread crumbs, flour, thyme, tarragon, and salt and pepper. Dredge the chicken breasts in the Parmesan mixture.

In a heavy skillet, heat the butter and oil and sauté the chicken over moderately high heat until golden brown on both sides. Transfer to a baking dish. To the same skillet in which the chicken was cooked, add the wine or champagne and the chicken broth, bring to a boil, and cook for 5 to 10 minutes, or until reduced by one third. Pour over the chicken and let sit for a few minutes. Sprinkle the chicken with the remaining ¼ cup of Parmesan cheese and bake uncovered in a preheated 325° oven for 20 minutes.

Serves 8

Greek Chicken

2 chicken breasts, halved and skinned
½ teaspoon ground cinnamon
Salt and pepper to taste
Lemon juice
3 tablespoons olive oil
1 onion, chopped
2 cloves garlic, minced
1 sweet red pepper, seeded and cut into strips
6 mushrooms, sliced
1 cup dry white wine
¼ cup chopped cilantro (coriander)
⅓ cup sliced black olives
1 lemon, sliced
1 teaspoon honey
Pinch of cayenne pepper

Wash and dry the chicken breasts. Season with the cinnamon, salt and pepper, and a little squeeze of lemon juice. In a large skillet, sauté the chicken breasts in 1½ tablespoons of the olive oil until golden, about 4 to 5 minutes on each side. Remove to a warm platter.

Add the remaining 1½ tablespoons of olive oil and sauté the onion, add the garlic and red pepper, then the mushrooms. Add the white wine and simmer for about 10 minutes. Add the cilantro, olives, lemon slices, and honey. Simmer until reduced by one half. Taste for seasoning. Add the cayenne. Keep the sauce warm and, just before serving, slip the chicken breasts back into the sauce to warm through. Serve with Steamed Sliced Potatoes (page 225).

Serves 2 to 4

Chicken Rolls with Chilies and Cheese

This is a pure California dish. Occasionally I have been accused of having an asbestos palate because I do love the flavor of our moderately hot chilies out here, so I use jalapeños for this dish—roasted, peeled, seeded, and then stuffed with mild Monterey Jack cheese. It makes a piquant and spicy dish. I suggest you prepare your chicken rolls with both hot and mild peppers and give your guests a choice. After you have seeded the peppers, there's not very much difference unless you come across one of those freaky chilies that happens to be really pungent. Place a large pimiento strip on the fold of the chicken to identify the hot ones. Believe me, your guests will know the difference.

6 small whole California chilies or any mild to semi-hot chilies (such as jalapeños), according to your taste, roasted, peeled, and seeded

12 ounces Monterey Jack cheese, cut into 6 finger-size pieces to fit inside the chilies

3 large whole boneless chicken breasts, halved

½ cup all-purpose flour for dredging

¼ cup clarified butter* mixed with olive oil

SAUCE

1 small whole California chili, roasted, peeled, seeded, and minced

1 small onion, minced

1 clove garlic, minced

2 cups dry white wine

8 tablespoons cold unsalted butter

1 teaspoon chili powder or to taste

1 teaspoon ground cumin

Salt and black pepper

Guacamole (optional)

Red Tomato Salsa (page 83)

Stuff the chilies with the Monterey Jack cheese. Place the chicken breasts between sheets of waxed paper and flatten with a mallet or the flat side of a cleaver. Lay a stuffed chili in the center of each chicken breast, roll and seal with toothpicks or tie with string, and dredge the roll lightly in the flour.

In 1 or 2 large heavy skillets, heat the butter over moderately high heat until it is hot but not smoking, and in it sauté the chicken for 2 minutes on each side until it is browned lightly.

In a baking dish large enough to hold the chicken in one layer, bake the chicken in a preheated 350° oven for 7 to 10 minutes, or until the cheese is just melted.

Make the sauce while the chicken is baking. In a heavy saucepan, combine the chili, onion, garlic, and wine. Bring the wine to a boil, and boil the mixture over moderately high heat until the wine is reduced to about 1 tablespoon. Reduce the heat to low and whisk in the butter, one piece at a time, lifting the pan from the heat occasionally to cool the mixture and adding each new piece before the previous one has melted completely. (The sauce should not become hot enough to liquefy; it should be the consistency of hollandaise.) Stir in the chili powder, cumin, and salt and black pepper to taste, until the sauce is well combined. Spoon the sauce over the chicken and serve the chicken—after removing toothpicks or string—with the guacamole and the salsa.

Serves 6

*Clarified butter is butter melted in a saucepan on top of the stove. When white froth appears on top, skim it off. This butter won't burn, and any that you have left over will keep for weeks in the refrigerator.

❋ *Chicken Breasts in Wine Sauce with Tomato and Tarragon*

Of course, the secret diet queen of the western world here used whole milk, or at the very most half and half instead of the heavy cream in this recipe. She also used the optional Cognac for zest!

6 thin, flattened boneless and
   skinless chicken breast
   halves
Salt and pepper to taste
½ cup flour
1 tablespoon olive oil
4 tablespoons butter or
   margarine
⅓ cup Cognac (optional)
1 tablespoon minced shallot or
   scallion

5 or 6 tomatoes, peeled, seeded,
   juiced, and cut into ½-inch
   pieces (about 1½ cups)
2 teaspoons dried tarragon
½ cup dry white wine or
   vermouth
½ cup chicken broth
½ cup heavy cream
2 to 3 tablespoons chopped
   fresh parsley

If the chicken breasts are too thick, pound them with a mallet between 2 sheets of waxed paper. Season the chicken breasts lightly with salt and pepper, dredge them in the flour, and shake off the excess.

Put the oil and 2 tablespoons of the butter or margarine in a large heavy skillet and heat until the butter foam begins to subside but is not browning. Add as many chicken breasts as will fit easily in one layer, and sauté for a minute or two on one side, until lightly browned. Turn and sauté on the other side only until the meat is light and springy when you press it with your finger. Remove the sautéed chicken breasts and continue with the rest, adding more oil and butter as necessary to keep the pan filmed. If you wish to flame them in Cognac, return the chicken breasts to the pan, pour in the Cognac, and, when bubbling, avert your face and ignite the liquid with a match; shake the pan for several seconds, then pour the contents into a side dish.

Add another tablespoon or so of the butter, stir in the minced shallot or scallion and cook for a moment, then add the tomatoes and tarragon, and cook over high heat for 2 to 3 minutes more. Pour in the wine, chicken broth, and cream. Boil hard for a few minutes until the liquids have reduced and the sauce has thickened slightly. Taste and correct the seasoning. Return the chicken breasts to the pan and baste with the sauce.

Cover and reheat for 3 to 4 minutes at below the simmer to warm the meat through without overcooking it. The breasts are done when the juices run clear when pricked with a fork. Arrange the chicken breasts on a hot platter, swish the parsley into the sauce, and spoon it over the meat. Serve immediately.

Serves 6

✤ A Sage Chicken (and Tasty Too)

I guess it's all in what you're used to, but I don't like turkey stuffing with sage. It's usually too wet and overpowering. (Try my Corn Bread Stuffing [page 137] for what I think should bless that holiday turkey.) But this summer I discovered the beauty and subtlety of fresh sage, and you will find it all through the book. Try this one—it's guaranteed.

4 boneless and skinless chicken breasts	1 tablespoon instant flour or a scant amount regular flour
Salt and white pepper to taste	3 fresh sage leaves, chopped, or
Lemon juice	½ teaspoon dried
4 fresh sage leaves, coarsely cut	1 cup chicken broth
Flour for dredging	½ cup dry white wine
1 tablespoon good olive oil	2 tablespoons very cold butter
2 tablespoons butter or	Fresh sage leaves or fresh
margarine	parsley sprigs for garnish
2 shallots, minced	

Place the chicken breasts between sheets of waxed paper and flatten them with a mallet or the side of a cleaver. Sprinkle with salt and white pepper, a little lemon juice, and the cut sage leaves. Let them sit in the refrigerator until ready to use.

Fifteen minutes before you are ready to cook them, pick off the sage, dredge the chicken lightly in flour, and shake off the excess. Heat the butter and oil in a large skillet, add the shallots, and sauté until they begin to soften. Add the chicken breasts (be sure the oil-butter is hot), brown them on one side approximately 2 to 3 minutes or until just golden, turn once, and brown on the other side. *Please* don't let them overcook. When springy to the touch, remove the chicken to a warm platter while you make the sauce.

If you need more butter or oil, be sparing, using the goodies in the bottom of the skillet. Add the instant or regular flour, chopped sage leaves, chicken broth, and white wine. Bring to a boil, lower the heat, and reduce the sauce by half. Taste for seasoning, adding salt and white pepper if necessary. Whisk in the cold butter in slivers. Each sliver should just melt and be absorbed before the next is added. The heat under the sauce should be medium but never too high, or the sauce will separate. Pour the sauce over the chicken breasts or, if you like, slip them back into the warm sauce to heat through for a few seconds. Serve garnished with fresh sage leaves or lots or parsley.

Serves 2 if you're really hungry,
4 if you're comfortably dieting

❖ *Poached Chicken Breasts on Spinach*

This little dish is delicious, simple, beautiful, dietetic, and healthy. It's great for a special luncheon or dinner—one to a customer if they're willing to settle, but be prepared for seconds.

4 thin boneless and skinless chicken breasts	2 tablespoons lemon juice
Salt and pepper to taste	1½ cups chicken broth
2 tablespoons chopped fresh dill	½ cup white wine
	1 tablespoon cornstarch
	Spinach (see below)

Marinate the chicken breasts in salt and pepper, 1 tablespoon of the dill, and the lemon juice as long as you can before dinner.

Bring 1 cup of the chicken broth to a simmer in a skillet. Slip the chicken breasts into the broth. When white on one side, turn over and cook on the other side, 4 to 5 minutes in all, depending on the thickness of the chicken breasts. Don't let them overcook. Slip the cooked breasts onto a warm plate and cover with foil to keep warm while you make the sauce.

To the skillet in which the chicken was cooked, add the remaining

½ cup of the chicken broth and the white wine. Bring to a boil and lower the heat. Scoop 2 tablespoons of broth into a cup and add the cornstarch to make a thin paste. Add this to the chicken broth in the skillet and, when thickened slightly, add the remaining tablespoon of dill and taste for seasoning. Slip the chicken breasts back in to finish cooking, 2 or 3 minutes. Serve over a bed of spinach.

SPINACH
1 bunch spinach, cleaned, chopped, and seasoned with salt, pepper and a dash of grated nutmeg

Cook in a minimum amount of water (there is so much liquid in spinach itself) until just tender, 2 or 3 minutes; drain and taste for seasoning. If using frozen spinach, defrost, season, and cook in the same manner.

Serves 4

❃ Chicken with Asparagus and Bean Sprouts

This is one of those lovely, healthy, Asian-flavored dishes you cook in a hurry and serve in a leisurely way with Japanese or Chinese Rice (page 240) or Pork or Hearty Fried Rice (page 238 or 239) and a bright green broccoli or snow peas, et cetera. If you like the bean sprouts a little less crisp, add them before the asparagus, cover for thirty seconds, and then add the aparagus and chicken.

2 whole boneless, skinless chicken breasts, cut into 1½-inch strips
1 teaspoon salt
1 egg white
1 tablespoon cornstarch
2 to 4 cups vegetable oil for deep-frying
1 slice fresh ginger, about the size of a quarter, finely minced

1 scallion, shredded
1 clove garlic, minced
1 pound asparagus, peeled and cut diagonally into 1-inch lengths
½ pound bean sprouts, washed and drained

SAUCE

6 tablespoons chicken broth
4 tablespoons oyster sauce
1 tablespoon sherry

1 tablespoon light soy sauce
1½ teaspoons cornstarch
1 teaspoon sugar

Combine all the sauce ingredients and set aside.

Mix the chicken, salt, egg white, and cornstarch together by hand.

Heat the oil in a wok to 350°. Deep-fry the chicken until golden. Quickly remove the chicken from the wok and drain it on paper towels. Drain the oil from the wok, leaving only about 2 tablespoons or less. Add the ginger, scallion, and garlic and stir-fry for about 30 seconds. Add the asparagus and stir-fry over high heat for 1 minute. Add the chicken and bean sprouts. Pour the sauce over all and bring to a boil. Serve immediately.

Serves 4

❧ Chicken with Five Cheeses

4 tablespoons butter or
  margarine
½ yellow onion, finely chopped
2 stalks celery, chopped
  medium fine
½ green pepper, seeded and
  chopped medium-fine
½ sweet red pepper, seeded and
  cut into strips (optional)
1 can artichoke hearts, drained
  and cut into 6 pieces
6 medium mushrooms, sliced
3 tablespoons flour
1 cup chicken broth
¾ to 1 cup nonfat milk
4 tablespoons plain low-fat
  yogurt

4 tablespoons low-fat cottage
  cheese
¼ cup finely grated Parmesan
  cheese
½ cup grated Cheddar cheese
½ cup grated Monterey Jack
  cheese
1 tablespoon Dijon mustard
½ teaspoon dried basil
Salt and white pepper
Dash of Tabasco sauce
1 teaspoon Worcestershire
  sauce
2 cups cubed cooked chicken
3 tablespoons grated
  mozzarella cheese

Melt 1 tablespoon of the butter in a skillet and sauté the onion until soft. Add the celery, green pepper, red pepper, and artichoke hearts and lightly sauté. Stir in the mushrooms and set aside.

Melt the remaining 3 tablespoons of butter in a saucepan, add the flour, and mix well. Slowly whisk in the chicken broth, stirring until the sauce is fairly smooth. Add the milk, stirring, until you have a medium béchamel sauce. Stir in the yogurt, then add the cottage cheese, Parmesan, Cheddar, and Monterey Jack. Mix well. Add the sautéed vegetables, Dijon mustard, basil, salt and white pepper, Tabasco, and Worcestershire. Taste for seasoning—it should not be too bland. Add the chicken, mix well and, again, taste for seasoning. (You may do all of this ahead of time and refrigerate it until 30 minutes before baking time.)

Preheat the oven to 350°. Pour the the mixture into 2 baking dishes or 1 large one and sprinkle with the mozzarella cheese. Bake for 35 to 45 minutes, until the casserole is bubbly and the cheese is melted on top.

Serves 4 to 6

❧ Chicken Breasts with Kielbasa à la Cordon Bleu

I was afraid our French cousins would blanch at the thought of kielbasa in their very French cordon bleu, hence the cop-out "à la cordon bleu," but Polish sausage has a rich, full flavor that gives us a whole new taste to our longtime friend.

6 boneless and skinless chicken
  breasts
Salt and white pepper to taste
¼ cup flour
1 egg
¾ cup water
½ cup bread crumbs
½ cup freshly grated Parmesan
  cheese
3 tablespoons olive oil
¼ cup chicken broth or white
  wine

Sauce (see below)
1 pound chicken kielbasa,
  thinly sliced diagonally and
  crisped in 1 tablespoon olive
  oil (you may substitute
  prosciutto or thinly sliced
  Virginia ham)
1 cup freshly grated
  mozzarella cheese

If the chicken breasts are too thick, cut them in half crosswise. Lightly salt and pepper the chicken breasts. Place them between sheets of waxed paper and gently flatten with the smooth side of a mallet. Dredge lightly in flour and shake off the excess. Mix the egg and water together and dip the chicken breasts in the mixture. Then dredge in the bread crumbs mixed with ¼ cup of the Parmesan cheese.

Heat the olive oil in a large skillet, and quickly sauté the chicken breasts, several at a time, lightly browning them on both sides. Set aside and keep warm. Deglaze the skillet with chicken broth or white wine, scraping up all the little browned bits. Set aside to use in the sauce.

In a flat baking dish lightly brushed with olive oil, ladle small amounts of sauce (the size of the chicken breasts). Place the browned breasts on top of the sauce and cover with the crisped kielbasa. Cover with the rest of the sauce. Sprinkle generously with mozzarella and the remaining ¼ cup of Parmesan cheese. Bake in a preheated 300° oven for 10 to 13 minutes, until the cheese is melted and lightly browned. Serve immediately.

SAUCE

2 tablespoons olive oil
½ medium-size yellow onion, chopped
4 cloves garlic, finely chopped
1 large can Italian tomatoes with their juice

3 to 4 basil leaves, chopped
3 tablespoons chopped fresh parsley
Salt and white pepper to taste
Reserved deglazing liquid

Heat the olive oil in a large skillet, add the onion and garlic, and sauté very slowly for 10 to 15 minutes. Don't let them brown if you can help it. Add the tomatoes, basil, parsley, salt, and white pepper. Bring to a simmer and add the reserved liquid from the deglazing. Simmer slowly until ready to use.

Serves 6

❧ Sort of Chinese-American Leftover Chicken

All right, so this isn't a pure use for leftover chicken. Hot creamed chicken on toast didn't seem too appealing at the moment, and I couldn't think of a really good Chinese variation for my already cooked chicken— so I threw this together. Everyone loved it. I served it with the Broccoli and Cashews (page 177).

1 tablespoon butter or
  margarine
2 tablespoons peanut oil
6 ounces cooked ham, cut into
  thin strips
2 stalks celery, chopped
3 small scallions, chopped
  (white and green parts)
½ green pepper, seeded and
  chopped

6 mushrooms, sliced
3 water chestnuts, chopped
3 tablespoons drained, chopped
  bamboo shoots
2 tablespoons cornstarch
2½ cups chicken broth
2 tablespoons soy sauce
White pepper
1½ to 2 cups cubed cooked
  chicken

Heat the butter and oil in a large sauté pan. Add the ham and sauté lightly. Remove the ham, drain on paper toweling, and keep warm. Add the celery, scallions, green pepper, and mushrooms. Sauté until soft, then add the water chestnuts and bamboo shoots and mix thoroughly. Add the cornstarch mixed with ½ cup of the broth and cook over low heat for 5 to 10 minutes, stirring frequently to make sure there are no lumps. Slowly pour in the remaining 2 cups of chicken broth and the soy sauce. Season to taste with white pepper. Add the ham and chicken and cook until warmed through.

Serve over hot rice or crisply toasted English muffins, depending on which way your palate is leaning that day.

Serves 4

✢ Shrimp and Chicken Fajitas

This is a nice Cal-Mex dish. The kids love it.

1 small clove garlic, finely
  chopped
½ medium onion, sliced
2 tablespoons vegetable oil
2 medium jalapeño peppers,
  seeded and finely chopped
½ green pepper, seeded and cut
  into strips
1 bay leaf
1 tablespoon finely chopped,
  fresh cilantro (coriander) or
  ½ teaspoon dried
1 tablespoon fresh parsley,
  chopped

1 medium Italian plum
  tomato, peeled, chopped, and
  seeded if you like
Salt and pepper to taste
Juice from ½ lemon
Dash of Tabasco sauce
¾ pound medium uncooked
  shrimp, shelled, deveined,
  and chopped
¼ pound cooked chicken
  breasts, cut into strips
8 small flour tortillas, warmed

Sauté the garlic and onion in the oil until soft and translucent. Add the jalapeños, green pepper, bay leaf, cilantro, parsley, tomato, salt and pepper, lemon juice, and Tabasco. Cook until well blended, about 10 to 12 minutes. Remove the bay leaf and add the shrimp. Cook just until the shrimp turns pink. Add the chicken and heat through.

Serve in the warmed tortillas with Red Tomato Salsa (page 83) on the side, and pinto beans if desired.

Variation: You can replace the chicken with an equal amount of leftover cooked beef or pork.

Serves 6 to 8

✿ *Santa Fe Chicken*

Chicken, corn, okra, and hominy give me a very comforting feeling. The cilantro and the cumin made me think of this as Santa Fe-ish.

Salt and freshly ground pepper to taste
One 2- to 3-pound chicken, cut up
½ cup plus 2 tablespoons vermouth
2 tablespoons vegetable oil
3 tablespoons butter or margarine
One 16-ounce can white hominy
3 ears fresh corn, kernels cut off the cob
1 medium onion, finely chopped
1 sweet red pepper, seeded and finely chopped

1 carrot, finely chopped
6 mushroom caps, finely chopped
¾ cup thinly sliced okra
3 to 4 jalapeño peppers, seeded and finely chopped
1 teaspoon ground cumin
1 tablespoon chopped fresh oregano or 1 teaspoon dried
1 bay leaf
½ cup finely chopped cilantro (coriander)
2 tablespoons half and half, warmed (optional)

Generously salt and pepper the chicken and marinate it, refrigerated, in the 2 tablespoons of vermouth for about 1 hour. Turn it a couple of times to coat the pieces well. Remove the chicken and pat it dry. In a heavy oven-proof casserole with a lid, heat the oil and 1 tablespoon of butter and sear the chicken quickly on both sides to seal in the juices. Set it aside on paper towels to drain.

Rinse the hominy, drain it, and rinse again. Spoon it into the casserole. Add the corn and then layer the chicken pieces over the bottom of the casserole. Layer the onion, pepper, carrot, mushrooms, okra, and jalapeños on top. Sprinkle lightly with salt and pepper, the cumin, and oregano. Place the bay leaf on top. Pour the remining ½ cup of vermouth into the casserole. Dot with the remaining 2 tablespoons of butter or margarine, cover, and bake in a preheated 325° oven for 45 to 50 minutes.

When the chicken is done, remove the casserole from the oven. Remove the bay leaf. Add the cilantro and warmed half and half (if you like) to the casserole. Stir to combine all the ingredients and taste for seasoning. Serve the chicken with the hominy-corn mixture and the juices from the casserole.

Serves 4

✾ *Gloria's Celebration Chicken Mole*

For weddings, births, graduations, confirmations, bris, birthdays, anniversaries, I recommend this glorious dish. It's worth the trouble—trust me.

The Mexican chocolate for the Mole Sauce can be purchased in specialty food stores.

2 whole chickens, cut into serving pieces
2 stalks celery, including tops
1 onion, halved
2 sprigs parsley
8 peppercorns
2 carrots

In a large saucepan, cover the chicken with water. Add the remaining ingredients and bring to a boil, skimming constantly. When the water looks clear, reduce heat and cook until the chicken is tender, about 1½ hours. When done, set the chicken aside and reserve the broth.

MOLE SAUCE

10 pasilla chilies
3 California chilies
1¾ cups vegetable oil
2 cups reserved chicken broth
2 corn tortillas
2 slices sourdough bread
⅓ cup raisins
5 tomatillos, outer skins removed
½ Ibarra chocolate bar (45 grams), cut into small pieces
3 cloves garlic
1 whole clove
½ cinnamon stick (break from top)
6 whole peppercorns
1 tablespoon sesame seeds
1 tablespoon reserved pasilla seeds
⅓ cup unsalted peanuts
1½ tablespoons pumpkin seeds
2 tablespoons sugar
¾ teaspoon salt or more if needed

Wash the chilies. Remove the seeds and reserve those from the pasillas. Place the chilies on paper towels to dry.

In a large skillet, heat 1 cup of the oil over medium heat. Fry the chilies very carefully 1 or 2 at a time for about half a second on each side. They brown easily and will get bitter if too brown. When the color of the chilies deepens slightly, remove them to a medium saucepan. Add the chicken broth to cover the chilies and set aside. In a skillet with ¼ cup oil, fry the tortillas whole. When light brown and crispy (don't burn), remove and place them in another saucepan. In the same skillet, fry the whole sourdough bread slices. Place them in the saucepan with the tortillas. Fry the raisins in the same skillet until they puff up, adding more oil if necessary. Turn them in the oil and remove them to the saucepan with the chilies. In the same skillet, fry the tomatillos until they get soft. Place in the saucepan with the chilies. Boil the chilies, raisins, and tomatillos for 15 to 20 minutes. Allow them to cool for a few minutes, then add the chocolate, stirring carefully (don't let it burn) while the chocolate melts. Set aside.

Pulverize the garlic, clove, cinnamon stick, peppercorns, sesame seeds, and chili seeds with a mortar and pestle, or in a blender or mini-chopper. Add a little water to make a paste. Add this to the chili mixture, place in a food processor fitted with a metal blade and puree. Fry the peanuts and pumpkin seeds in a skillet with about 2 tablespoons of oil and then add them to the bread mixture. Place in a food processor fitted with a metal blade and process until smooth.

In a large saucepan, heat 4 to 5 tablespoons of the oil over medium heat. Add the chili mixture and reduce the heat. Cook, stirring constantly, for 10 to 15 minutes. Add the bread mixture, stirring constantly over very low heat so it won't stick. Add the sugar and salt. Taste for seasoning. If the sauce appears too thick, add a little chicken broth. Cook and stir for about 20 minutes.

RICE

3 cups raw extra-long-grain
   white rice—not instant
4 to 5 cups boiling water
½ onion, coarsely chopped
3 medium very ripe tomatoes,
   coarsely chopped
¾ cup corn oil

3 cloves garlic (1 for each cup
   of rice)
2 cups cold water
4 cups hot chicken broth
5 or 6 sprigs parsley
3 teaspoons salt

Place the rice in a bowl. Cover with the boiling water and set aside for 15 minutes only. Place the rice in a sieve. Wash and rinse, and then spread it out to dry a little.

Place the onion and tomatoes in a food processor fitted with a metal blade and puree.

In a large skillet, heat the oil over medium-high heat. Place the whole garlic cloves in the oil; then add the rice. When the rice is browned, reduce the heat. Stirring constantly, cook the rice until it is golden. Remove the garlic and excess oil. Add the tomato-onion mixture with its juice to the rice. Cook until the liquid is absorbed. Add the cold water and bring to a boil. Add the chicken broth, parsley, and salt. Reduce the heat, cover tightly, and cook over very low heat for 20 to 25 minutes.

Most of the liquid will be absorbed. If you need more, add a little hot chicken broth.

Serve the Mole Sauce over the chicken pieces with the rice on the side.

Serves 8

❋ *Cornish Hens in Lemon Sauce*

Four 1-pound Cornish hens

MARINADE

2 tablespoons light soy sauce   *1 cup chicken broth*
2 tablespoons dark soy sauce
2 tablespoons sherry   *Cilantro (coriander) for*
1 teaspoon sesame oil   * garnish*
Juice of 1 lemon   *Lemon slices, for garnish*
1 tablespoon sugar
2 tablespoons peanut oil

Wash and dry the hens. Remove the gizzards and liver, wash and dry them, and cut them in half.

Combine the light soy, dark soy, sherry, sesame oil, lemon juice, and sugar in a large bowl. Add the hens, gizzards, and liver and marinate for 1 hour.

Heat the oil in a wok, add the hens, gizzards, and livers and fry until lightly browned. Stir in the remaining marinade and add the chicken broth to make a sauce. Bring to a boil, lower the heat, and simmer for 20 minutes.

Remove the hens and cut them into quarters. Place the hens, gizzards, and livers on a warm serving platter. Bring the sauce to a boil again and pour over all. Garnish with the cilantro and lemon slices.

Serves 4

✾*Herbed Cornish Hens*

This is one of the most delicious recipes I've served. Forget just that dainty half chicken, most people want the whole thing. Please try and marinate them overnight or at least two or three hours before cooking. The flavor penetrates beautifully.

Six 1- to 1½-pound fresh Cornish game hens
Unsalted butter, melted
Salt and pepper to taste
Sprigs watercress, for garnish

MARINADE

⅓ cup fresh lemon juice
⅓ cup olive oil
3 cloves garlic, minced
2 teaspoons minced fresh thyme or ¾ teaspoon dried
1 bay leaf, crumbled
¾ teaspoon salt
6 large sprigs rosemary or 2 teaspoons dried, crumbled

Have your butcher cut the hens along the backbone from neck to tail, in order to butterfly them.

Combine all the marinade ingredients except the rosemary in a bowl and mix well.

Arrange the hens in 2 flat dishes in a single layer and brush them with the marinade. Place a sprig of rosemary under each hen or sprinkle the undersides of the hens with the crumbled dried rosemary. Marinate the hens, covered and refrigerated, for at least 2 hours or overnight.

Transfer the hens to a plate, reserving the rosemary sprigs if you used them, and pat them dry. Reserve the marinade for broiling. Brush the hens on all sides with the melted butter and season them with salt and pepper. Top each hen with a reserved rosemary sprig and broil the hens, skin side down, under a preheated broiler about 4 inches from the heat, basting every 5 minutes or so with the reserved marinade, turning them once. Broil for 20 to 25 minutes, or until the juices run clear when a thigh is pricked with the tip of a sharp knife.

Transfer the hens to a heated platter and garnish with the watercress.

Serves 6 to 8

❧ *Orange-Chili Duck*

I had a hard time selling duck to some friends until this recipe came along. All that unwelcome fat is drained off and the duck is crispy without being dried out.

One 5- to 5½-pound duck
Salt and pepper
¼ cup vegetable oil
2 cups chicken broth
12 whole cloves
1 fresh hot chili, about 1½ to 2
   inches long, stemmed and
   seeded

½ cup fresh orange juice,
   strained
2 tablespoons fresh lime juice,
   strained
½ cup finely chopped sweet red
   pepper
2 oranges, cut into wedges

Preheat the oven to 350°. Pat the duck completely dry inside and out with paper towels, and remove the large chunks of fat from the cavity. Cut off the loose neck skin, and prick the surface around the thighs, the back, and the lower part of the breast with a fork or the point of a sharp knife. Season well, inside and out, with salt and pepper.

In a heavy 5- to 6-quart Dutch oven, heat the oil over moderate heat until a light haze forms. Add the duck and, turning it frequently with a slotted spoon or tongs, cook for about 15 minutes, or until it browns deeply on all sides. Transfer the duck to a plate and discard the fat remaining in the Dutch oven. Pour in 1 cup of the chicken broth and bring to a boil over high heat, scraping in any brown particles that cling to the bottom and sides of the pan. Stir in the cloves and chili, then return the duck and the liquids that have accumulated around it to the Dutch oven. Cover tightly with foil and braise in the middle of the oven for 1½ hours. Remove the foil for the last 15 to 20 minutes.

Place the duck on a plate, and, with a large spoon, skim as much fat as possible from the surface of the cooking liquid. Discard the cloves and chili.

Add the remaining cup of chicken broth to the Dutch oven and, stirring and scraping the brown bits that cling to the pan, bring to a boil on top of the stove. Mix in the orange and lime juices, red pepper, and ¼ teaspoon of salt.

Place 4 or 5 of the orange wedges in the cavity of the duck. Return the duck to the Dutch oven, and baste it with the simmering sauce. Cover loosely with foil and return the duck to the oven for about 15 minutes. To test for doneness, pierce the thigh of the duck with the point of a small, sharp knife. The juice should trickle out a clear yellow; if it is slightly pink, cook the bird for another 10 to 15 minutes.

Place the duck on a heated platter and pour the sauce over it. Garnish the platter with the remaining orange wedges and serve at once.

Serves 4 to 6

❈ Corn Bread Stuffing

This bears repeating, not only because it's "perfect" (a subjective point of view), but I mentioned on page 000 my aversion to a wet sage dressing for Thanksgiving and Christmas, and I believe it only fair to present an alternative.

1 green pepper, seeded and
  finely chopped
2 cups coarsely chopped celery
2 cups finely chopped carrots
2 large onions, finely chopped
  or grated
½ cup chopped fresh parsley
1 cup butter or margarine

½ loaf stale bread, toasted and
  finely crumbled
1 pan Buttermilk Corn Bread,
  crumbled (page 137)
Turkey or Chicken Stock (see
  below)
Salt and pepper

Sauté the vegetables and parsley in the butter or margarine until soft. Slightly moisten the crumbled breads with the stock and add to the vegetable mixture. Season to taste with salt and pepper. Use this to stuff your favorite chicken or turkey.

Makes 10 to 12 cups

TURKEY OR CHICKEN STOCK

Neck, gizzard, and heart of
  turkey or chicken
1 whole onion
1 carrot

1 stalk celery
1 whole tomato
1 whole potato (optional)
Freshly ground black pepper

Place all the ingredients in a saucepan and add water to cover. Bring to a boil and simmer an hour or until the giblets are tender. (I use this stock for gravy, too.)

Fish

If you compare dipping a timid toe into the pool, as I did with fish and seafood (nine recipes) in my first cookbook for dear old Doubleday, to taking the plunge into the big waters (a little play on words here) with the thirty-five or so recipes listed here, you'll see how much I've come to know and appreciate this healthy, varied product with which we have been so generously surrounded and provided by nature. I'm sure I've mentioned to you before that I'm from the middle of a land-bound state, Tennessee—beautiful lakes and rivers, with trout and bass and catfish, but shrimp, crab, lobster, and oysters had to be imported from the Gulf or the Atlantic coast. My mother was daring. I did learn to love fried oysters (the raw came later), crab-meat salad, shrimp Creole, along with any and all river fish one could fry, but they weren't in our everyday budget, recipe repertoire, or diet. I've made up for whatever I missed, as you can see. Just go through the recipes here and try them— I'm proud of them.

❊ *Hot Scallops Cold Vinaigrette*

1½ pounds large fresh sea
scallops
Salt and freshly ground pepper
to taste
2 tablespoons olive oil

3 sprigs fresh rosemary,
chopped, or 1 tablespoon
dried
⅛ teaspoon red pepper flakes
Vinaigrette Sauce (see below)

One half hour before broiling, put the scallops in a bowl and marinate with salt and pepper and a mixture of the olive oil, rosemary, and red pepper flakes. Cover with plastic wrap. Since it's only a half hour, you don't have to refrigerate.

Preheat the broiler to high. Arrange the scallops on a rack in a single layer and place them about 6 inches from the heat. Broil for 2 minutes, turn, and broil for about 2 minutes more. Don't overcook, or they'll be rubbery. They'll be white and sort of opaque. Place the scallops on a hot plate and pour the cold vinaigrette over them, turning a little to coat. Serve a little of the sauce on the side.

Serves 4

VINAIGRETTE SAUCE

1 small sweet red pepper, cored, seeded, and cut into large chunks or slices
½ cup coarsely chopped white onions
1 clove garlic, peeled
½ cup loosely packed fresh cilantro (coriander)

½ cup olive oil
1 tablespoon red wine
1 tablespoon red wine vinegar
½ teaspoon salt
¼ teaspoon freshly ground black pepper

Combine all the ingredients in a blender or food processor and pulse to blend to a semicoarse texture for a few seconds.

✽ *Sea Scallops with Orange-Butter Sauce*

The ocean and sky at Malibu can be great deceivers. For instance, in the evening before the sun sets or as it is just about to, we gather on the upper deck after a long day's experimenting with all kinds of dishes and, drunk with the beauty of it all (and perhaps with a little help), we have one of our taste-testing dishes and it tastes WONNDDEERRFFUULLL! This scallop dish was one of those. I hope it's as delicious as it was at sunset in Malibu, but if it isn't—imagine you're there and you'll love it!

1½ pounds sea scallops
Salt and white pepper
2 tablespoons olive oil
4 sprigs fresh thyme or 1 teaspoon dried
1 tablespoon fresh rosemary or 2 teaspoons dried

2 teaspoons finely chopped garlic
⅛ teaspoon red pepper flakes
2 tablespoons lemon juice

ORANGE-BUTTER SAUCE

½ cup freshly squeezed orange
   juice, pulp included
4 tablespoons butter or
   margarine, at room
   temperature
¾ cup peeled, seeded, and
   diced tomatoes

¼ cup fresh cilantro
   (coriander) or parsley,
   chopped
Salt and pepper to taste
1 tomato, peeled and coarsely
   chopped

Place the scallops in a mixing bowl with salt and white pepper to taste, the olive oil, thyme, rosemary, garlic, red pepper flakes, and lemon juice. Blend well and refrigerate for 1 hour.

Meanwhile, place the orange juice in a saucepan and cook over high heat until it is reduced by half. Add the butter or margarine, tomatoes, and cilantro and cook briefly until the combination is well blended. Season with salt and pepper. Keep warm.

Heat a broiler or grill until it is quite hot.

Divide the scallops into 4 equal batches and place them on 4 skewers. Brush with the marinade. Place the skewers on the grill or under the broiler and cook for 2 to 4 minutes. Turn the skewers and cook for 2 to 4 more minutes on the other side, or until they are opaque.

Add the coarsely chopped, uncooked tomato to the warm sauce. Serve immediately with the Orange-Butter Sauce.

Serves 4

❦ Scallops, Fennel, and Dill

I never quite knew what to do with those big, beautiful, pale green bulbs of fennel without abusing their delicate flavor. I do now.

1 cup finely chopped white
   part of leek, washed well
   and drained
1 cup thinly sliced fennel bulb
Salt and pepper
1½ tablespoons olive oil
½ cup dry white wine
¼ cup water
1 pound bay scallops, rinsed
   and patted dry

1½ tablespoons butter,
   softened
1½ tablespoons flour
¼ cup plain low-fat yogurt
2 tablespoons snipped fresh
   dill
½ cup grated Gruyère cheese
   (about 2 ounces)
Fresh dill sprigs and lemon
   wedges, for garnish

In a skillet, cook the leek and the fennel with salt and pepper to taste in the oil over moderately low heat, until the fennel is tender, 10 to 15 minutes. Add the wine and water and bring the liquid to a boil.

Meanwhile, make a beurre manie by putting the butter and flour in a small bowl and kneading them together until well combined.

When the liquid is reduced by half, add the scallops, and cook over moderately high heat, stirring, for 1 to 2 minutes, or until they are opaque. Add the beurre manie, a little at a time, to the scallop mixture, stirring, and bring the mixture to a boil. Simmer, stirring for 2 minutes. Stir in the yogurt and salt and pepper to taste, and continue to simmer, stirring, for 1 minute.

Stir in the dill, divide the mixture among 6 large scallop shells or small gratin dishes, and top each gratin with some of the Gruyère.

Arrange the gratins on a jelly-roll pan, broil them under a preheated broiler about 4 inches from the heat for 3 to 5 minutes, or until the Gruyère is melted and golden, and garnish each gratin with a dill sprig and a lemon wedge.

Serves 6

❁ *Vodka Shrimp*

This is delightful and, again, Oriental.

8 to 10 uncooked jumbo
  shrimp
1 cup cold water
¼ teaspoon salt
1 scallion, cut crosswise (white
  part only)
1 thin slice fresh gingerroot,
  minced

1 tablespoon light soy sauce
1 tablespoon vodka
Scant 2 tablespoons peanut oil
1 teaspoon sugar
Whole lettuce leaves to use as
  serving cups

Shell the shrimp, leaving the tails on. Make a shallow cut down the back of each shrimp and remove the black vein. Rinse and soak in a cup of cold water to which you have added ¼ teaspoon salt.

Mix together the scallion and gingerroot. Set aside. Mix together the soy sauce and vodka. Set aside.

Heat a 9- or 10-inch skillet over medium heat, add the oil, using just enough to cover the bottom of the skillet. When hot, add the shrimp in one batch and sauté until almost cooked through and crisped on the outside, turning once or twice, about 3 to 4 minutes. Sprinkle lightly with the sugar and turn the shrimp a few times while the sugar is caramelizing. Turn the heat to high and add the scallion-ginger and vodka combinations. Cook for about 30 seconds to 1 minute. Serve hot, in lettuce leaf cups.

Serves 4 to 5

❋ *Jalapeño Shrimp*

Hot, spicy, and utterly wonderful.

1 clove garlic
½ teaspoon salt
6 long green chilies
½ cup sliced onion
2 fresh jalapeño chilies, seeded and sliced
1 tablespoon minced fresh cilantro (coriander)

2 tablespoons butter
1 tomato, cored and diced
Dash of sugar
2 dozen uncooked medium shrimp, peeled, washed, deveined, and butterflied
4 to 6 tablespoons vegetable oil

Mash the garlic in the salt. Coarsely chop 2 of the long green chilies and set them aside.

Sauté the garlic, onion, jalapeño chilies, and cilantro in 2 tablespoons of butter over low heat until tender. Add the tomato, chopped chilies, and sugar to the onion mixture and cook, stirring, for 3 minutes. Set the sauce aside.

Char the remaining 4 long green chilies under the broiler or over a gas flame, turning them frequently. Peel the chilies and, leaving the stems intact, split them from tip to stem.

For each serving, sauté 6 shrimp in 1 to 2 tablespoons of oil for 3 to 4 minutes, or until the shrimp turn pink. Add sauce to taste and cook for 1 minute longer. Arrange the shrimp over the long green chilies and serve with rice. This is fairly spicy. If you have a sensitive palate, use fewer chilies in the sauce or serve with a generous amount of rice.

Serves 4

❦ *Shrimp-and-Crumb-Stuffed Artichokes*

The hardest part of this is preparing the artichoke without its falling apart on you—but try it. It's worth the trouble.

4 artichokes
Lemon juice
½ teaspoon dried dill
½ teaspoon dried basil
½ teaspoon dried oregano
2 cups water

¼ cup olive oil
2 cloves garlic, halved
Salt and white pepper
Stuffing (see below)
Butter (optional)

Wash the artichokes, peel off 2 outer layers of leaves, and set them aside. Cut off the sharp points of the remaining leaves with a sharp knife. Rub all the cut points with lemon juice. Spread the artichokes carefully from the center and cut out the purple, prickly choke. (This ain't easy, but, again, it's worth it.) Sprinkle the dill, basil, and oregano over the artichokes.

Place the artichokes in a large pot, flower end down, stem end up. Add the water, olive oil, garlic, and salt and white pepper to taste. Cook covered for 20 minutes, or until just tender. Drain, reserving the cooking liquid. Set aside to cool.

Gently pull apart the leaves of the cooled artichokes and generously stuff with the shrimp mixture. Place the stuffed artichokes in a large baking dish and surround with the reserved leaves. Pour a little of the reserved cooking liquid over all, dot with a little butter if you like, and bake in a preheated 300° oven for 10 minutes or until warmed. Serve warm.

Serves 4

STUFFING

2 tablespoons olive oil
2 tablespoons butter or
  margarine
2 shallots, chopped
2 tablespoons finely chopped
  green pepper
1 tablespoon finely chopped
  pimiento
2 tablespoons finely chopped
  fresh parsley
½ cup unflavored bread crumbs

½ pound uncooked shrimp,
  peeled, deveined, and cut
  into bite-size pieces
¼ teaspoon dried marjoram
1½ teaspoons chopped fresh
  basil or ½ teaspoon dried
¼ teaspoon dried oregano
Dash of Tabasco sauce
Dash of Worcestershire sauce
Salt and pepper

Heat the oil and butter or margarine in a skillet. Lightly sauté the shallots, green pepper, pimiento, and parsley. Stir in the bread crumbs. Add the shrimp, marjoram, basil, oregano, Tabasco, Worcestershire, and salt and pepper to taste. Mix well. Taste for seasoning. Remove from the heat and set aside until cool enough to handle.

❧ Seafood Potpie

This looks long and difficult. It isn't either. Much can be done ahead of time. I wanted to give you all the lovely details so you could relax and fully appreciate the oobs and aabs when you serve it. Don't expect a standing ovation after the meal, your guests will be too contented to be overenergetic.

Puff pastry (available in the
    frozen-food section of most
    supermarkets)
1½ cups hot clam juice (with
    lemon juice and peppercorns
    added, to taste) or Fish Broth
    (see below)
2 lobster tails, cut into chunks
1½ pounds uncooked medium
    shrimp, cleaned, shelled,
    deveined, and halved
    (reserve shells for Fish Broth)
1½ pounds sea scallops,
    quartered
Salt and black pepper to taste
One 10-ounce box of frozen
    peas (petits pois)
5 tablespoons butter or
    margarine
2 large or 3 small cloves
    garlic, finely chopped
½ green pepper, seeded and
    chopped
Scant 1 tablespoon peeled and
    chopped fresh ginger
    (optional)

2 stalks celery, chopped
2 scallions, chopped
8 shitake mushrooms, halved
6 medium mushrooms, halved
5 tablespoons flour
1 cup plus 2 tablespoons milk
    (half and half, if you feel
    thin) or half low-fat and
    half whole milk if you feel
    like I do
Scant ½ cup good dry sherry
    (Tio Pepe) or your favorite
    dry white wine
1 teaspoon of salt
White pepper to taste
1 teaspoon ground cumin
2 teaspoons Tabasco sauce or
    red pepper flakes
Scant 2 tablespoons good fresh
    curry powder (optional)
½ cup slivered toasted
    almonds
3 tablespoons pimiento strips,
    drained
1 egg beaten with 2
    tablespoons water

Defrost the puff pastry in the refrigerator a couple of hours before using it. Using the casserole in which you will be cooking and serving as your guide (the casserole should be fairly deep), make a template of waxed paper 1 inch larger than the casserole. On a lightly floured board, roll out the puff pastry to a thickness of ¼ inch. Using the template, cut the pastry to size. Place between sheets of waxed paper and return it to the refrigerator until ready to use.

Bring the clam juice or fish broth to a boil. Plunge the lobster tails into the broth and remove them when the shells turn red, about 1 or 2 minutes. Remove the meat from the shells and return the shells to the broth. Set aside the meat in a bowl. Plunge the shrimp into the broth and cook until the shrimp just turn pink. Remove with a slotted spoon and place in the bowl with the lobster. Drop the scallops into the broth and cook until opaque, about 1 or 2 minutes. Remove with a slotted spoon and place in the bowl with the other shellfish. Salt and pepper if needed.

Place the peas in a strainer and cook briefly in the hot fish broth. Remove and set aside.

In a large skillet, melt 2 tablespoons of the butter. Lightly sauté (do not brown) the garlic, green pepper, ginger, celery, scallions, shitake, and other mushrooms. Add the remaining 3 tablespoons butter and melt. Reduce the heat to low and gradually add the flour, stirring constantly until the flour is thoroughly incorporated with the vegetables. Slowly add the heated clam juice or broth, the milk, and the sherry. This should make a fairly thick béchamel sauce. Add 1 teaspoon of salt, white pepper, cumin, Tabasco, and curry powder (if using). Taste for seasoning. Add the reserved lobster, shrimp, and scallops, and the almonds, pimiento, and peas. Mix well.

Pour into the casserole and cover with the puff pastry, pulling the pastry as firm and straight across as possible without tearing it. Seal the edges well with the egg-water mixture. Decorate the crust with extra pastry you have braided or cut into small fish shapes. Brush with the egg-water mixture.

Bake in a preheated 350° oven for 20 minutes, or until the crust is brown and the casserole is hot and bubbly. Serve with steamed rice.

Serves 6 to 8

FISH BROTH

3 cups water	*8 white peppercorns*
½ lemon, quartered	*Salt*
1 bay leaf	*3 whole scallions*
2 stalks celery, tops and all	*Reserved shells from shrimp*

Combine all the ingredients, bring to boil, and simmer for an hour or so.

❋ *Hot and Cold Shellfish Salad*

Yin and yang—the hot and the cold. The bland and the piquant, etc.—whatever, you'll love it.

Salad greens torn into bite-size
   pieces (small romaine,
   spinach, Bibb lettuce,
   whatever you like—
   watercress is nice)
½ small onion, finely chopped
1 clove garlic, finely chopped
¼ green pepper, seeded and
   finely chopped
1 stalk celery, finely chopped
4 medium mushrooms, finely
   chopped
1 teaspoon good fresh olive oil
1 teaspoon butter or margarine
½ pound uncooked shrimp,
   peeled, deveined, and halved
   or quartered

½ pound uncooked sea
   scallops, halved or quartered,
   depending on size
Salt and white pepper
¼ cup chicken broth
Your favorite salad dressing
   (French or Italian)
2 slices bacon, fried crisp and
   crumbled, or 2 tablespoons
   slivered toasted almonds
   (optional)
Chopped parsley, for garnish
Lemon wedges, for garnish

In the morning, prepare your greens: Wash, tear, and dry them, then place in a kitchen towel in a bowl in the refrigerator.

Sauté the onion, garlic, green pepper, celery, and mushrooms in the oil and butter. If pressed for time, the vegetables can be sautéed ahead of time and reheated. Just before serving, heat the vegetables, add the shrimp (be sure the skillet is hot), and when they are just turning pink, add the scallops. When the scallops are white and opaque, slip the shellfish out of the skillet. Season to taste with salt and white pepper.

Keep the heat high and add the chicken broth to deglaze the pan. While you are deglazing, mix the greens with the dressing and portion out onto nice-size plates—not too small. Slip the shellfish back in the sauce, which should be slightly reduced. Be careful in deglazing that the liquid does not completely cook away; if it does, a little more chicken broth will help.

When the shellfish is heated through, check for seasoning and portion it out on top of the greens. Sprinkle with bacon or almonds, and garnish with chopped parsley and a lemon wedge. If you like, or if you have it, a little hot Red Tomato Salsa (page 83) on top of the seafood is nice.

Serves 6 to 8

✿ *Catfish and Shrimp*

Have I told you about my friends who claim they won't eat catfish even if it's buried in caviar? They don't know the little, much maligned, dickens has been elevated to breeding farms and no longer hovers on the bottom of the river scrounging around for the world's leftovers. Rather than explain, I serve them this little number, calling it before dinner by any other name that would make it taste as sweet—filet of sole, orange roughy, red snapper, and so on. Then, after the applause and cheers have subsided (well, I can dream can't I!?!), I admit to them that it was catfish and I have thereupon made converts—or earned distrust forever after.

Six 8-ounce catfish filets	*1 tablespoon olive oil*
Salt and pepper to taste	*1 tablespoon margarine, or*
Juice of 2 lemons	*more if needed*
1 cup flour	*Shrimp Sauce (see below)*

Salt and pepper the catfish. Pour the lemon juice over all. Marinate for 2 hours if possible.

Roll the filets in flour and sauté in a large skillet in the olive oil and margarine. When the filets are brown and slightly crisp on one side, turn and brown on other side.

Pour the sauce over the catfish filets, dividing the shrimp equally among the filets.

Serves 6

SHRIMP SAUCE

½ pound uncooked medium	*2 scallions, finely chopped*
shrimp, peeled and deveined	*(green part also)*
Salt and pepper to taste	*1 tablespoon flour*
Juice of ½ lemon	*1 teaspoon chicken broth*
2 tablespoons olive oil	*concentrate mixed with 1*
2 tablespoons margarine, or	*cup hot water, or 1 cup*
more if needed	*chicken broth*
8 mushrooms, thinly sliced	*½ cup white wine*

Salt and pepper the shrimp and pour the lemon juice over them. Marinate for 30 minutes or longer if possible. Remove the shrimp from the lemon juice with a slotted spoon, reserving the juice to add to the sauce.

In a large skillet, sauté the shrimp in the olive oil and margarine until just pink. Remove the shrimp and set aside. When cool, cut them in half crosswise. Add the reserved lemon juice to the skillet. Sauté the mushrooms and scallions until soft, adding more margarine if necessary. Sprinkle the flour over the mushrooms and scallions and cook, stirring constantly, for 5 minutes. Add the chicken broth and wine and continue cooking, stirring constantly, until all the flour is dissolved. Raise the heat and reduce the sauce by one half. Add the shrimp and cook just until the shrimp is warmed through.

❃ *Catfish Stew*

This is another one of those things that was first enhanced by ocean breezes, a glorious sunset, and good company—all intoxicants without wine or beer or whatever your pleasure. The dish turned out to be every bit as good the next day.

3 slices lean uncooked bacon
1½ cups finely chopped onions
6 medium-size firm-ripe tomatoes, washed, cored, and cut into 1½-inch pieces
2 large boiling potatoes, peeled and cut into 1-inch cubes (about 3 cups)
1 pound catfish trimmings—the head, tail, and bones reserved from fileting the fish (these can be obtained from your fish merchant)
2 tablespoons Worcestershire sauce
½ teaspoon Tabasco sauce
2 teaspoons salt
Freshly ground black pepper
2 pounds catfish filets, cut into 1½-inch pieces

In a heavy 4- to 6-quart casserole, fry the bacon slices over moderate heat, turning them with tongs until they are crisp and brown and rendered of all their fat. Transfer them to paper towels to drain, then crumble into small bits and set aside.

Add the onions to the fat remaining in the casserole and, stirring frequently, cook over moderate heat for about 5 minutes, until they are soft and translucent but not brown. Stir in the tomatoes, potatoes, catfish trimmings, Worcestershire, Tabasco, salt, and a few grindings of pepper, and bring to a boil over high heat. Reduce the heat to low, cover tightly, and simmer for 30 minutes.

With tongs or a slotted spoon, remove and discard the catfish trimmings. Add the catfish filets and reserved bacon to the stew and mix well. Cover the casserole tightly again and continue to simmer over low heat for 8 to 10 minutes, or until the fish flakes easily when prodded gently with a fork. Taste for seasoning and serve the stew at once, either directly from the casserole or in large heated bowls.

Serves 4

❊ *Broiled Halibut with Pesto in Tomato Sauce*

Six 8-ounce ³/₄-inch-thick
  halibut filets
Salt and pepper to taste
Lemon juice
Pesto Sauce (see below)
2 Japanese eggplant, sliced
  lengthwise at an angle

2 zucchinis, sliced lengthwise
  at an angle
2 tablespoons olive oil
Fresh Tomato Sauce (see
  below)
Fresh tomato, peeled and
  coarsely chopped for garnish

Marinate the fish in the salt, pepper, and a little lemon juice if you like, for 30 minutes. Pat dry.

Arrange the filets on a rack in a broiler pan and broil until the fish is opaque on top. Turn carefully. Brush a layer of the Pesto Sauce over each fish portion. Broil without turning 3 to 4 minutes, or until the fish is opaque and flakes when pierced with a fork.

Season the eggplant and zucchini with salt and pepper and set aside for 10 minutes. Sauté in 2 tablespoons of olive oil for 7 to 10 minutes, or until browned on both sides.

To serve, place the cooked fish with the remaining pesto on a bed of Fresh Tomato Sauce. Surround with fresh chopped tomato and decorate with the sautéed eggplant and zucchini slices.

Serves 6

PESTO SAUCE
3 cloves garlic
4 walnut halves
Generous ¹/₂ cup fresh basil
  leaves

2 tablespoons olive oil
1 teaspoon grated Parmesan
  cheese
Salt and pepper

Combine the garlic, walnuts, and basil in a blender and chop fine. Add the oil in a stream, slowly blending until well mixed and slightly thickened. Add the Parmesan cheese and blend just enough to mix. Season to taste with salt and pepper.

FRESH TOMATO SAUCE

6 medium-large ripe tomatoes, peeled and coarsely chopped, plus 2 medium-large ripe tomatoes, peeled and coarsely chopped (set aside)
1 tablespoon olive oil
½ teaspoon finely chopped garlic
1 tablespoon finely chopped sweet red pepper

Generous 1 tablespoon mixed chopped fresh basil, parsley, tarragon, and chervil (if you don't have fresh herbs, use a mixture of dried herbs)
4 pimiento-stuffed green olives, minced or thinly sliced
Salt and pepper

Blend the 6 tomatoes in a food processor until smooth. Add the olive oil, garlic, red pepper, chopped herbs, and olives. Season to taste with salt and pepper. Simmer over medium heat until the sauce is reduced by half. You should have 2½ to 3 cups sauce. Season the tomatoes you have set aside with salt and pepper and add to the cooked tomato sauce just prior to serving.

❈ *Halibut with Salsa*

Four 1-inch-thick halibut steaks
Salt and pepper to taste
Lemon juice

8 tablespoons Red Tomato Salsa (page 83)

Season the halibut well with salt and pepper. Sprinkle lemon juice over all and marinate as long as you can before cooking.

Place 2 tablespoons of salsa on each steak and broil until the fish flakes easily when pierced with a fork.

Serves 4

✿ *Baked Halibut*

You may notice an inordinate number of halibut recipes in these few pages. Each one is so different from the other that I couldn't quite eliminate any of them. (You should see the dozens I didn't put in.) Besides, I'm on this health kick and permanent diet and fish handles both deliciously. If you're tired of halibut or find it not easy to get at the moment, use any firm white fish (your fish merchant can be quite helpful here), such as white fish, orange roughy, cod, scrod, et cetera. Take the word of a onetime reluctant fish eater—these recipes are wonderful and easy.

Juice of 1 lemon
Six ¾-inch-thick halibut filets
   approximately 8 ounces each
2 tablespoons chopped fresh
   dill
1 tablespoon olive oil
1 large tomato, coarsely
   chopped
½ green pepper, seeded and
   coarsely chopped
½ cup coarsely chopped onion
1 stalk celery, coarsely chopped

2 cloves garlic, chopped
3 sprigs parsley, coarsely
   chopped
2 sprigs basil, coarsely
   chopped, or 1½ teaspoons
   dried
1 sprig tarragon, coarsely
   chopped, or 1 teaspoon dried
1 sprig rosemary, coarsely
   chopped, or 1 teaspoon dried
Salt and pepper

Squeeze the lemon juice over the halibut filets. Sprinkle them with the chopped dill. Let stand in the refrigerator at least 1 hour. (The fish will cook a little faster when marinated in lemon juice.)

Heat the olive oil in a skillet. Sauté the vegetables and herbs until the vegetables are soft and the flavors are well mixed. Add salt and pepper to taste.

Place the halibut filets in a glass oven-proof baking dish. Pour the vegetable mixture over the fish and bake for 20 minutes in a preheated 350° oven, or until the fish flakes when pierced with a fork.

Serves 6

❀ Halibut with Chayote "Noodles" and Black Beans

2 chayote squash
2 tablespoons vegetable oil
2 tablespoons olive oil
Four 4-ounce halibut filets
Salt and pepper to taste
Flour for dredging fish
½ cup dry white wine
2 cups clam juice
1½ cups half and half
3 cloves garlic, roasted and
   pureed (roast in a small pan
   at 350° until soft, then mash
   or puree in a food processor)

1 serrano chili, seeded and
   diced
5 tablespoons butter or
   margarine
¾ cup cooked black beans
2 tablespoons diced sweet red
   pepper
2 teaspoons minced shallots
½ teaspoon chopped cilantro
   (coriander)
½ teaspoon lime juice

Peel the chayote. Cut it in half lengthwise, then cut each half in half, and cut into thin slices or "noodles." Blanch the "noodles" in boiling water for 2 minutes, then refresh in ice water. Drain and set aside.

In a large skillet, combine the oils and heat until lightly smoking. Season the filets with salt and pepper and coat lightly with the flour. Sauté the filets until golden brown on both sides, about 3 minutes per side. Remove from the skillet and keep warm while preparing the sauce.

Deglaze the skillet with the wine and reduce by half. Add the clam juice and reduce again by half. Add the half and half, roast garlic puree, and serrano chili and reduce once more by half. Whisk in 3 tablespoons of the butter and season with salt and pepper. Add the black beans and diced red pepper. Heat through.

In a small skillet, heat the remaining 2 tablespoons of butter and add the shallots. Sauté for 1 minute, then add the cooked chayote, the cilantro, and lime juice. Season with salt and toss gently until heated through. Put a portion of the chayote noodles on each of 4 warm plates and place the fish filets on top. Spoon the sauce generously over all.

Serves 4

❋*Stuffed Filet of Sole*

8 sole filets or other firm white
   fish (filets should be as
   uniform in size as possible)
Salt and pepper to taste
3 tablespoons olive oil
1 medium yellow onion, sliced
3 large or 4 medium cloves
   garlic, chopped
1 green pepper, seeded and cut
   into thin strips
2 stalks celery, sliced
6 sprigs parsley, chopped
1 medium tomato, thinly
   sliced

One 16-ounce can Italian
   plum tomatoes, juice and all
¼ teaspoon dried basil
4 basil leaves
1 bay leaf
½ teaspoon dried oregano
½ cup chicken broth or ½ cup
   red wine
1 medium eggplant, peeled,
   thinly sliced, salted, and
   placed in a colander to
   drain

Wash the filets and pat them dry with paper towels. Season with salt and pepper and set aside.

Heat 1½ tablespoons of the olive oil in a large skillet. Add the onion, garlic, green pepper, and celery. Sauté until soft. Add the parsley, sliced tomato, canned tomatoes, dried basil, basil leaves, bay leaf, oregano, and salt and pepper. Mix well, breaking up the tomatoes as you mix. Taste for seasoning. Add the broth or red wine, bring to a boil, reduce the heat, and simmer uncovered while you prepare the eggplant.

Pepper the eggplant and quickly sauté it in the remaining 1½ tablespoons of olive oil until just softened. Add to the sauce, breaking up the eggplant as you mix. Deglaze the pan with a bit of chicken broth and add the deglazing to the sauce. Let the sauce simmer uncovered over low heat for another 10 to 15 minutes. Remove the bay leaf and taste for seasoning.

Place 1 sole filet on a large square of foil. Cover the filet with a generous amount of vegetables from the sauce (use a slotted spoon). Cover with another filet and spoon some sauce over all. Seal the foil. Repeat with the remaining filets.

Bake in a preheated 400° oven for 20 to 30 minutes. To serve, slice the stuffed filets into individual portions.

Serves 8

CLOCKWISE FROM TOP: Tecate Bread p. 258 Fresh Tomato Soup p. 54 Carrots with Mint p. 180 Poached Filets on Greens p. 164

CLOCKWISE FROM TOP: Shrimp-Scallop Soup-Stew for Company p. 48 Cold Tomato-Vegetable Soup p. 59 Winter Wonder Soup p. 46 Emerald Soup p. 51 Five Bean Soup p. 42 Almond Soup p. 56 Cucumber Soup with Fresh Herbs p. 58

CLOCKWISE FROM TOP: A Whole Meal Salad—A Real Mexican Treat p. 62 Black-Eyed Peas Like Mother Never Made p. 80 Warm Potato and Sausage Salad p. 61 Molded Chicken Salad p. 70

❧ Lime-Marinated Filet of Sole

4 thin sole filets, 4 to 6 ounces
    each
¼ cup lime juice
3 tablespoons grated onion
Salt and pepper to taste
⅓ cup finely chopped toasted
    almonds

¼ cup freshly grated Parmesan
    cheese
¼ cup chopped fresh parsley
½ cup white wine (optional)
½ cup clam juice (optional)

Brush the filets with the lime juice and grated onion. Sprinkle with salt and pepper and let stand an hour or so.

Preheat the broiler. Brown the filets quickly on one side about 4 inches from the flame. Turn them over. Dust with the almonds and Parmesan cheese, sprinkle with parsley, and brown quickly to crisp the almonds and melt the cheese a little. The fish is done when it flakes easily when pierced with a fork.

Or you can poach the filets in white wine and clam juice. When done, remove them from the poaching liquid, dust with almonds and Parmesan cheese, sprinkle with parsley, then broil quickly in a preheated broiler 4 inches from the flame to crisp the almonds and melt the cheese a little.

Serves 4

❧ Orange Roughy with Spinach

2 pounds orange roughy filets
    or any other firm-fleshed
    filets
Salt and pepper to taste
Juice from ½ lemon
Scant 1 tablespoon margarine
    or butter, or more if needed
2 tablespoons olive oil, or
    more if needed

¼ cup pine nuts (pignolia)
2 packages frozen chopped
    spinach, partially defrosted,
    or you can use fresh spinach
    or fresh mustard greens, kale
    and collard greens
Pinch of grated nutmeg

Wash the filets, pat dry, and season both sides with a generous sprinkling of salt and pepper and a squeeze of lemon juice. Let stand in the refrigerator until ready to assemble.

Melt the margarine or butter in a large skillet. Add 1 tablespoon olive oil and the pine nuts; then add the spinach or greens. Season with salt and pepper, and a little squeeze of lemon juice, and a pinch of nutmeg. Cook until warmed through—no more.

Place the spinach or greens in a 14-inch glass oven-proof baking dish with 2-inch sides, each portion should be a little bigger than a filet of fish. Place the filets on top of the spinach. Drizzle with the remaining very fresh good olive oil. (Easy here—I don't think I used more than 1 tablespoon for all the filets.)

Bake in a preheated 400° oven for 20 minutes, or until the fish flakes with a fork. Lift each portion of spinach and filet with a large spatula and place on a warmed plate.

This is a lovely dish served with sweet green, red, and yellow peppers and boiled dilled potatoes.

Serves 4

❀ Steamed Rock Cod or Bass with Soy Dipping Sauce

This has a light, Oriental touch. Be sure to serve a small bowl of dipping sauce with each portion.

One 4- to 5-pound whole rock cod or sea bass
1 teaspoon salt
4 tablespoons good dry sherry (I used Tio Pepe)
8 thin slices fresh gingerroot, peeled and shredded on the coarsest blade of a grater
4 large scallions, cut into ½-inch slivers, white part only

¼ sweet red pepper, seeded and cut into thin strips
¼ green pepper, seeded and cut into thin strips
4 tablespoons vegetable oil
Lemon slices, for garnish
Dipping Sauce (see below)

Have the fish cleaned and scaled (of course), leaving the head and tail on if you have the nerve—it enhances the taste. Rinse and dry the fish thoroughly. Mix together the salt and sherry. Rub over the fish, inside and out. Make 3 diagonal slices in the fish; this helps it to cook and absorb the seasoning.

Place the fish in a heat-proof baking dish and sprinkle with the grated ginger. Bring 2 inches of water to boil in a steamer. Place the dish on the rack of the steamer 1 inch above the boiling water. Cover and steam for about 25 minutes, or until the fish flakes easily when pierced with a fork. (Cooking times will vary depending on the size of the fish.) Have more boiling water ready in case the water in the steamer gets too low.

Place the steamed fish on a warm serving platter and sprinkle with the scallions and peppers. Heat the oil (careful here) and pour it over the fish. Serve on a platter garnished with lemon slices. Serve the Dipping Sauce on the side.

Serves 8

DIPPING SAUCE
2 tablespoons light soy sauce
2 tablespoons white vinegar

1 teaspoon peeled and minced
fresh gingerroot

Mix all the ingredients together in a small bowl.

❋ *Grilled Salmon Steaks with Watercress-Mustard Butter*

Definitely outdoor summer fare—or indoor if you want to reminisce about summer. Salmon steaks are available just about all year round, and they are delicious.

WATERCRESS-MUSTARD BUTTER
1 cup minced watercress leaves
8 tablespoons unsalted butter,
* at room temperature*
1 tablespoon minced shallot
1 tablespoon Dijon mustard or
* to taste*
¼ teaspoon salt or to taste
Freshly ground pepper

Six 8-ounce salmon steaks,
* 1-inch thick*
Salt and freshly ground pepper
* to taste*
Watercress sprigs, for garnish
Light Mustard Sauce (see
* below)*

For the butter: Thoroughly combine the ingredients in a small bowl. Adjust the seasoning. Refrigerate for at least 1 hour. (This can be prepared a day ahead.)

Adjust a barbecue rack (if grilling) 4 inches from the fire. Prepare the barbecue grill or preheat the broiler. Season the salmon with salt and pepper. Dot with slightly less than half the watercress butter. Arrange, buttered side up, on the barbecue or broiler rack. Grill for 5 minutes. Turn, dot with the remaining butter, and cook until just opaque, about

5 minutes. Transfer to individual plates, garnish with watercress sprigs, and serve immediately with the Light Mustard Sauce on the side.

Serves 6

LIGHT MUSTARD SAUCE

3 tablespoons butter	*½ teaspoon freshly ground*
1 tablespoon flour	*black pepper*
½ teaspoon dry mustard	*1 cup fish stock or clam juice*

Melt the butter over medium-high heat. Add the flour and the mustard and stir until well blended. Add the pepper and stir in the stock or clam juice gradually, stirring constantly, over medium heat. When it comes to a boil, boil for 2 minutes and no more

Makes about 1 cup

❋ *Marinated Swordfish*

I always thought swordfish was dry and tasteless. I've changed my mind. You'll never believe why: On a long plane flight going somewhere, Delta Airlines gave us a choice of three entrées. I thought if I ordered the swordfish I wouldn't eat much of it and be slim and gorgeous when I landed. It was juicy and delicious! So is this recipe and the one that follows.

Six 7-ounce swordfish steaks	*¼ cup extra-virgin olive oil*
(or tuna or snapper filets)	*2 tablespoons fine dry bread*
Salt and freshly ground pepper	*crumbs*
1 cup dry white wine	*3 tablespoons chopped capers,*
1 fresh rosemary sprig, finely	*drained*
chopped	*Juice of 1 lemon*
4 cloves garlic, finely chopped	*Pepper Sauce (see below)*

Place the swordfish steaks in a bowl and season with salt and pepper. Add the wine, rosemary, and garlic. Coat steaks well and marinate for at least 1 hour.

Drain the fish, reserving the marinade. Brush a skillet with a little of the oil and heat it. Sprinkle the fish with bread crumbs and capers, add to the skillet and cook on both sides until nearly cooked through, basting from time to time with the reserved marinade.

Whisk the remaining oil with the lemon juice in a small bowl. Pour it over the fish and cook a few minutes more. Serve hot, with the Pepper Sauce.

Serves 6

PEPPER SAUCE

1 teaspoon whole peppercorns, finely chopped or pounded
½ cup white wine
½ cup half and half
½ cup clam juice

Simmer the peppercorns in the wine. Reduce the liquid to one half or less. Add the cream mixed with the clam juice. Boil up at once and simmer for a few minutes. Strain.

Makes about 1½ cups

❧Another Marinated Swordfish

Six 7-ounce swordfish steaks
Salt and freshly ground white pepper
2 tablespoons vegetable oil
2 tablespoons soy sauce
2 tablespoons Worcestershire sauce
2 cloves garlic, minced

Place the swordfish steaks in a bowl and season with salt and white pepper to taste. Combine the oil, soy sauce, Worcestershire sauce, and garlic and pour over the steaks. Marinate for at least 1 hour.

Remove the steaks from the marinade and place on a broiler pan. Broil about 6 inches from the heat, basting occasionally with the marinade, until the fish flakes easily when pierced with a fork.

Serves 6

❧Steamed Trout

4 small 12-ounce whole trout, heads and tails removed and fileted
Salt and pepper to taste
¼ cup white wine
2 tablespoons lemon juice
1 tablespoon olive oil
¼ cup chopped fresh parsley
2 tablespoons butter or margarine, melted
¼ cup pecan pieces

Carefully wash the trout and pat them dry. Place the trout on a heat-proof plate—I used a Pyrex pie plate. Salt and pepper generously, pour the wine, lemon juice, and olive oil over the trout and sprinkle with the parsley.

Wrap the plate completely with foil. Place the plate in a steamer, cover the steamer, and let the water come to a rolling boil. Reduce the heat and simmer for 18 minutes. If the trout flakes easily when touched with a fork, it's ready to serve.

Drizzle the fish with melted butter or margarine in which you've crisped the pecan pieces, if you're so inclined—I am. (I can only be totally disciplined up to a point.) Serve very hot, with small boiled parsleyed potatoes and your favorite green vegetable.

Serves 4

✤ *Trout Amandine*

3 small 4- to 6-ounce trout,
 boned and opened flat
Lemon or lime juice
Salt and pepper
Flour for dredging
3 tablespoons olive oil or
 butter or margarine or a
 mixture of oil and butter or
 margarine

¼ cup slivered almonds
Lemon or lime wedges, for
 garnish

Soak the trout in ice water for a few minutes. Pat dry, sprinkle inside the filets with lemon or lime juice, and salt and pepper to taste. Dredge the filets in flour, shaking off the excess.

In a large skillet, heat the oil or combination of butter and oil until hot. Add the filets and brown quickly until golden and crisp on both sides. Remove to a warm platter. In the same skillet, sauté the almonds until lightly browned. Sprinkle over the trout. Garnish with lemon or lime wedges.

Serves 3 people, 4 if somebody is willing to share

❖ *Tony's Filet Mignon of Tuna*

For other delicious recipes from Tony's restaurant see Vincent Bommarito's Pasta Primavera from Tony's (page 220) and Sesame–Poppy Seed Ring (page 256).

Six 2-inch-thick 7-ounce tuna steaks
¼ to ½ cup fresh virgin olive oil
3 cloves garlic, 2 halved, 1 minced
Freshly ground black pepper
1 leek, thinly sliced (white and green parts)
1 medium tomato, peeled, seeded and chopped

1 whole fennel bulb, thinly sliced
2 tablespoons butter or margarine
1¾ cups fish stock
¾ cup white wine
Salt and white pepper
Pinch of saffron

Marinate the tuna steaks in the olive oil, halved garlic cloves, and black pepper to taste for at least 1 hour, longer if you have time.

In a heavy skillet, sauté the leek and fennel slices and tomato in the butter or margarine for 1 or 2 minutes, until slightly softened. Add the minced garlic and sauté for 1 minute. Add the fish stock and wine, bring to a boil, and reduce by ½ cup. Add salt and freshly ground white pepper to taste and saffron.

Preheat the broiler or charcoal grill. Salt and pepper the tuna steaks and sprinkle them with chopped sage. Broil about 6 inches from the heat for about 6 minutes on each side. If the steaks are 1 inch thick, broil for about 3 minutes on each side or until they flake when pierced with a fork. Please don't overcook. Pour the leek-fennel mixture over the broiled tuna. Serve on very hot plates.

Serves 6

❋ *Your Favorite White Fish Baked with Cashews and Mango-Ginger Sauce*

Though they're not exactly a staple in my house, when mangoes are in and wonderful in the summer out here in California—and not so frightfully expensive—this is a lovely, intriguing combination of the usual and the unusual.

¼ pound unsalted cashews, roasted and ground medium-fine
½ cup fine dry bread crumbs
Four 6-ounce filets of firm white fish (halibut, cod, orange roughy, preferably halibut)

Salt and pepper to taste
3 to 4 tablespoons peanut oil
Mango-Ginger Sauce (see below)

Preheat the oven to 375°.

Combine the ground cashews and bread crumbs and spread them on a small plate. Season the fish generously with salt and pepper, and press the filets into the crumb mixture until completely coated.

Heat the oil in an oven-proof sauté pan over medium heat. Carefully place the breaded fish in the pan and cook until lightly browned on one side. Do not let them burn or blacken. Turn the fish and place the pan in the oven for about 5 minutes or until the fish are firm and flake when the underside is pierced with a fork. Do not overcook. Place the fish on warm dinner plates, surround with the Mango-Ginger Sauce, and serve immediately.

Serves 4

MANGO-GINGER SAUCE

2 very large ripe mangoes, peeled, seeded, and coarsely chopped
4 teaspoons grated fresh ginger
2 cups chicken stock

4 fresh basil leaves, rinsed and dried
Salt to taste
Juice of ½ lime
1½ teaspoons maple syrup

Combine the mangoes, ginger, and chicken stock in a heavy saucepan. Bring to a boil, reduce the heat, and simmer for about 20 minutes, or until the liquid is reduced by half.

Pour the mixture into a blender or food processor and blend until very smooth. Place the basil leaves in the sauce and pour into the top half of a double boiler over hot water. Steep for at least 20 minutes. Just before serving, remove the basil leaves and season to taste with salt and lime juice. Stir in the maple syrup—that little taste of sweetness is delicious.

❃ *Baked Fish with Cashews*

This recipe and the one that precedes it both call for cashews, but don't for a moment think these dishes are alike. They are different, both delicious, and really worth a company try.

2½ pounds red snapper filets
Juice of 3 limes or 1 large lemon
Salt to taste
1½ cups finely chopped unsalted cashews
½ cup grated Monterey Jack cheese
1 small onion, very finely grated
1 small clove garlic, crushed
½ cup milk
½ teaspoon grated nutmeg
Cayenne pepper to taste
1 bay leaf, finely ground
½ cup fine dry bread crumbs
Scant 3 tablespoons butter or margarine

Brush the fish on both sides with lime or lemon juice and sprinkle with salt. Let it sit in the refrigerator as long as possible, 3 to 4 hours is best.

Mix the nuts with the cheese, onion, and garlic, moistening it with milk to form a stiff paste. Add salt, the cayenne, nutmeg, and bay leaf, and mix well.

Grease your baking dish well. If you have a pretty oven-proof dish, use it to bake and serve in. Place the fish in the dish. Carefully pat and spread the cashew-cheese mixture over the fish, sprinkle with bread crumbs, and dot with the butter or margarine.

Bake in a preheated 375° oven for about 45 minutes, basting with drippings from the pan or extra margarine if you need it. The fish is cooked when it flakes easily when pierced with a fork (do this in an inconspicuous place—don't spoil the picture).

Serves 4 to 6

❋ *Poached Filets on Greens*

I think I mentioned earlier that I was never a "fish" person. Growing up in Nashville, if it didn't come out of the Cumberland River and it wasn't fried, I just didn't know it existed. (Actually, nothing is better than crisply fried fish and fried potatoes, but there comes a time ...) I've found more incredibly succulent fish dishes, now that I've put my mind to it, than I ever dreamed possible. Try the Lime-Marinated Filet of Sole (page 155), and the Orange Roughy with Spinach (page 155), both guaranteed low calorie, low cholesterol, high in health, and definitely a dieter's soul food. This recipe is a little less virtuous, but if you've had the above-mentioned "good guys" for a week or two, you owe it to yourself.

1¼ pounds orange roughy or
  any delicate white fish
Salt and pepper
½ cup lime juice
½ cup water
½ bunch mustard greens
½ bunch kale
2 bay leaves, tied together
1 teaspoon cayenne pepper or
  to taste

¼ pound mushrooms, chopped
3 tablespoons butter or
  margarine
¾ tablespoon flour
⅓ cup sour cream
¾ cup clam juice
½ cup cooked shrimp

Season the fish with salt and pepper to taste. Mix the lime juice with the water and marinate the fish for an hour, then drain.

Meantime, cover the mustard greens and kale with water, and add a little salt, the bay leaves, and the cayenne pepper. Boil for 10 minutes, then add the drained fish to the greens and poach slowly for about 10 minutes, or until the fish flakes easily. When tender, place the fish and greens on a warmed plate and set aside. While the fish poaches, make the sauce.

Chop the mushrooms very fine and sauté them in 2 tablespoons of the butter or margarine. Remove the mushrooms and set aside. In the same saucepan, mix the remaining 1 tablespoon of butter or margarine with the flour. When smooth, return the mushrooms to the saucepan, add the sour cream and clam juice, and simmer until hot. Add the shrimp. Serve the filets on warmed plates over the greens, with the sauce.

Serves 3 to 4

❧ Fish Provençale

"Provençale" simply means somebody in a provincial area thought of a sensational way to combine tomatoes, vegetables, and herbs with chicken or fish or a light meat of some kind. It's easy and a whole meal for the greatest gourmands.

FISH STOCK

3 pounds meaty fish bones (preferably with head and tails on and gills removed)	4 sprigs parsley
	1 bay leaf
	½ teaspoon dried thyme
8 cups water	6 peppercorns
1½ cups dry white wine	Salt to taste
1 cup coarsely chopped onion	½ cup green part of leeks
1 cup coarsely chopped celery	(optional)

Combine all the ingredients in a stockpot, bring to a boil, and simmer for 20 to 30 minutes. Remove from the heat, strain, and set aside. You should have about 7½ cups of stock.

3 tablespoons olive oil	¼ teaspoon fennel seed
1 large onion, sliced	½ teaspoon bottled orange peel
1 carrot, sliced	1½ teaspoons salt
1 leek, sliced	2 pinches of saffron
2 quarts Fish Stock (see above) (clam juice may be used)	1 pound shrimp
	1 pound lobster tails
1 cup dry white wine	(optional)
One 19-ounce can plum tomatoes with juice	1 pound sea scallops
	3 to 4 pounds assorted lean
2 cloves garlic, halved	white fish (cod, perch,
1 bay leaf	halibut, snapper, bass), cut
¼ teaspoon dried thyme	into 3-inch chunks

Heat the olive oil and sauté the onion, carrot, and leek. Add the fish stock , white wine, and tomatoes. Stir in the garlic, bay leaf, thyme, fennel seed, orange peel, salt, and saffron. Bring to a boil and simmer for about 15 minutes. Taste for seasoning. About 10 to 15 minutes before serving, add the seafood and fish in the order listed, cooking each one for 10 to 15 seconds before adding the next. When all have been added, continue to cook 9 to 14 minutes longer.

Serve with salad and garlic bread.

Serves 8

✱ *Mixed Seafood Provençale*

Something quite wonderful and buttery happens to this sauce when those tomatoes and vegetables and herbs come together—and there's not a smidgen of butter in it. You won't gain weight on this one unless you eat as much of it as I did.

I first cooked it when Beautiful Daughter Missy and her three equally beautiful children, Jennefer, Adam, and Alex (age two but already possessing a fine palate) came to visit Meemah (me) at the beach one week. I actually served it in soup bowls so we wouldn't waste a drop of the sauce.

Crusty French bread and a nice green salad are all you need to go with it, but we had already decided to have the Pecan Caramel Chocolate Chip Ice Cream (page 290)—oh well.

⅓ cup finely chopped onion
2 tablespoons olive oil
2 cloves garlic, minced
¼ pound uncooked fresh
   shrimp, cleaned, shelled, and
   deveined
2 pounds Italian plum
   tomatoes, peeled, seeded, and
   chopped, or one 28-ounce
   can Italian plum tomatoes
   with juice
5 flat anchovies, rinsed and
   chopped
⅔ cup dry white wine
¼ teaspoon red pepper flakes
   (more if you like—I do)
1 tablespoon chopped fresh
   thyme or scant 1 teaspoon
   dried

1 tablespoon chopped fresh
   sage or scant 1 teaspoon
   dried
1 tablespoon chopped fresh
   tarragon or scant 1 teaspoon
   dried
1 pound boneless sea bass, cut
   into chunks
1 pound boneless red snapper,
   cut into chunks
½ cup black niçoise or
   Kalamata olives
1 tablespoon capers, drained
Salt and pepper to taste
Fresh basil leaves, coarsely
   chopped, for garnish

In a large skillet, sauté the onion in the olive oil until softened; add the garlic and then the shrimp. When the shrimp turn pink, remove and place them on a warm platter. Add the tomatoes and anchovies to the skillet and cook for 5 minutes. Add the white wine, red pepper flakes, thyme, sage, and tarragon. Bring to a boil and add the sea bass, then the red snapper. Cook for 4 to 5 minutes, until just done. With a slotted spoon, remove the fish to the platter with the shrimp and keep warm.

Bring the sauce to a boil and cook until thickened. Add the olives, capers, salt, and pepper, and simmer for 1 or 2 minutes. Spoon the sauce over the fish and sprinkle with chopped basil leaves.

Serves 6 to 8

❀ *Corn Crab Cakes with Jalapeño-Tartar Sauce*

¼ *cup mayonnaise*
1 *egg plus 1 egg white*
⅓ *cup cooked corn kernels*
¼ *cup finely diced sweet red pepper*
½ *cup finely diced California chilies*
2 *tablespoons finely diced red onion*
1 *teaspoon dry mustard*
½ *teaspoon freshly ground white pepper*
A *few drops of Worcestershire sauce*

Pinch of cayenne pepper
1 *cup bread crumbs (made from dry French bread)*
½ *pound crab meat, picked over and cleaned*
1 *tablespoon butter*
1 *tablespoon vegetable oil*
Pickled baby corn, for garnish
Lemon wedges, for garnish
Pickled jalapeño chilies, for garnish
Jalapeño-Tartar Sauce (see below)

Blend the mayonnaise and egg and egg white in a large bowl. Mix in the corn kernels, red pepper, chilies, onion, mustard, white pepper, Worcestershire sauce, and cayenne. Stir in the bread crumbs and fold in the crab meat. Shape the mixture into 12 patties, using ¼ cup for each.

Melt the butter and oil in a large, heavy skillet over high heat. Add the crab cakes (in batches if necessary) and cook until lightly browned, 2 to 3 minutes on each side. Garnish with baby corn, lemon wedges, and chilies. Serve with the tartar sauce.

Serves 4

JALAPEÑO-TARTAR SAUCE

2 cups mayonnaise

3 tablespoons chopped red
onion

2 tablespoons chopped fresh
parsley

2 tablespoons seeded and
chopped jalapeño chilies

1 tablespoon chopped
cornichons

¾ teaspoon dry mustard

Dash of Tabasco sauce

Combine all the ingredients in the bowl of a food processor and
blend, using on/off turns, until the ingredients are finely diced. Transfer
to a bowl, cover, and refrigerate.

❊ Salt Cod Cakes

*I love croquettes—egg croquettes, chicken croquettes, salmon cro-
quettes—and a long time ago in Nashville, I remember having this wonderful croquette Mother used to make out of codfish. It's flaky, and has
character and tastes like the sea.*

*You get codfish in the frozen-food section of your local supermarket.
I've repeated the directions for preparing it pretty much the way they are
on the package—you'll enjoy it. Sometime, make small 1½- to 2-inch
codfish cakes, crisped and served as an hors d'oeuvre. Serve them with
the Pepper Sauce on page 159. Or, if you prefer a spicier one, use the
sauce following this recipe or any tartar sauce.*

One 16-ounce box frozen salt
cod

3 potatoes, peeled and
quartered

2 tablespoons finely chopped
onion

2 tablespoons finely chopped
green pepper

2 tablespoons finely chopped
celery

2 tablespoons finely chopped
fresh parsley

1 tablespoon finely chopped
cilantro (coriander)

1 tablespoon finely chopped
fresh mint

Salt and pepper to taste

Tabasco sauce to taste

Generous dash of
Worcestershire sauce

2 tablespoons milk

1 egg yolk

2 tablespoons unflavored bread
crumbs

Vegetable oil

Soak the cod in cold water for 15 to 30 minutes or overnight. Drain. Place in a saucepan, add cold water, and bring to a boil. Drain and repeat the process 3 times. (It's not as much trouble as it sounds and gets that metallic salt taste out and it's worth it).

Boil the potatoes for about 20 minutes or until tender, drain, and place them in a large bowl with the cod. Add the onion, green pepper, celery, parsley, cilantro, mint, salt and pepper, Tabasco, and Worcestershire. Mix well. I use a potato masher to get a good texture. Form the mixture into cakes about 3 inches in diameter.

Mix together the milk and egg yolk. Dip the patties in the milk mixture and then into the bread crumbs. Heat about 1½ to 2 inches of oil in a skillet. Sauté the patties until golden brown and crispy on both sides. Place on paper towels to drain. Serve hot, with the following sauce or another of your choice.

Serves 4 to 6 unless it's an hors d'oeuvre

SAUCE
3 tablespoons mayonnaise　　　　*1 teaspoon Red Tomatilla Sauce (page 31)*

Mix together in a small bowl.

✣ *Tuna Salad Soufflé*

The nice thing about this dish is that the ingredients are so flexible. For instance, if you don't have the shrimp on hand—or the ham, or the bacon—not to worry, it will still be a treat for the ever-faithful tuna salad sandwich lover. Chopped water chestnuts, a few almonds, a little grated onion, any of these goodies added to the salad to give it a little extra zest make the soufflé a surprisingly delicious supper or luncheon dish. Do it all ahead except, of course, the egg white and baking part.

TUNA SALAD

4 stalks celery, chopped
½ green pepper, seeded and chopped
Scant 2 teaspoons finely grated onion
2 tablespoons butter or margarine
¼ pound medium shrimp, shelled and deveined and cut into 3 pieces
Two 6½-ounce cans water-packed tuna fish, drained
2 strips lean country ham, chopped, or 2 strips lean bacon, crisply fried, drained, and crumbled
1 teaspoon capers, drained
2 eggs, hard-boiled, chopped
1 tablespoon Worcestershire sauce
Couple of dashes of Tabasco sauce
4 ripe olives, diced
Salt and pepper to taste

Sauté the celery, green pepper, and onion in the butter until translucent. Add the shrimp, then the tuna, and cook until the tuna is heated through. Remove from the heat. Add the remaining ingredients, taste for seasoning, and set aside.

SOUFFLÉ

*4 tablespoons butter plus extra
 for soufflé dish
4 tablespoons flour
1 teaspoon salt
Dash of paprika
Dash of cayenne pepper or
 Tabasco sauce
¼ teaspoon mustard
1 cup milk*

*1 cup coarsely grated Monterey
 Jack cheese
4 egg yolks, well beaten
Reserved tuna salad
5 egg whites, beaten with a
 wire whisk until stiff but not
 dry
Freshly grated Parmesan cheese*

Melt the butter in a double boiler. Add the flour, salt, paprika, cayenne or Tabasco, and the mustard and blend well. Add the milk and cook until thickened. Add the cheese and stir until melted. Cool, and add the egg yolks. Stir in the reserved tuna salad. Stir ¼ cup of the beaten egg whites into the flour-egg-cheese-tuna mixture. Then fold in the remainder of the egg whites, gently and carefully, so as not to lose the air you beat into them.

Butter and dust with Parmesan cheese a 6-cup soufflé dish. Pour the mixture into the dish and bake in a preheated 475° oven for 10 minutes, then reduce the heat to 400° and bake for about 25 minutes longer. Serve at once or sooner.

Serves 4

Vegetables

I learned to love vegetables dearly—the long, hard way. I'd always thought green beans had to be slightly gray in color and cooked with a little "side meat" to be really significant, broccoli pretty much the same. Then I went through the nouvelle totally al dente phase. I've decided not to waste myself on either one. Vegetables can be gloriously emerald green or yellow or golden—neither soggy nor so underdone you might as well serve them with a dip. There's a doneness in between that's perfect and full of flavor—nice to look at, no trouble at all to cook, less to serve, and makes you the resident wonder because where it is almost a cinch to produce a fine, tasty entrée, it takes a real flair to get an unusual flavor for an accompanying, less glamorous partner. Try some of these recipes. On occasion I've served them all by themselves as a special course—they were that interesting.

❧ Baked Asparagus Parmesan

1 pound asparagus, peeled	*Salt*
3 tablespoons butter, softened	*½ cup grated Parmesan cheese*

Boil the asparagus until just al dente. Drain at once. Butter the bottom of a baking dish and arrange a row of asparagus side by side. Be sure the tips all face in one direction and remain uncovered. Sprinkle with salt to taste and Parmesan cheese. Dot with butter. Continue making layers until all the asparagus is used. Bake for 15 minutes on the top shelf in a preheated 450° oven.

Serves 4

❧ *Asparagus Crepes*

12 asparagus spears, peeled
   and trimmed (reserve the
   ends)
¾ cup chicken broth
1 tablespoon butter or
   margarine
1 tablespoon flour

¾ cup low-fat milk
Salt and pepper
4 crepes (your own or
   available in frozen food
   section)
Freshly grated Monterey Jack
   cheese

Cook the asparagus ends for about 15 minutes, or until almost done, in well-seasoned chicken broth. Add the asparagus spears and cook until al dente. Drain, reserving the cooking liquid. (There should be about ¾ cup left.)

Meanwhile, melt the butter or margarine over low heat, add the flour, and mix well. Add the milk, stirring constantly to avoid lumps. Add the reserved ¾ cup cooking liquid to the roux, and season with salt and pepper to taste. Add the asparagus, and cook slowly until tender. Do not overcook or they will become mushy. Taste for seasoning—the sauce should have a healthy asparagus flavor by now.

When ready to serve, place the open crepes on hot dinner plates. Place a portion of asparagus and a little sauce on one half of each crepe. Fold the tops over, pour a little sauce over all, sprinkle with 1 tablespoon cheese, and put under the broiler until the cheese is melted. Serve hot.

Serves 4

❧ *Harvard Beets*

I wish I could think of a way to improve on this and name it Vanderbilt Beets after my alma mater. On second thought—why not? See the P.S. on this recipe for the old college try.

12 medium-size firm young
   beets
⅓ cup sugar
1½ teaspoons cornstarch

½ teaspoon salt
⅓ cup red wine vinegar
2 tablespoons butter, cut into
   ½-inch bits

With a small, sharp knife, cut the tops from the beets, leaving about 1 inch of stem on each. Scrub the beets under cold running water and place them in a 4- to 5-quart saucepan. Pour in enough cold water to cover them by 2 inches, bring to a boil over high heat, and cover the pan tightly. Reduce the heat to low and simmer until the beets are tender. This may take from 30 minutes to 1 hour for young beets to as long as 2 hours for older ones. The beets should be kept constantly covered with water; add boiling water if necessary during the cooking.

Drain the beets in a colander set over a bowl and reserve ½ cup of the cooking liquid. Slip off the skins, cut the beets crosswise into ¼-inch-thick slices, and set them aside.

Combine the sugar, cornstarch, salt, and vinegar in a 2- to 3-quart enameled or stainless-steel saucepan and stir until the mixture is smooth. Add the reserved beet liquid and, stirring constantly, cook over moderate heat until the sauce comes to a boil and thickens. Swirl in the butter bits and then add the beets, turning the slices with a spoon to coat them evenly with the sauce. Simmer for 2 or 3 minutes to heat the beets through. Taste for seasoning and serve from a heated bowl.

P.S. Add 3 tablespoons of sour cream or yogurt to make it even more beautiful and to alter the taste somewhat. So there you are, unless you thought of it first—it's Vandy Beets.

Serves 6

❖ *Yale Beets*

I tasted this recipe at a lovely New England restaurant, which called it Yale Beets, and said they got it out of someone's book. If this is the same as yours, wherever you are, I apologize, and I thank you—as will everyone else who tastes them.

So—three prominent universities, the student bodies and faculties of which I'm sure enjoy principally cheeseburgers and hot dogs, are hereby represented in a way as classic as their jerseys.

1 or 2 medium-size oranges
1 medium-size lemon
3 tablespoons butter, 1 softened, 2 cut into bits
12 medium-size firm young beets, trimmed, peeled, and sliced crosswise into ⅛-inch-thick rounds (about 6 cups)

2 tablespoons flour
½ cup sugar
½ teaspoon salt

Peel 1 orange and the lemon, being careful not to cut too deeply so you do not include the bitter white pith. Reserve the fruit. Cut the orange and lemon peels into strips about 1 inch long and ⅛ inch wide and drop them into enough boiling water to cover them completely. Boil briskly uncovered for 5 minutes. Drain in a colander and run cold water over the strips of peel to set their color. Set aside to drain thoroughly.

Meanwhile, preheat the oven to 350°. With a pastry brush, spread the 1 tablespoon of softened butter over the bottom and sides of a 13-x-8½-x-2-inch baking dish. Spread the sliced beets evenly in the buttered dish and set aside.

Squeeze the peeled lemon and strain 2 tablespoons of the juice into a small bowl. Add the flour and stir until it dissolves completely. Then squeeze the peeled orange and strain the juice into another bowl. There should be ½ cup of juice; if necessary, squeeze and strain a second orange. Add the orange juice, sugar, and salt to the lemon-flour mixture and stir until the sugar dissolves. Pour the entire contents of the bowl over the beets. Scatter the 2 tablespoons of butter bits on top.

Cover the dish tightly with foil and bake in the middle of the oven for 1½ hours, or until the beets are tender and show no resistance when pierced with the point of a small knife.

Transfer the beets and sauce to a heated bowl, sprinkle with the reserved strips of orange and lemon peel, and serve at once.

Serves 6 to 8

❋ *Broccoli*

Broccoli is beautiful just about everywhere all year round. It was difficult not to overload the vegetable section with broccoli recipes—but it is wonderfully adaptable. Here are a few ideas that worked for me.

❋ *Sautéed Broccoli and Red Peppers*

Red pepper strips and pine nuts make this a party dish.

1 bunch broccoli, cut into flowerets
2 tablespoons butter or margarine
2 tablespoons olive oil

1 sweet red pepper, seeded and sliced into thin strips
2 cloves garlic, minced
2 tablespoons toasted pine nuts (pignolia)

In a large skillet, sauté the broccoli in the butter or margarine and oil for 3 to 4 minutes. Add the pepper, garlic, and pine nuts. Sauté for 2 to 3 minutes more, or until the vegetables are tender-crisp.

Serves 4 to 6

❧ *Broccoli with Cashews*

Serve this Chinese-flavored vegetable dish with an all-Chinese menu or with your regular pork, beef, lamb, or chicken entrée.

1 tablespoon peanut oil
1 teaspoon chopped fresh ginger
1 teaspoon chopped fresh garlic
1 tablespoon soy sauce (preferably light)
½ teaspoon sugar
2 tablespoons dry sherry or Chinese cooking wine
2 tablespoons chicken broth

Dash of Chinese hot sauce (available in specialty markets) or Tabasco, if you like (I do)
1 bunch broccoli, stems peeled, and cut into flowerets
¼ sweet red pepper, seeded and cut into thin strips
Salt and pepper
Generous ¼ cup whole or halved cashews, toasted a little

Heat the oil in a wok or a deep skillet with a tight-fitting lid. Add the ginger and garlic. When the flavor is released, after 1 or 2 minutes, add the soy sauce, sugar, sherry, chicken broth, and hot sauce or Tabasco. Add the broccoli and red pepper, and mix well to coat with sauce. Add salt and pepper to taste. Cover and cook for about 5 minutes, or until almost done, shaking the pan from time to time. Stir in the cashews and continue to cook another 5 minutes, until the broccoli is tender.

Serves 6

❧ *Steamed Piquant Broccoli*

2 tablespoons Dijon mustard
Juice of ½ lemon
½ teaspoon paprika
¼ teaspoon cayenne pepper
1 tablespoon olive oil
Salt

1 bunch broccoli (approximately 1½ pounds), stems trimmed, peeled, and cut into ½-inch pieces, top cut into flowerets

Combine the mustard, lemon juice, paprika, cayenne, and olive oil. Steam the broccoli for 10 or 15 minutes, or until tender. Remove to a bowl and season with salt to taste. Add the mustard mixture and toss until thoroughly coated.

Serves 4

❊ *Orange-Lemon Broccoli*

This unusual way of cooking broccoli seems to bring out every ounce of flavor, and it's definitely a party dish too.

3 tablespoons sugar
1 bunch broccoli, stems peeled, cut into flowerets
2 quarts boiling water
3 tablespoons butter or margarine
3 tablespoons flour
1 cup milk (low-fat is okay)
Salt to taste

Cayenne pepper to taste
2 tablespoons half and half
2 tablespoons lemon juice
2 tablespoons orange juice
½ cup freshly grated Parmesan cheese
¼ cup slivered almonds or cashews

Place the sugar in a heavy saucepan over medium-high heat. When the sugar begins to caramelize, add the broccoli and stir to coat lightly. Pour the boiling water over all and cook for 5 to 7 minutes; the broccoli will be bright emerald green. Drain in a colander and rinse with cold water to stop the cooking. Place the broccoli in an oven-proof baking dish and set aside.

Melt the butter or margarine, stir in the flour, and cook for about 1 minute. Slowly, stirring with a wire whisk, pour in the milk. Add the salt and cayenne pepper to taste. Stir in the half and half, lemon juice, and orange juice. Carefully pour the sauce over the broccoli. Sprinkle with the Parmesan cheese and the almonds or cashews. Bake in a preheated 400° oven for 10 minutes or until browned and bubbly. Serve piping hot.

Serves 4 to 6

✿ Broccoli in Crab Meat Sauce

...And still another. This is a perfect luncheon dish all by itself.

1 bunch broccoli, cut into
  medium-size flowerets
Salt and pepper
2 tablespoons olive oil
1 tablespoon butter or
  margarine
2 small scallions, chopped (use
  some of the green part)
3 water chestnuts, chopped
  medium-fine*

2 tablespoons bamboo shoots*
Scant 3 tablespoons flour
1¾ cups chicken broth
¼ pound crab meat, picked
  over, cleaned, and coarsely
  chopped
1 tablespoon plus 2 teaspoons
  good soy sauce
Generous grinding of white
  pepper

Cook the broccoli for 10 to 15 minutes in boiling water to which you have added salt and pepper. The broccoli should be bright green but not too underdone.

Heat the olive oil and butter or margarine in a sauté pan. Add the scallions, water chestnuts, and bamboo shoots and sauté until lightly warmed. Add the flour, reduce the heat to low, and cook for 5 to 10 minutes (do not let the roux brown). Slowly add the chicken broth, stirring constantly to remove all lumps. The sauce should be smooth. Add the crab meat and heat through. Stir in the soy sauce and white pepper.

Pour the sauce over the cooked, well-drained broccoli just before serving. Serve hot—please.

Serves 4 to 6

*Store the remaining water chestnuts and bamboo shoots in jars in the refrigerator for future use. They're lovely for extra texture and flavoring in salads and other dishes.

❀ *Creamy Cabbage with Dill*

1 small firm head of cabbage
1 tablespoon coarse salt
3 tablespoons butter
1 large onion, chopped

One 3-ounce package cream
 cheese
2 tablespoons chopped fresh
 dill or 1 teaspoon dillseed
Salt and white pepper

Remove the outer leaves of the cabbage and slice it into quarters, cutting out the hard core at the bottom of each quarter. Shred the cabbage coarsely and place it in a large bowl. Cover with boiling water, stir in the coarse salt, and let stand for 5 minutes. Drain in a colander and refresh under cold running water. Drain well again and then chop.

Melt the butter in a large, heavy pot and sauté the chopped onion over medium-low heat for 5 minutes, then add the drained cabbage. Cut the cream cheese into pieces and stir it into the cabbage until blended. Simmer until the cheese melts. Add the dill, season with salt and white pepper to taste, and simmer for another minute or so. Serve hot.

Serves 4

❀ *Carrots with Mint*

This is so simple. Those little mint leaves give our golden—taken for granted—year-round nuggets a flavor you'd never expect.

2 pounds carrots, peeled and
 cut diagonally into ¼-inch
 rounds
1½ cups water
1 teaspoon salt

3 tablespoons butter, cut into
 slices
Freshly ground black pepper
4 tablespoons coarsely cut
 fresh mint leaves

Place the carrots in a saucepan and add the water and salt. Cover and bring to a boil over high heat. Reduce the heat and simmer 15 minutes or until the carrots are done.

Drain the carrots and return them to the saucepan. Stir in the butter and the pepper. Remove the saucepan from the heat and toss lightly with the mint leaves.

Serves 6

❧ Cauliflower with Cheese

1 large cauliflower, cut into
 flowerets
¼ cup margarine or butter,
 melted

¼ cup grated Parmesan or
 mozzarella cheese

Cook the cauliflower in salted water for 15 to 20 minutes, or until just tender. Preheat the oven to 350°. Arrange the cauliflower in a casserole, cover evenly with the margarine or butter, and sprinkle with the grated cheese. Heat in the oven until warmed through. Then place under the broiler to lightly brown the cheese.

Serves 4 to 6

❧ Braised Celery with Almonds

Celery is treated like some taken-for-granted poor cousin of the vegetable family. It perks up dishes such as stews and salads—and it helps you diet virtuously (at least you're munching on something). But it's a great low-calorie dish all on its own. I made this simple braised celery one day for lunch when everybody else in the house was cooking something to test for tasting at dinner. It was a smashing success. Try it—you'll give it an executive position of its very own.

1 bunch celery
2 sprigs parsley
1 bay leaf
1¼ cups chicken broth
1½ tablespoons butter or
 margarine

1½ tablespoons flour
1 cup milk
½ teaspoon salt
⅛ teaspoon white pepper
2 tablespoons half and half
¼ cup slivered and crisply
 toasted almonds

Wash the celery and cut the stalks in half lengthwise and then crosswise into 2-inch lengths. Reserve the tops. Put the celery tops, parsley, and bay leaf in a cheesecloth bag. Bring the chicken broth to a boil and drop in the celery and bag of herbs. Boil the celery for about 15 minutes, or until just tender; don't let it overcook. Drain, reserving the cooking liquid, and place on a warm platter. Cover the celery with foil while you are making the sauce.

Melt the butter or margarine over low heat in a saucepan. Add the flour and cook, stirring constantly for 2 to 3 minutes, until the flour loses its raw taste. Add the milk slowly, stirring with a small wire whisk to dissolve any lumps. Pour in the reserved celery cooking liquid and season with salt and white pepper, then add the half and half. Taste for seasoning. Pour the sauce over the hot celery and sprinkle with the almonds.

Serves 6

❋ *Creamy Noncreamed Corn*

I love corn—on and off the cob, yellow or white, creamy or non-creamy. Just to help us get off the heavy cream kick, here's a lovely compromise: summertime with fresh corn, wintertime with the frozen—though it's worth waiting through the winter for this special treat.

5 to 6 ears fresh corn or two
   10-ounce boxes frozen,
   thawed
1 stalk celery, chopped
2 tablespoons each chopped
   red and green bell peppers

2 tablespoons margarine
Salt and white pepper to taste
½ to ¾ cup milk

Remove the corn from the cob. Lightly sauté the celery and peppers in the margarine. When the peppers are soft, add the corn, salt, and pepper. When the corn begins to soften, add the milk, cover, and simmer until the liquid is reduced and absorbed. Taste for seasoning. Cover, and continue to cook over low heat for about 5 minutes, or until the corn is cooked through.

Serves 4 to 6

❋ *Corn and Tomato Casserole*

As I said, nothing is better than corn—unless it's tomatoes—and how about the two together? If you add a cup of okra I'd like to come to dinner.

3 tablespoons butter or
   margarine, 1 softened, 2 cut
   into ¼-inch bits
2 cups fresh corn kernels or 2
   cups thoroughly defrosted
   frozen corn
5 medium-size firm ripe
   tomatoes, peeled, seeded, and
   coarsely chopped

1 egg, lightly beaten
1 teaspoon light brown sugar
1 teaspoon salt
Freshly ground black pepper
1 cup soft fresh bread crumbs

Preheat the oven to 325°. Spread the 1 tablespoon softened butter evenly over the bottom and sides of a 1½-quart baking dish.

In a large bowl, combine the corn, tomatoes, egg, sugar, salt, and a few generous grindings of black pepper and mix gently but thoroughly. Pour the corn mixture into the buttered dish and press it down with a spatula or the back of a large spoon until it is smooth and compact. Sprinkle the top with the bread crumbs and dot with the 2 tablespoons of butter bits.

Bake in the middle of the oven for 1 hour, or until the bread crumbs are a rich golden brown. Serve hot, as a vegetable course or a main dish at lunch.

Serves 4 to 6

✤ Herb-Roasted Corn

Nothing tastes better than fresh corn on the cob in season, simply boiled for five to seven minutes and served hot with butter and salt and pepper. Now that I've ventured that bold statement as fact, this herb and corn combination is really, really delicious, especially if you have a few guests over to share it with you. Though I've used this blend of herbs, almost any fresh ones you have on hand will do.

4 to 6 ears of corn
8 tablespoons butter or
   margarine, softened
4 teaspoons chopped fresh
   parsley
4 teaspoons chopped fresh
   chives

2 teaspoons chopped fresh
   basil
2 teaspoons chopped fresh sage
Dash of Tabasco sauce
Dash of Worcestershire sauce
¾ teaspoon salt

Pull the corn husks down, leaving them attached to the cob. Remove all the silks.

Mix the butter or margarine with the herbs, Tabasco, and Worcestershire. Spread a scant 1 tablespoon on each ear of corn and sprinkle with salt. Pull the husks up and wrap each ear in foil. Roast under a preheated broiler or over charcoal 4 inches from the heat, turning them from time to time to cook evenly until the corn is tender, about 30 minutes.

Remove the foil and the husks and brush the corn with the remaining herb butter.

Serves 4

❀ Cucumbers with Mint

Fresh mint and cucumbers—it sounds, and is, refreshing and cooling, even if it does taste better served hot.

3 large cucumbers
¼ cup butter or margarine
Salt and pepper

1½ teaspoons chopped fresh
*   mint*
¼ cup rice wine vinegar

Peel the cucumbers and cut them in half lengthwise. Scoop out the seeds with the tip of a spoon. Cut the cucumbers into ½-inch chunks. Place in boiling salted water and cook for 4 to 5 minutes, or until tender. Drain well, return to the pot, and shake over the heat to get rid of the excess moisture. Transfer the cucumber to a warm bowl and set aside.

Melt the butter or margarine in the pot the cucumbers cooked in, add salt and pepper to taste, and the mint; sauté for 1 minute. Return the cucumbers to the pot and toss until well coated. Add the vinegar and bring to a boil. Cook until the vinegar is evaporated, leaving the mint and butter. Serve hot.

Serves 4

❀ Eggplant-Mushroom Casserole

A delightful summer or winter vegetable casserole. The eggplant adds its own little zesty surprise. It reheats well, which makes it easy if you need the oven for something else that has to be served immediately.

¾ *cup freshly grated Parmesan*
cheese
½ *cup grated mozzarella*
cheese
Oil for the baking dish
4 medium potatoes, unpeeled,
thinly sliced
1 parsnip, scraped and thinly
sliced (optional)
1½ *tablespoons flour*
¾ *teaspoon salt*
½ *teaspoon black pepper*

1 pound mushrooms, sliced
2 tomatoes, thinly sliced
1 small eggplant, peeled, sliced
¼ *inch thick, salted, and*
placed in a colander to
drain, rinsed lightly and
patted dry
2 tablespoons butter or
margarine
1 cup low-fat milk
1 tablespoon chopped fresh
parsley

Mix the grated cheeses together.

Lightly oil the bottom of a shallow 1½-quart baking dish. Cover the bottom of the dish with a layer of potatoes and parsnip. Sprinkle with flour, salt, and pepper. Add a layer of mushrooms, tomatoes, and eggplant. Sprinkle with the grated cheeses. Dot with the butter or margarine. Repeat the layers in the same order until all the ingredients are used.

Pour the milk over all. Cover and bake in a preheated 375° oven for 45 minutes. Remove the cover and continue baking until the potatoes are tender and the top of the casserole is browned. Sprinkle with chopped parsley.

Serves 6

✽ Stuffed Eggplant

This is very popular out here in California. It's unusual, pretty, and the garlic doesn't bother anybody. Once they've seen and nibbled this dish, there are no holdouts, so we all breathe happily on each other.

2 small eggplants
2 tablespoons olive or
vegetable oil
1 small clove garlic, chopped
2 shallots, finely chopped
¼ *cup very finely minced*
onion
2 teaspoons finely minced fresh
parsley

3 tablespoons whole pine nuts
(pignolia)
Salt and pepper
½ *cup water*
Parsley sprigs or cilantro
(coriander) leaves for
garnish
Crisp slices of pita bread or
buttered rye toast

Sauté the whole eggplants in the oil, turning them often and carefully, for about 5 minutes. Remove the eggplants from the oil, make slits all over them, and set aside in a baking dish. In the same oil (you may have to add a little more, as those eggplants just soak it up), sauté the garlic, shallots, onion, parsley, and pine nuts for 2 or 3 minutes, until softened and blended. Add salt and pepper to taste. Stuff the vegetable mixture into the slits in the eggplants. Place the ½ cup water (or enough to come halfway up the sides of the eggplant) in the baking dish and bake in a preheated 350° oven for 30 minutes.

Serve right in the baking dish, if it's a pretty one, with a few pine nuts sprinkled on top and garnished with parsley sprigs or cilantro leaves. Have crisp slices of pita bread or buttered rye toast handy.

Serves 4

❖ Escarole with Bacon

An easy, light vegetable dish with an unusual look and texture.

2 pounds escarole, endive, and sorrel (combined) or any one of these	3 cloves garlic, chopped
	Salt and freshly ground black pepper
¼ cup extra-virgin olive oil	¼ cup crumbled cooked bacon

Trim the escarole, endive, and/or sorrel, discarding any tough stems and damaged or wilted leaves. Cut each bunch into quarters. Wash and pat dry.

Heat the oil in a skillet, add the garlic, and brown lightly over medium heat. Add the escarole, endive, and sorrel; cover, reduce the heat, and cook for 5 minutes. Season with salt and pepper to taste, scatter the bacon on top, and cook uncovered for another minute or two before serving.

Serves 6

❖ Braised Fennel in White Wine

Fennel is a nice, anise-flavored vegetable that looks like a big onion. It doesn't need a lot of help—it has a strong, unusual flavor. But don't pass it by because you can't figure out what to do with it. Here's a suggestion: A little added to your vegetable soup makes people wonder how you arrived at that special flavor. And then there's this delicious recipe, which you'll love on its very own.

4 medium fennel bulbs
1 large onion, sliced
2 tablespoons olive oil
1 small clove garlic, minced
1 small carrot, finely diced

1 stalk celery with tops, finely chopped
1 cup white wine
1 sprig fresh thyme
Salt and pepper

Remove the fronds from the fennel and quarter the bulbs. Sauté the onion in the olive oil until translucent. Add the garlic, carrot, and celery and sauté for 2 or 3 minutes, or until slightly softened and blended. Add the fennel quarters and sauté until they look glazed. Add the wine, thyme sprig, and salt and pepper to taste. Bring to a boil, reduce the heat, cover, and simmer until the fennel is tender, about 25 minutes depending on size.

Remove the thyme sprig before serving. Serve with a little dollop of butter if you like, but it doesn't need it.

Serves 6

✿ *Chinese Snow Peas and Peppers*

1 clove garlic, halved
1 slice fresh ginger, about the size of a quarter
2 tablespoons peanut oil
1 pound snow peas, topped and tailed
½ sweet red or green pepper, seeded and cut into strips

1 tablespoon soy sauce
1 teaspoon sugar
½ cup chicken broth
2 teaspoons dry sherry
1½ tablespoons cornstarch

Sauté the garlic and ginger in a heated wok with the oil for about 1 or 2 minutes. When the flavor and aroma are released, add the snow peas, turning to coat them with oil. Lift out and discard the garlic and ginger. Add the green or red pepper and mix well. Mix the soy sauce, sugar, ¼ cup of the chicken broth, and the sherry and pour over the vegetables. Turn and stir the vegetables to coat them with liquid. Cover and cook for a minute or two. Mix the cornstarch with the remaining chicken broth and add to the liquid in the wok. Turn the vegetables frequently and cook for about 1 minute. Serve hot.

Serves 4

❋ Grilled Peppers, Onions, and Eggplant

This is a warm and comforting side dish or a vegetable all unto itself. I make double the amount—it keeps well, and is a real treat with almost any meal, or as a snack before dinner. It sounds a little difficult because of the peeling process, but it isn't. It's not too spicy, not too bland—just mellow.

2 green peppers
2 sweet red peppers
1 tablespoon lemon juice
Olive oil
Salt and pepper
1 clove garlic, halved

1 large sweet onion, peeled
  and quartered
½ medium eggplant, cut into
  sticks as you would for
  French fries

Line a heavy skillet with foil and roast the peppers until blistered and charred, or broil them close to the flame (about 4 inches), turning frequently until blistered and charred. Wrap the peppers tightly in plastic wrap, or place them in a paper bag to steam. When cool, the skins will slip off easily. Cut the peppers in half, remove the seeds and white membranes, and cut into strips.

In a bowl, combine the lemon juice, 2 tablespoons olive oil, ½ teaspoon salt, ½ teaspoon pepper, and the garlic. Add the peppers and let stand for 15 minutes or so.

Thread the onion and eggplant onto skewers. Sprinkle with salt and pepper, drizzle a little oil over them, and broil close to the flame, turning often until tender, about 20 minutes. Place them in the bowl with the peppers and marinade and turn to coat well. Taste for seasoning. Serve warm. Or, if you prefer, heat some olive oil in a heavy skillet, add salt and pepper to taste, and sauté the onions, then the eggplant—the eggplant cooks quickly. When they are tender, place them in the bowl with the peppers and marinade. Turn well to coat. Taste for seasoning. Serve warm.

Serves 6 to 8

❋ Sweet Pepper Sauté

I serve this as a side dish with almost any fish, poultry, pasta, or meat dish. If you want to serve it cold, add the juice of half a lemon or to taste, and a little more olive oil and salt and pepper.

2 tablespoons olive oil
1 large sweet red pepper,
   seeded and cut into strips
1 large green pepper, seeded
   and cut into strips

1 large yellow pepper, seeded
   and cut into strips
2 cloves garlic, halved
Salt and pepper to taste

Heat the oil in a large skillet with high sides. Sauté the peppers and garlic until the peppers are slightly softened. Season well with salt and pepper. Remove the garlic prior to serving.

Serves 6

❋ Marinated Red Peppers

3 sweet red peppers
Salt to taste
½ cup olive oil
Squeeze of lemon juice

2 cloves garlic, pressed or
   chopped
2 tablespoons chopped fresh
   parsley

Place the whole peppers on a gas burner, a barbecue, or under the broiler and roast until black, turning frequently. After roasting, place the peppers in a brown paper bag or wrap them in plastic until cool. The skins will slip off easily. Seed under running water and cut into thin strips.

Combine the remaining ingredients. Add the peppers and chill.

Serves 4

❋ Dill Pickles

Your local deli, like Nate N' Al's here in Beverly Hills, probably has great dill pickles—but when the dill is in and the cucumbers are fresh I love to make my own.

36 to 40 good fresh cucumbers,
   about 3 to 3½ inches in
   length
6 quart jars with tight-fitting
   seals, sterilized
½ carrot, sliced
6 small cloves garlic

1 small hot red pepper, seeded
   and diced
Sweet onion, sliced into rings
   (if you like)
Scant 1 tablespoon kosher salt
Gobs of fresh dill

Place the cucumbers in the jars. To each jar add some carrot, a garlic clove, some hot red pepper, onion, and kosher salt. Pack the dill around the cucumbers. Add boiled water to fill the jars and cover the cucumbers, seal, and let stand for at least 2 weeks. (I usually can't wait that long—so open one and see how you're doing. Add more dill if you like—it can't hurt.) Place in the refrigerator before serving if it's a hot day.

Makes 6 quart jars

✤ Southern-Style String Beans

I love these string beans. I was raised on them and every once in a while it's good to go back—if only with your taste buds. Bake a little Buttermilk Corn Bread (page 253) to serve with them. Ummmmm.

4 slices lean raw bacon, cut into 1-inch dice
½ cup thinly sliced scallion rounds
1 pound green beans, washed and trimmed
1 tablespoon cold water

1 teaspoon salt
¼ teaspoon freshly ground black pepper
1½ teaspoons red wine vinegar
2 tablespoons finely cut fresh mint leaves for garnish (optional)

Fry the bacon in a 10- to 12-inch skillet, turning frequently until it is brown and crisp and has rendered all its fat. Remove with a slotted spoon and drain on paper towels. Drop the scallions into the fat and, stirring occasionally, cook over moderate heat for 3 to 4 minutes, until they are soft but not brown. Remove 1 tablespoon of fat from the skillet and add the beans, stirring until they are coated with the remaining fat. Add the water and cover the pan tightly. Cook over low heat for 5 minutes, then uncover the pan and continue to cook until the beans are tender but still resistant to the bite. Sprinkle with the salt and pepper, stir in the vinegar, and remove from the heat.

Serve in a heated dish, garnished with bacon bits and, if you like, with the cut mint leaves. Make this recipe only when the string beans are good and tender.

Serves 4 to 6

❀ String Beans and Salsa

½ pound green beans
Salt and white pepper
1 tablespoon Red Tomatillo
  Sauce (page 131)

½ fresh tomato, coarsely
  chopped
1 tablespoon margarine
1 teaspoon olive oil

Cut or break off the ends of the green beans. Cut the beans in half lengthwise. Bring to a boil enough water to cover the beans. Add salt and white pepper to taste. Add the beans. Simmer for 10 minutes, or until the beans are tender. Drain well in a colander.

In the same saucepan, combine the sauce, chopped tomato, and the margarine mixed with olive oil. Cover and cook until the sauce is hot. Add the beans and cook, stirring, until the beans are piping hot.

Serves 2

❀ String Beans with Yogurt or Sour Cream

1 pound string beans, washed
  and trimmed
Salt and pepper to taste
2 tablespoons chopped
  scallions
½ pound mushrooms, sliced
1 tablespoon olive oil

2 tablespoons butter or
  margarine
4 tablespoons canned pimiento
  strips
Pinch of grated nutmeg
2 tablespoons plain low-fat
  yogurt or sour cream

Cook the string beans in boiling salted and peppered water until just done. Sauté the scallions and mushrooms in the olive oil and butter or margarine, then add the pimientos. Stir in the cooked, drained string beans, add salt, pepper, and nutmeg, and taste for seasoning. Just before serving, add the yogurt or sour cream and stir to coat the string beans well. Serve hot.

Serves 4

❉ *String Beans with Carrots and Salami*

Try this one first as a side dish or for a luncheon. It is a little spicy and certainly a different way of treating your familiar summer standby.

1 pound string beans, washed
  and trimmed
2 teaspoons minced garlic
2 tablespoons olive oil
1 tablespoon unsalted butter
½ pound carrots, peeled and
  cut into 4-x-¼-inch sticks
¼ pound Genoa salami, cut
  into ¼-inch sticks

2 tablespoons minced fresh
  marjoram or 2 teaspoons
  dried
⅓ cup water
3 tablespoons minced scallions
  or to taste
Salt and pepper

Blanch the string beans in boiling water for 30 seconds. Drain the beans in a colander, refresh them under cold running water, and drain them well.

In a large, heavy skillet, cook the garlic in the oil and the butter over moderately low heat, stirring until it is softened. Add the beans, the carrots, salami, and marjoram, and cook over moderate heat, stirring, for 1 minute, or until all the ingredients are coated with the oil and butter. Add the water and steam the mixture, covered, for 5 minutes, or until the beans and carrots are just tender. Toss with the scallions and salt and pepper to taste and transfer to a heated serving dish.

Serves 6 as a first course or a side dish

❉ *Squash Casserole*

Here's a great Nashville dish. While we were back home taping some shows for my series and the great "Grand Ole Opry" with Minnie Pearl (Mrs. Henry Cannon), Roy Acuff, and Eddy Arnold, Brenda Hall and her husband David, good friends, entertained us royally. David is a constantly traveling network executive who can't wait to get home to Brenda and their baby girl. Who could blame him? This is just one little number we had for dinner one night.

2 pounds yellow squash,
  trimmed and cut into ½- to
  ¾-inch cubes
1 medium onion, coarsely
  chopped
2 cloves garlic, peeled
Salt and pepper

3 tablespoons butter or
  margarine
1 cup Saltine cracker crumbs
1 cup grated Cheddar cheese
½ cup milk
1 egg

Cook the squash, onion, and garlic in boiling salted and peppered water until the squash is just tender, about 10 minutes. Remove from the heat and drain. Discard the garlic cloves.

Place the vegetables in a large mixing bowl. Add ½ teaspoon salt, a dash of pepper, the butter or margarine, cracker crumbs, ½ cup of the Cheddar cheese, the milk, and egg. Stir until well blended. Pour into a buttered oven-proof casserole and sprinkle the remaining ½ cup of cheese over all. Bake in a preheated 350° oven for 20 to 30 minutes.

Serves 4 to 6

❊ Stuffed Summer Squash

This is beautiful, delicious, and easy.

6 to 8 green or yellow summer
  squash (do not remove the
  stems)
Salt and pepper
¾ cup fresh bread crumbs
¼ cup freshly grated Parmesan
  cheese

1 teaspoon finely chopped fresh
  sage (or your favorite herb if
  fresh sage isn't available; the
  dried version comes on a
  little strong for this dish)
4 tablespoons butter or
  margarine, melted

In a large saucepan, cook the squash in boiling salted and peppered water until just soft, about 10 minutes. Drain, and run cold water over the squash. When the squash is cool enough to handle, carefully cut off the tops and set aside.

Scoop out the cooked pulp, being careful not to break the outer skin. Place the pulp in a mixing bowl, stir in the bread crumbs, Parmesan cheese, and sage and mix well. Return the squash mixture to the scooped out shells, drizzle with the melted butter, and place on a baking sheet or shallow baking pan. Bake in a preheated 375° oven for 10 to 15 minutes, or until the tops are lightly browned and crisp. When ready to serve, place the reserved squash tops on the filling.

Serves 6 to 8

❀ *Spaghetti Squash with Vegetables (A Vegetable Pasta Primavera)*

This is pretty, different, and a nice surprise when the pasta turns out to be spaghetti squash.

2 cups coarsely chopped
    tomatoes
½ cup plus 3 tablespoons olive
    oil
1 cup finely chopped fresh
    basil leaves
1 cup finely chopped fresh
    parsley
3 tablespoons freshly grated
    Parmesan cheese
3 cloves garlic, finely minced
Salt

One 3½-pound spaghetti
    squash
3 tablespoons butter, melted
Freshly ground black pepper
2 cups broccoli flowerets
½ pound carrots, peeled and
    cut into 1-inch rounds
1 zucchini, halved lengthwise
    and cut crosswise into ¼-
    inch slices
½ cup finely chopped scallions

In a bowl, combine the tomatoes, ½ cup of olive oil, the basil, parsley, Parmesan cheese, garlic, and 2 teaspoons of salt. Let stand at room temperature, covered, for 1 hour.

Bake the squash in a preheated 350° oven for 1¼ to 1½ hours, or until it can be easily pierced with a fork. Let stand for 15 minutes and halve lengthwise. Remove the seeds carefully with a fork and scrape the flesh into a large bowl. Add the melted butter and salt and pepper to taste.

While the squash is baking, prepare the vegetables. In a large saucepan of boiling salted and peppered water, boil the broccoli for 1 minute or until just tender. Remove with a slotted spoon, and set aside to cool. In the same saucepan boil the carrots and zucchini for 3 minutes, or until just tender. Drain and set aside to cool.

In a large skillet, cook the scallions in the 3 tablespoons of olive oil over moderate heat, stirring until softened. Add the blanched vegetables with salt and pepper to taste, and heat, tossing for 3 to 4 minutes, or until heated through. Add the vegetable mixture to the spaghetti squash, combine with the tomato mixture, toss, and transfer to a serving dish. Serve warm or at room temperature.

Serves 6 to 8

❧ Caramelized Turnips

2 pounds turnips, peeled and
  sliced
2 tablespoons butter
Salt and freshly ground black
  pepper

1 whole clove
2 tablespoons sugar

Place the turnips in a saucepan. Add the butter, salt and pepper to taste, the clove, and a small amount of water. Cover the saucepan and cook the turnips over medium-low heat until tender, stirring from time to time and adding more water as necessary. When all the liquid has evaporated and the turnips are cooked through, add the sugar and cook over medium heat, stirring gently, for another 2 minutes. Serve immediately.

Serves 6

❧ Zucchini and Yellow Squash

I know you've all thought of combining these two squashes, but try my way. That little bit of thyme gives it a piquancy.

1 pound small zucchini
1 pound small yellow squash
4 slices raw bacon, diced
½ cup chopped scallions

½ teaspoon salt
⅛ teaspoon dried thyme leaves
Dash of pepper

Wash the zucchini and squash. Cut, on the diagonal, into slices ½ inch thick.

In a large skillet, sauté the bacon and scallions until golden, about 5 minutes. Add the zucchini, yellow squash, salt, thyme, and pepper; toss lightly. Cook over low heat, covered, for 15 to 20 minutes, or just until the vegetables are tender.

Serves 6

❋ *Zucchini and Carrots with Oyster Sauce*

A Chinese variation on a couple of old standbys. It's good to look at, and, of course, delicious.

1 pound zucchini
2 tablespoons peanut oil
1 tablespoon minced fresh
  ginger
1 scallion, minced
1 clove garlic, minced
1 cup shredded carrots

3 tablespoons oyster sauce
4 tablespoons chicken stock
1 teaspoon sugar
1 teaspoon cornstarch
  dissolved in 2 teaspoons
  water

Wash and dry the zucchini, then trim off the ends. Cut crosswise into 1½-inch-long sections, then cut the sections lengthwise into ¼-inch-thick slices.

Heat the oil in a wok, add the ginger, scallion, and garlic and stir-fry over moderate heat until aromatic, about 30 seconds. Add the zucchini and stir-fry over high heat for 1 minute. Add the carrots and stir-fry briskly for about 1 minute. Pour in the oyster sauce, chicken stock, sugar, and cornstarch and water and stir-fry for about 1 minute more, until thoroughly heated.

Serves 4 to 6

❋ *Zucchini and Tomatoes with Shallots*

2 tablespoons olive oil
1 pound zucchini, trimmed
  and cut into ⅛-inch slices
  (about 4 cups)
⅓ cup finely minced shallots
¾ pound ripe plum tomatoes,
  peeled and cut into ½-inch
  cubes (about 1½ cups)

Salt and freshly ground pepper
8 fresh basil leaves, coarsely
  chopped, or fresh parsley,
  chervil, or tarragon

Heat the oil in a nonstick skillet. When it is quite hot, add the zucchini. Cook over high heat, shaking the skillet and tossing the zucchini pieces gently with a spatula, about 4 minutes. Add the shallots and cook for 1 minute. Add the tomatoes, salt and pepper to taste, and the basil. Cook and toss for 2 minutes more. Serve immediately.

Serves 4

✤ *Mixed Vegetables with Bulgur*

I always have whole grains—bulgur, kasha, wheat, berries, et cetera—in the pantry. They keep well and are a crunchy addition to stir-fried vegetables. Almost any vegetable can be cooked in this way, if you prefer celery, onions, green or red pepper, whatever. The vegetable juice cocktail and the bulgur give the dish a beautiful texture and color.

3 tablespoons vegetable oil
1 cup raw bulgur
1 cup thinly sliced carrots
2 cups broccoli or cauliflower
flowerets
1 clove garlic, minced
1 teaspoon crushed oregano
leaves
1 tablespoon sesame seeds
1¾ cups vegetable juice
cocktail (Snappy Tom, V-8,
or tomato juice spiced up
with Tabasco, Worcestershire,
and lemon juice)

1 cup thinly sliced zucchini
1 cup sliced small mushrooms
Salt and pepper
1 cup shredded Monterey Jack
or Swiss cheese
½ cup sliced scallions
(including green part)

Heat the oil in a 10-inch skillet, making sure the bottom of the pan is well covered so the vegetables will not stick. Add the bulgur, carrots, broccoli or cauliflower, the garlic, oregano, and sesame seeds, stirring quickly and frequently, about 2 minutes. Add the vegetable juice, zucchini, mushrooms, and salt and pepper to taste. Heat to boiling, then reduce the heat to low. Cover and simmer for 15 minutes or less, until the liquid is absorbed.

Stir in the cheese and sprinkle the scallions over the top.

Serves 12

❀ *Vegetable Pie in Crisp Potato Crust*

Fresh vegetables in a smooth sauce surrounded by a crisp potato pancake. What more can you want?

1 cup broccoli flowerets
1 cup cauliflower flowerets
1 cup 2-inch pieces asparagus
Salt and white pepper
2 medium baking potatoes
1 small onion, very finely
  grated
1 egg white
1 tablespoon olive oil, plus oil
  to grease the pan
2 tablespoons butter or
  margarine

2 tablespoons flour
½ to 1 cup reserved vegetable
  cooking liquid
½ cup nonfat milk
Dash of grated nutmeg
¼ teaspoon Dijon mustard
Dash of Tabasco sauce
Dash of Worcestershire sauce
1 egg plus 2 egg whites, lightly
  beaten
½ cup shredded mozzarella
  cheese

Blanch all the vegetables in boiling salted water. Drain, reserving the cooking liquid. Set both aside.

Grate the potatoes very coarsely—they should be as thick as if you had julienned them—and place them immediately in a bowl of ice water. Remove from the water, wrap them in a towel, and squeeze as much excess moisture from them as you can. Combine the potatoes, onion, egg white, and salt and pepper to taste in a mixing bowl.

Oil a 9-inch round baking dish well. Press the potato mixture into the bottom of the dish and up the sides. Dot with 1 tablespoon of the butter or margarine. Bake in a preheated 400° oven for 20 minutes, or until the crust is golden brown.

While the crust is baking, heat the remaining tablespoon of butter or margarine and the oil in a skillet. Stir in the flour and mix well. Do not brown. When thickened, whisk in the reserved vegetable cooking liquid and the milk. If the sauce seems too thick, add a little more vegetable liquid. Add the nutmeg, Dijon mustard, ⅛ teaspoon of white pepper, ¼ teaspoon of salt, the Tabasco, and the Worcestershire. Add a few teaspoons of sauce to the beaten egg and whites. Whisk the egg mixture back into the sauce, but do not boil. Taste for seasoning. Stir the blanched vegetables into the sauce. Remove from the heat.

When the crust is done, remove it from the oven and pour the vegetables and sauce into the crust. Sprinkle with mozzarella cheese, return to the oven, and bake for another 10 minutes.

P.S. Please do not expect this to come out in nice, neat slices.

Serves 6 to 8

✤ A Vegetable Dinner Dish

Salt and pepper
1 chicken broth cube
  (optional)
2 carrots, thinly sliced
  crosswise
2 stalks celery, thinly sliced
  crosswise
½ green pepper, seeded and cut
  into strips

1 cup broccoli flowerets
1 cup cauliflower flowerets
2 medium zucchini, sliced
¼ medium head cabbage,
  shredded
2 small Italian plum tomatoes,
  quartered
¼ cup coarsely chopped water
  chestnuts (optional)

Into boiling water well seasoned with salt, pepper, and the chicken broth cube if you wish, plunge the carrots, and cook for a minute or two; then add celery and green pepper. Cook for about 3 minutes. Remove the vegetables with a slotted spoon and place in a colander to drain. Add the broccoli, cauliflower, zucchini, cabbage, tomatoes, and water chestnuts, and cook for about 2 minutes. Drain into the same colander, reserving some of the liquid, and set aside.

SAUCE
1 medium onion, finely
  chopped
2 cloves garlic, finely chopped
1 tablespoon margarine or
  butter
1 tablespoon olive oil
½ cup sliced mushrooms
1 teaspoon salt
1 teaspoon pepper
½ teaspoon dried dill

½ teaspoon dried oregano
½ teaspoon dried basil
1 cup plain low-fat yogurt
½ cup sour cream
1 tablespoon soy sauce
2 tablespoons brandy
¼ cup vegetable cooking broth,
  if needed
4 ounces spaghettini, cooked al
  dente

Sauté the onion and garlic in the margarine or butter and the olive oil until translucent and soft. Then add the mushrooms and seasonings. Stir in the yogurt, sour cream, soy sauce, brandy, and vegetable cooking broth if needed for thinning. Taste for seasoning. It may need a little more soy sauce and brandy.

Carefully stir in the vegetables and heat through. All this may be done ahead of time and reheated (do not boil) at time of serving.

Serve over hot spaghettini.

Serves 4

❋ *Vegetable Casserole*

3 to 4 tablespoons butter or
margarine
½ large sweet onion, sliced
into thin rings
4 ears corn, cooked and cut off
the cob
4 tomatoes, peeled and sliced
1 beefsteak tomato, peeled and
sliced, reserving 4 thin slices
1 teaspoon seeded and finely
chopped jalapeño pepper

½ teaspoon seeded and finely
chopped hot red pepper
1 cup sliced okra
Salt and pepper
2 slices stale thin bread,
broken into five pieces
1 thick slice fresh bread,
processed into crumbs

Heat 2 tablespoons of the butter or margarine in a large skillet. Sauté the onion until just soft. Lift it out with a slotted spoon and set aside. Add the corn, tomatoes, peppers, and okra. Sauté gently for 5 to 7 minutes, or until the tomatoes get juicy and the okra is slightly tender. Salt and pepper to taste. Return the onion to the skillet and mix with the other vegetables.

In a large buttered casserole, place a layer of vegetables. Add salt and pepper and lightly dot with some butter or margarine. Add another layer of vegetables. Salt and pepper and dot with more butter or margarine. Layer thin pieces of bread over the vegetables. Cover with the reserved tomato slices, sprinkle with the bread crumbs, and season well with salt and pepper to taste.

Place the casserole in a preheated 350° oven for 30 minutes, or until all the vegetables are cooked.

Serves 4 to 6

❊ Eggplant Cilantro

1 eggplant, peeled and sliced
   lengthwise ½ inch thick
Salt
1 tablespoon olive oil
4 tablespoons unsalted butter,
   melted
2 tablespoons finely chopped
   cilantro (coriander)

1 teaspoon ground coriander
   seeds
2 tablespoons lime juice
1 garlic clove, minced
¼ teaspoon red pepper flakes

Lightly salt the eggplant and set aside. Mix together the remaining ingredients. Lightly brush the eggplant with the sauce, place it on a baking sheet, and broil for 7 minutes, turning and basting often with the sauce.

Serves 4 to 6

Pasta, Potatoes, and Rice

This chapter hits me where I live and love. Name one group of foods without which I could not happily spend the rest of my life and it would be my pastas and potatoes and my rice. The hardest decisions in the process of elimination were letting go of any one of these veritable treasures I wanted you to taste. The combinations of flavors and textures are limitless. I mean, I just heard of a pasta five minutes ago, and tasted one two nights ago I just couldn't bear to leave out—except the two Shirley Secretaries, on whom I rely deeply, swore they'd quit, after dropping this chapter on my golfing fingers, if I added one more word to their already neatly assembled, carefully recorded account of my carbohydrate obsessions.

✿ Pasta

My close Italian friends tell me pasta is really, really good for you. Pasta: It will lower your cholesterol, lower your weight and raise your spirits. A day without pasta is no day at all. I believe them—but then I believed the guy who told me that my pet rock would grow hair.

✿ Lasagna with Ricotta

1 pound lasagna, cooked al
   dente according to package
   directions
3/4 pound ricotta cheese
Salt and freshly ground black
   pepper

2 tablespoons chopped fresh
   parsley
8 tablespoons butter or
   margarine
1/2 cup freshly grated Romano
   cheese

When the pasta is cooked, drain, reserving some of the cooking liquid. Drain the ricotta in a sieve and mix the cheese with a wooden spoon until it becomes a smooth paste. Add a few tablespoons of hot water from the lasagna, salt and pepper to taste, and the chopped parsley. Add 3 tablespoons of the butter to the cooked pasta and grease a 9-x-13-inch baking dish with 1 tablespoon of the butter or margarine. Put a layer of one third the lasagna on the bottom of the baking dish, cover with half the ricotta, sprinkle one third of the Romano, and dot with a third of the remaining butter. Add a second layer of lasagna, ricotta, and Romano and then a final layer of lasagna. Dot with the remaining butter, sprinkle with the remaining Romano, and bake in a preheated 400° oven until just brown, about 10 minutes.

Serves 6

✤ *Lasagna with Red Wine*

I have two great lasagna recipes here. I don't mean to confuse you— it's called indecision. Each is perfect in its own way. This lasagna with red wine and chicken is just right with an antipasto salad. The one with white wine that follows, on the other hand, is lighter, as delicate as a meat lasagna can be, and as a result, I usually eat twice as much of it. It's good for winter, spring, and fall, with a salad and great crusty bread. (Remember, it's lighter.)

MEAT SAUCE

1 large carrot, finely chopped
1 large red onion, finely chopped
1 celery stalk, finely chopped
6 to 8 sprigs Italian parsley, finely chopped
1 clove garlic, finely chopped
3 tablespoons olive oil
1/4 pound ground pork
1/2 pound ground beef
1/2 a chicken breast, cut into strips
1/2 cup dry red wine
1 tablespoon tomato paste mixed with 1 cup hot chicken broth

1 cup chicken broth
1/2 pound small fresh mushrooms, thinly sliced through the caps and stems, or 1 ounce dried porcini mushrooms, soaked in water for 20 minutes
Salt and freshly ground pepper
1/4 pound prosciutto or boiled ham, finely chopped
Freshly grated nutmeg
Sprinkle of red pepper flakes (optional)

Place the carrot, onion, celery, parsley, and garlic in a saucepan with the olive oil and sauté very gently until light golden brown; don't let the vegetables burn. Add the pork, beef, and chicken breast, and sauté for 15 to 20 minutes more, then add the wine and cook until the wine is reduced to about 1 tablespoon, about 15 minutes. Add the tomato paste mixed with the broth and cook for 15 minutes. Add the second cup of broth, the mushrooms, which have been drained, if dried, and salt and pepper to taste. Cook for about 15 or 20 minutes, until the sauce is quite thick, then add the prosciutto. Taste for seasoning.

Remove the pan from the heat. Add the nutmeg and a sprinkle of red pepper flakes if you like (I do). Set aside to cool.

BÉCHAMEL SAUCE

6 tablespoons butter or margarine
½ cup flour

3 cups whole milk or 1 cup low-fat and 2 cups whole milk
Salt and freshly grated nutmeg and pepper

Melt the butter or margarine in a heavy saucepan over a medium-low flame. When the butter is bubbling a little, add the flour. Mix very well with a wooden spoon, then cook until the color is golden brown, not too dark. Remove the pan from the heat and let the mixture rest for 10 or 15 minutes.

While the butter-flour mixture is resting, heat the milk in another pan until it is very close to the boiling point. Put the first saucepan back on the flame and very quickly add all the hot milk. Begin mixing with a wooden spoon while you pour and keep mixing, always stirring in the same direction, to prevent lumps from forming. Or, add the milk very slowly, stirring it constantly into the flour mixture to get rid of all the lumps. (A wire whisk helps here.) Let the sauce simmer and bubble, and when it reaches the boiling point, add salt, nutmeg, and pepper to taste. Lower the heat and continue to stir gently with a wooden spoon while the sauce cooks slowly for 12 to 14 minutes more. Remove from the heat. The sauce is ready to use.

CHEESE

8 ounces mozzarella, coarsely grated

1½ cups freshly grated Parmesan cheese
½ cup ricotta

Mix the cheeses together with a wooden spoon, cover, and place in the refrigerator until needed.

ASSEMBLY

*½ pound yellow lasagna
noodles*
*½ pound green lasagna
noodles*

Butter for the dish
Grated Parmesan cheese

Cook the lasagna according to package directions just until al dente. They should be very firm. Drain the noodles and drop them in cold water. Remove with a slotted spoon and place gently on dry kitchen towels in a single layer so the lasagna will not stick together.

Heavily butter a rectangular glass oven-proof baking dish (13 x 9 inches). Spread 1 tablespoon of Meat Sauce over the bottom of the dish; then add enough lasagna noodles to cover the bottom of the baking dish and to allow about 1 inch of overhang at each end; sprinkle with the cheese mixture. Add another layer of lasagna, this time covering only the inside of the dish. Cover with the Béchamel Sauce. Keep alternating the 3 fillings (Meat Sauce, Béchamel, and cheese), covering each layer of filling with a layer of lasagna. The last layer should be either cheese or Béchamel covered with a layer of lasagna noodles.

Take the lasagna ends hanging over the edges of the baking dish and fold them in over the top layer of lasagna. Sprinkle with grated Parmesan cheese. Then place the dish in a preheated 400° oven for about 25 minutes; the top layer should be lightly golden brown and crisp. Remove from the oven and cool for 15 minutes before serving.

Serves 8 to 10

❧ *Light Lasagna with White Wine Sauce*

Buy the best and lightest lasagna noodles you can find. The more delicate the noodles, the more delicious the dish. There are some fresh pasta places listed in the yellow pages—better still, make your own. There's nothing quite like freshly made pasta.

The meat sauce can be made the day before and reheated.

MEAT SAUCE

2 tablespoons finely chopped yellow onion
3 tablespoons olive oil
3 tablespoons butter or margarine
2 cloves garlic, finely minced
2 tablespoons finely chopped celery
2 tablespoons finely chopped carrot
1 pound lean beef, cut into chunks and chopped in a food processor, or ¾ pound beef and ¼ pound veal is a nice combination of meats

Salt and pepper
1 cup dry white wine
½ cup low-fat milk
⅛ teaspoon grated nutmeg
2 cups roughly chopped canned Italian tomatoes with their juice

In a large skillet, sauté the onion in the olive oil and butter or margarine over medium heat until just translucent. Add the garlic and sauté until soft. Add the celery and carrot and cook gently for 2 minutes. Add the ground beef or beef and veal, 1 teaspoon of salt and pepper or to taste, and cook, stirring, to crumble the meat. Cook only until the meat has lost its red color. Do not let it brown. Add the wine, turn the heat up to medium-high, and cook, stirring occasionally, for about 3 minutes. Reduce the heat to medium, add the milk and nutmeg, and cook, stirring constantly, until the milk has been incorporated into the sauce. Then add the tomatoes and stir thoroughly. When the sauce starts to bubble, reduce the heat to the lowest simmer and cook uncovered for 3½ to 4 hours, stirring occasionally. Taste and correct for salt and pepper. If the sauce starts to get too thick, add a little more wine or chicken broth.

CHEESE

1 pound mozzarella cheese, grated
½ cup ricotta cheese

⅓ pound freshly grated Parmesan cheese

Mix the cheeses together and set aside, reserving some Parmesan for the top of the lasagna.

BÉCHAMEL SAUCE

1 tablespoon butter or
   margarine
3 tablespoons olive oil
4 generous tablespoons flour

3 cups low-fat milk or 1 cup
   low-fat milk and 2 cups
   whole milk
Salt and white pepper

Melt the butter or margarine in a large skillet and add the olive oil. Add the flour, stirring constantly until the mixture is fairly smooth. Slowly add the milk, stirring constantly with a wire whisk to avoid lumps. When the mixture is smooth, cook for 10 to 15 minutes over low heat until the sauce is almost as thick as it's going to get. Add salt and pepper and taste for seasoning.

ASSEMBLY

1 pound lasagna noodles

Butter or margarine

Cook the lasagna according to package directions just until al dente. The noodles should be firm, not mushy. Drain and drop the lasagna in cold water. Remove the noodles with a slotted spoon and place gently on dry kitchen towels in a single layer so the lasagna will not stick together.

In a well-greased 9-x-13-inch lasagna pan, place a layer of pasta, then a layer of Meat Sauce, a layer of Béchamel Sauce, a layer of pasta, and a layer of mixed cheeses. Repeat, ending with a layer of Béchamel Sauce. Sprinkle the reserved Parmesan over all and dot sparingly with butter or margarine.

Bake in a preheated 450° oven for 10 to 15 minutes.

Serves 8 to 10

❀ *Cannelloni with Lump Crab Meat*

I have a friend who introduced me by phone to a friend of his—a great chef and restaurant owner named Jimmy Moran, spelled as in Moran's of New Orleans. Don't be fooled by the Irish name, he knows more about Italian food than Vittorio Di Gormese de Pasquirtano (whoever that is). Jimmy's origins are Italian, and we've had more fun talking food on the phone—I keep threatening to fly down to New Orleans to "student" in that great kitchen of his, but then this whole book would have been pasta and a thousand other great things to serve with it. One day Jimmy sent me a picnic cooler full of the lightest, most delicate lasagna and fettucine noodles possible, exquisite fresh Parmesan cheese, and some lump crab meat to go with it. I called to thank him and to tell him Barbara and Frank Sinatra were coming to dinner, and he volunteered his cannelloni recipe. It was too good to waste on mere mortal palates, but there were no gods among my neighbors that day so I elevated us all to some kind of celestial state. Try it—it's good company up there—to the tune of "Come Fly With Me."

8 ounces flat lasagna noodles, as wide as you can get
1 pound lump crab meat, picked over and cleaned
Salt and freshly ground black pepper

2 tablespoons cream
½ cup freshly grated Parmesan cheese
Marinara Sauce (see below)

In a large kettle, add the lasagna noodles to rapidly boiling water. The moment the lasagna noodles rise to the top, lift them out and place them in cold water. Then lay them on a kitchen towel to dry. Cut into 4-inch strips.

Mix the crab meat with salt and pepper to taste. Preheat the oven to 350°. Place 2 to 3 tablespoons of crab meat on each lasagna noodle strip, roll over, and seal.

Lightly grease a 9-x-13-inch glass oven-proof baking dish. Place the rolled up lasagna noodles, sealed side down, in the baking dish.

Add the cream and ¼ cup of the Parmesan cheese to the Marinara Sauce. Pour over the cannelloni (rolled lasagna noodles) and bake in the preheated oven, basting every 4 to 5 minutes with the Marinara Sauce for 20 to 25 minutes. Serve hot with the remaining ¼ cup of Parmesan cheese.

Serves 4

MARINARA SAUCE

1 large sweet onion or 2 medium yellow onions, finely chopped
2 tablespoons olive oil
2 cloves garlic, finely chopped
8 to 10 medium, very ripe tomatoes, peeled and coarsely chopped, or 4 cups canned Italian plum tomatoes with their juice

Salt and freshly ground black pepper
½ cup finely chopped fresh basil
½ cup whole fresh basil leaves

In a large skillet, sauté the onion in the olive oil until soft. Add the garlic and sauté until the onion and garlic are translucent. Add the tomatoes and salt and pepper to taste. Bring to a boil, reduce the heat, and simmer covered for about 1 hour. Add the chopped basil and simmer uncovered, stirring occasionally, for 10 to 15 minutes, until the flavors are blended. Just before serving, add the whole basil leaves.

Makes 3 cups

❧ *Balsamella Sauce for Crab Meat Cannelloni*

That same wonderful Jimmy Moran of New Orleans sent me more lump crab meat and instructions to try it with my favorite Balsamella-Parmesan Sauce. Here it is.

The Marinara in the preceding recipe is exquisitely creamy—it would be good on hardwood siding, I'm convinced. But this one really enhances the flavor of the crab meat. See what you think—they're both about as good as it gets.

1½ tablespoons each butter and margarine, mixed
4 tablespoons flour
1½ cups milk
Salt

¼ teaspoon Tabasco sauce
¼ cup chopped fresh basil (optional)
1 cup freshly grated Parmesan cheese

Melt the butter and margarine in a saucepan, and blend in the flour. Slowly add the milk, stirring constantly to avoid lumps. When the sauce thickens, add salt to taste, the Tabasco, and the basil. Add the Parmesan by handfuls, stirring constantly until the cheese is melted. Pour a wide strip of sauce down each cannelloni to *just* cover it well.

Makes approximately 2½ cups

❧ *Creamiest Fettucine*

This is one of the great treats of the whole golf tournament week. Like the Cannelloni with Lump Crab Meat (page 208), the recipe comes from Jimmy Moran, who owns Moran's great restaurant in New Orleans. The noodles I used were shipped to me by Jimmy, and I may be exag-

gerating slightly, but if you held up one of those cooked noodles to the light, you could see the view through the noodle. They are that delicate! So try to find the thinnest fettucine noodles you can, or if you are so inclined, make your own.

1 pound fettucine noodles (as thin as possible)	1 cup finely grated fresh Parmesan cheese, plus additional for serving
4 tablespoons butter or margarine	Salt and white pepper

Cook the fettucine al dente in boiling salted water according to the package directions. Drain, reserving some of the hot cooking liquid. In a very warm bowl, place half of the cooked noodles, 2 tablespoons of the butter or margarine, ½ cup of the Parmesan cheese, a little salt and white pepper, and start mixing. Then add the remaining fettucine with the remaining butter or margarine and Parmesan cheese.

Add ¼ cup of the reserved cooking liquid and keep turning the noodles gently. Add another ¼ cup of reserved cooking liquid and mix very gently. Serve on hot plates with extra Parmesan cheese, and sprinkle salt and white pepper to taste over all.

Serves 4

✿ *Linguini with Ed Marinaro's Sauce*

Who'd believe a football star turned TV star could also be a great cook. You'd think every girl in sight would be cooking for him at every chance. I guess the girls do the salad and dessert. Ed and I were salivating over great ideas for recipes all the way home from President Ford's Vail, Colorado, golf tournament. By the time we landed, I was starving. I went home and tried this one of Ed's and it worked. It's simple and oh so good!

12 ripe Italian plum tomatoes, peeled and chopped into bite-size pieces	2 tablespoons capers, drained
	8 or 10 Greek or Italian olives, pitted and coarsely chopped
1 clove garlic, very thinly sliced	2 tablespoons chopped fresh basil
8 anchovies, rinsed and chopped	2 tablespoons chopped fresh oregano
2 tablespoons olive oil	Salt and pepper
8 or 10 Greek or Italian olives, pitted and coarsely chopped	1 pound linguini, cooked al dente in boiling salted water
	Freshly grated Parmesan cheese

Combine all the ingredients except the linguini and Parmesan in a large bowl and mix well. Let sit at room temperature for at least 2 hours.

Serve over hot linguini with Parmesan cheese and extra capers, if you like.

Serves 6 as a side dish, 4 as a main course

❀ Linguini with Smoked Salmon

A pasta with several unusual twists—this little number is delicious. None of the unusual ingredients is used in large enough amounts to "take over," but each contributes to a rather exotic, mysterious whole.

1 pound linguini
2 cloves garlic, finely chopped
4 tablespoons olive oil
4 ounces smoked salmon, cut into thin strips
2 ounces black olives, pitted and coarsely chopped
1 cup half and half

1 large tomato, peeled and finely chopped
2 tablespoons finely chopped fresh mint
1 teaspoon finely chopped fresh oregano or a pinch of dried
½ teaspoon salt or to taste

Cook the linguini al dente according to the package directions.

Cook the garlic in the oil and when it is just beginning to brown, add the smoked salmon. Stir gently, add the chopped olives, and stir in the half and half to make a sauce. Add the tomatoes (this gives the sauce a beautiful color) and season with the mint, oregano, and salt. Simmer for a few minutes and serve over the hot pasta.

Serves 6 as a side dish, 4 as a main course

❀ Pasta with Lobster Sauce

2 tablespoons olive oil
1 cup finely chopped onions
2 cloves garlic, minced
½ teaspoon sugar
3 large tomatoes, peeled and coarsely chopped
¼ cup coarsely chopped fresh basil
2 bay leaves

Dash of cayenne pepper
Salt and black pepper
10 ounces linguini
1 lobster tail, cooked in Fish Broth (see Seafood Potpie, page 145) and cut into 1-inch chunks
2 tablespoons good brandy

Heat 1 tablespoon of the olive oil in a large skillet. Add the onions and sauté until softened; then add the garlic and sauté until translucent. Add the sugar and mix well. Add the tomatoes, basil, bay leaves, cayenne pepper, and salt and pepper to taste. Bring to a boil, cover, and reduce the heat. Simmer for 30 to 45 minutes.

Meanwhile, cook the linguini al dente according to the package directions.

Just prior to serving, heat the remaining 1 tablespoon of oil in another skillet. Add the cooked lobster, seasoned with salt and pepper. Pour the brandy over all. (It's not wasted, I promise you.) Avert your face and light the brandy with a match. When the flame goes out, add the lobster to the sauce. Mix half of the sauce with the cooked and drained pasta and pour the remaining sauce over the top.

Serves 6 as a side dish, 4 as a main dish

❧ *Thin Spaghetti with Garlic-Flavored Olive Oil and Chili Peppers*

Simple, spicy, flavorful. I first tasted this many years ago when a lovely gentleman named Vincenzo Buonassisi cooked it on our show. This is the way I remember it from my scribbled notes—especially the dried chilies.

10 ounces spaghettini
Salt
3 to 4 cloves garlic, peeled and
    crushed
3 tablespoons olive oil, or
    more if necessary

2 small dried red chilies,
    crushed slightly with the side
    of a knife
1 to 2 tablespoons minced
    Italian parsley
Freshly grated Parmesan cheese
    (optional)

Bring a large pot of water to the boil. Add the spaghettini and salt to taste. Cook al dente, according to the package directions.

Place the crushed garlic in a large, warm bowl. Add the olive oil, chilies, and parsley. Drain the spaghettini, reserving about ¼ cup of cooking water. Pour the cooking water into the bowl with the olive oil, chilies, garlic, and parsley. Add the drained spaghettini and toss to coat the pasta and mix the chilies and parsley—or remove the chilies if they're too hot for you. Add more olive oil to taste, if you like.

Serve with Parmesan cheese on the side—but you won't need it.

Serves 4

✲ *Thin Spaghetti with Fresh Tomato Sauce*

This is the purest fresh tomato and basil sauce possible, and something to look forward to when summer finally rolls in. The tomatoes are bright deep red all the way through, and they taste like it. The basil is better than your favorite perfume.

TOMATO SAUCE

1 tablespoon olive oil
2 tablespoons butter or margarine
1 medium sweet onion, finely chopped
2 cloves garlic, minced
½ green bell pepper, seeded and finely chopped
3 sprigs fresh basil or 2 teaspoons dried, plus 3 tablespoons finely chopped fresh basil or 2 teaspoons dried

6 large ripe tomatoes, chopped
1 small serrano chili, seeded and finely chopped
Salt and freshly ground pepper
½ cup half and half (optional)
8 ounces spaghettini or angel hair pasta, cooked al dente

In a large skillet, heat the oil and butter or margarine and sauté the onion until just soft. Add the garlic and green pepper and sauté until just soft. Add the sprigs of basil or dried basil, the tomatoes, serrano chili, and salt and freshly ground pepper to taste. Cover and cook slowly for an hour or so. Uncover and continue cooking to let the sauce thicken, about 5 minutes over low heat.

You may add half and half just before serving if you like, but it really doesn't need it. At the last minute, add the 3 tablespoons fresh basil or 2 teaspoons dried. Mix half the sauce with the hot pasta. Pour the other half over the top.

Serves 4

✣ *Ziti or Rigatoni with Sweet Red Peppers*

¼ *pound lean raw bacon*
4 *sweet red peppers*
2 *tablespoons olive oil*
3 *tablespoons reserved bacon fat*
4 *whole garlic cloves, peeled and halved*
15 *large or 20 small basil leaves, rinsed and patted dry (if large, tear into smaller pieces)*

Salt
One 1-pound package ziti or rigatoni
1 *tablespoon margarine*
⅓ *cup ricotta cheese*
⅓ *cup freshly grated Parmesan cheese*

Cut the bacon into narrow strips. Place in a small sauté pan and cook until very lightly browned. Do not let the bacon become crispy. Drain and set aside, reserving 3 tablespoons of the fat. Wash the peppers in cold water. Cut them along their deep folds into lengthwise sections. Scoop out and discard the seeds and pulpy core. Peel away the skin and cut the peppers lengthwise into strips about ½ inch wide, then cut the strips in half.

Heat the olive oil and 1 tablespoon of the reserved bacon fat in a large sauté pan over medium-high heat. Add the garlic and sauté until light brown, then remove the garlic. Add the remaining 2 tablespoons of the bacon fat and the peppers to the pan and cook them at a high heat for 15 minutes or so. Add the basil leaves during the last 5 minutes of cooking. When the peppers are nearly done, salt them liberally.

Cook the pasta until al dente according to the package directions. While the pasta is cooking, melt the margarine over low heat. Crumble the ricotta cheese and add it to the melted margarine.

When the pasta is tender but firm to the bite, drain it thoroughly and put it in a warm serving bowl. Add the peppers and basil and the oil from the pan. Stir in the bacon, Parmesan, and ricotta mixed with margarine.

Serves 6 as a side dish, 4 as a main course

❋ *Pasta with Red Pepper Sauce*

That golf tourament of ours each April brings out the best in the best of people. Here's an example of each—an executive, a golfer, and, I found out, a cook, named Mike Masterpool, came up with this beautiful, tasty different red sauce for pasta with nary a tomato in it. It's like his momma made.

¼ *cup olive oil*
2 *large or 4 small cloves*
garlic, peeled
7 *large sweet red peppers,*
halved, seeded, and cut into
½*-inch strips*
2 *large onions, halved and*
thinly sliced

Salt and pepper
2 *tablespoons chopped fresh basil*
1 *tablespoon chopped fresh parsley*
2 *cups chicken broth*
Pinch of red pepper flakes (optional)
2 *pounds pasta, ziti, penne, or bow ties*
Locatelli cheese, grated

Heat the oil in a large skillet or Dutch oven over high heat, brown the garlic, and remove it from the oil. Add the peppers and onions and cook, stirring often, until the edges of the onions begin to brown, about 15 minutes. Lower the heat to medium, add salt and pepper to taste, the basil, and parsley. Add the broth, cover, and cook 5 minutes longer. If desired, add a pinch of red pepper flakes—maybe half a pinch.

Remove about 12 slices of red pepper and set them aside. Place the remaining mixture in a food processor or, working in batches, in a blender. Process to the consistency of thick tomato sauce. If the sauce is too thick, add more broth.

While the sauce is cooking, cook the pasta until al dente in a large pot of boiling water. Drain, then toss with the sauce in the skillet or Dutch oven. Serve garnished with the reserved strips of red pepper and grated locatelli cheese.

Serves 8

❋ *Pasta with Chicken, Broccoli, and Radicchio*

3 *cups broccoli flowerets*
2 *cups boiling water*
2 *large chicken bouillon cubes*
⅓ *cup butter*
⅔ *cup olive oil*

½ *teaspoon Italian seasoning*
2 *cloves garlic, minced*
Pepper
2 *tablespoons bottled*
marinara sauce

¾ to 1 cup flour
1 teaspoon salt
1½ pounds chicken breast, cut
   into strips
1 pound penne or other tube-
   shape pasta

Salt
1 cup sliced radicchio
½ cup grated Parmesan or
   Romano cheese

Blanch the broccoli flowerets 10 seconds. Plunge them into cold water to prevent further cooking. Set aside.

Combine the boiling water, bouillon cubes, butter, and ⅓ cup of the oil in a saucepan. Add the Italian seasoning, garlic, pinch of pepper, and marinara sauce. Simmer for 10 minutes, stirring occasionally. Set aside.

In a plastic bag, combine the flour and salt. Add the chicken pieces and shake in the bag until the strips are coated with flour. In a large skillet, heat the remaining ⅓ cup of oil over medium heat. Add the chicken, shaking off any excess flour. Do not crowd the pan. Cook, turning the chicken, until browned. Remove with a slotted spoon and drain on paper towels. Cool.

Cook the pasta until al dente in boiling salted water. Drain and transfer to a serving bowl. Pour the sauce over the pasta and mix well. Add the broccoli, chicken, and radicchio and mix again. Season to taste with salt and pepper, and serve with grated Parmesan or Romano cheese.

Serves 8

❖ Sausage with Pasta

4 hot or sweet Italian sausages
2 tablespoons butter or
   margarine
1 tablespoon olive oil
2 cloves garlic, finely minced
4 cups canned tomatoes with
   their juice, or 8 to 10 fresh
   tomatoes, peeled and
   chopped (if using canned
   tomatoes, puree slightly in a
   blender or food processor)

2 tablespoons finely minced
   fresh parsley
½ cup chopped fresh basil or 1
   tablespoon dried
½ cup beef broth
½ teaspoon red pepper flakes
Salt and pepper
8 ounces pasta of your choice,
   cooked al dente in boiling
   salted water
Freshly grated Parmesan cheese

Place the sausages in a small baking dish and bake in a preheated 325° oven for 25 minutes, or until the sausages are cooked through and browned. Cut them into chunks and set aside.

In a large skillet, melt 1 tablespoon of the butter or margarine, add the olive oil and heat. Add the garlic and sauté until just soft. Add the tomatoes, parsley, basil, beef broth, red pepper flakes, and salt and pepper to taste. Bring to a boil, reduce the heat, and simmer until ready to use, about 30 minutes.

When ready to serve, add the reserved cooked sausage and heat it through. Mix the cooked pasta with the remaining tablespoon of butter or margarine, salt and pepper to taste, and half the sauce. Pour the remaining sauce over all. Serve with Parmesan cheese on the side.

Serves 4

❁ *Toasted Ravioli*

3 tablespoons cooked chicken or turkey, chopped
4 tablespoons cooked and drained spinach, chopped
2 tablespoons ricotta cheese
1 egg
2 tablespoons walnuts, chopped
1 teaspoon fresh basil, finely chopped or $^1/_3$ teaspoon dried
Salt and pepper

Two 8- by 12-inch sheets of fresh pasta (available at Italian markets)
$^1/_4$ cup flour
1 egg mixed with 2 tablespoons water
$^1/_4$ cup bread crumbs
$^1/_2$ cup Parmesan cheese
1 tablespoon parsley, chopped
4 tablespoons olive oil for frying, or more if needed

Mix together the chicken or turkey, spinach, ricotta cheese, egg, walnuts, basil, and salt and pepper to taste.

Do not boil the pasta. Cut the pasta sheets into 2- to 2½-inch squares. Place a teaspoon or so of the chicken mixture on each square. Cover and seal the edges with the tines of a fork. Dust the ravioli in the flour and dip into the egg and water mixture. Mix together the bread crumbs, ¼ cup of Parmesan, parsley, and salt and pepper. Roll the filled ravioli in the mixture. Fry in olive oil until golden brown, about 5 to 7 minutes. Place fried ravioli in an oven-proof baking dish and sprinkle with the remaining Parmesan. Bake in a preheated 350° oven for 5 minutes or until cheese is melted.

Makes approximately 20 ravioli

CLOCKWISE FROM TOP: Skillet Potatoes p. 226
Braised Celery with Almonds p. 181 A Layered
Meat Loaf p. 111 Asparagus Soup p. 47

CLOCKWISE FROM TOP: Coleslaw with Peanuts p. 66 Catfish and Shrimp p. 148 Corn and Tomato Casserole p. 182 Dinah's Beer-Apple Fritters p. 247 Scalloped Potatoes p. 227 Barbecued Pot Roast p. 91 Southern-style String Beans p. 190 Beet and Onion Salad p. 67 Corn Muffins with Jalapeño Peppers and Fresh Dill p. 248

CLOCKWISE FROM TOP: Raisin-Saffron Rice
p. 240 Cucumbers with Mint p. 184 Lamb with
Couscous p. 96 Your Favorite White Fish Baked
with Cashews and Mango-Ginger Sauce p. 162
Grilled Peppers, Onions, and Eggplant p. 188

❖*A Great Pasta Primavera Without the Cream*

½ cup broccoli flowerets
½ cup cauliflowerets
¼ cup green pepper, seeded and cut into strips
½ cup fresh or frozen peas
2 small tomatoes, cut into chunks
Salt and pepper
4 tablespoons margarine
1 tablespoon olive oil
2 scallions, sliced
4 mushrooms, sliced
3 cloves garlic, halved
½ teaspoon red pepper flakes or to taste
¼ cup coarsely chopped fresh basil

1 teaspoon fresh oregano or ½ teaspoon dried (optional)
3 tablespoons flour
¾ cup hot chicken broth
¾ cup hot low-fat milk
1 cup bite-size pieces well-seasoned cooked chicken breast (optional)
2 tablespoons grated mozzarella cheese
½ pound linguini or other pasta
Grated Parmesan cheese
Grated Romano cheese

Quickly blanch all the fresh vegetables except the tomatoes in boiling salted and peppered water. Drain and set aside.

Heat 1 tablespoon of the margarine and the olive oil in a large skillet. Add the scallions, mushrooms, and garlic and sauté lightly. Add the red pepper flakes, basil, oregano, and salt and pepper to taste. Mix well. Add the remaining margarine and the flour and mix well. Slowly stir in the chicken broth and milk, stirring constantly to prevent lumps. Remove the garlic cloves and taste for seasoning. Stir in the blanched vegetables, the tomato chunks, and the chicken and mix thoroughly but lightly in order not to break the vegetables. Add the mozzarella.

Cook the pasta according to the package directions. Drain and return it to the pot along with a few tablespoons of the cooking water. Pour the sauce over the pasta and mix well.

Serve hot with Parmesan and Romano cheese on the side.

Serves 4 to 6

❋ *Vincent Bommarito's Pasta Primavera from Tony's*

A pasta primavera from my friend, Vincent Bommarito, at Tony's in St. Louis. This is different, as you'll see. Most pasta primaveras have cream and butter and loads of Parmesan and are made with a harder pasta, like a linguini. This is delicate, dietetic, if you're worried, and delicious. Be sure to save the broth drained from the vegetables and the pasta. It's terrific if you've seasoned it properly for the vegetables. Drain the broth into a bowl and ladle it into cups as a first course with this scrumptious luncheon dish. You'll feel satisfied and virtuous as you feel the pounds fall off.

1 cup cauliflowerets, chopped
   medium-fine
Salt and pepper
½ cup summer squash,
   chopped medium-fine
½ cup sweet red or green
   pepper, seeded and chopped
   medium-fine

½ cup mushrooms, chopped
   medium-fine
8 ounces cappellini pasta
   (angel hair)
½ cup tomatoes, chopped
   medium-fine
2 tablespoons butter or
   margarine

Add the cauliflower to boiling salted and peppered water. Let it cook for 1 or 2 minutes, then add the squash, red or green pepper, and mushrooms. Cook for 1 or 2 minutes more. Add the pasta and cook until almost done, about 3 minutes.

Drain off most of the water into a large bowl. (Don't forget, it makes a delicious vegetable broth.) Add the tomatoes and the butter or margarine and cook the pasta until done, about 1 or 2 minutes more. Season to taste with salt and pepper.

Serves 6

❋ *Scallop Pasta*

This is one of my best. You'll love it—I do. (So what else is new?) I've used shrimp with the scallops. Use fresh ones, peeled and deveined, and sprinkled with salt and pepper. Before cooking the scallops, cook the shrimp a minute or two, until they turn pink.

4 tablespoons olive oil
1 yellow onion, finely chopped
2 cloves garlic, finely chopped
½ sweet red pepper, seeded and
   cut into thin strips
1 zucchini, thinly sliced
6 large mushrooms, sliced
   medium-thin
1 medium tomato, sliced
   lengthwise and cut into
   small wedges
6 fresh leaves basil, chopped
1 sprig fresh oregano, chopped

Generous 6 parsley sprigs,
   chopped
Salt and white pepper
½ pound (or less) thin
   spaghetti
6 large sea scallops, halved
4 tablespoons flour
1 tablespoon margarine
½ cup chicken broth
¼ cup white wine
Grated Parmesan cheese
Freshly ground black pepper

Heat 1½ tablespoons of the olive oil in a large skillet and sauté the onion and garlic until soft but not brown. Add the red pepper and, when it begins to get soft, add the zucchini, mushrooms, tomato, basil, oregano, parsley, and salt and white pepper to taste. Sauté over low heat until well blended. Taste for seasoning and remove from the heat.

While the spaghetti is cooking, roll the scallops in 2 tablespoons of the flour. Shake off the excess. Heat the remaining 2½ tablespoons olive oil and the margarine in a skillet over medium-high heat and sauté the scallops, turning them carefully so as not to break them (they're delicate). When the scallops are crisp on the outside and almost done inside, remove them from the skillet and set aside in a warm bowl. (Don't worry—they'll continue to cook in the bowl and later in the sauce when mixed with the pasta.)

Drain the juice from the skillet, add the remaining 2 tablespoons of flour, stir, and then add the chicken broth and white wine. Bring to a boil. Add the liquid (if you have any) from the bowl in which you have placed the scallops to the sauce. Combine the sauce with the vegetable mixture and reheat. Taste for seasoning.

When the spaghetti is cooked until al dente, drain it. Place a few tablespoons of sauce in the hot spaghetti pot. Pour the hot spaghetti over the sauce, add the remaining sauce and the scallops, and mix gently. Serve immediately on warm plates with a little Parmesan and freshly ground black pepper on the side.

Serves 4

❧ *Fried Pasta*

Leftover spaghetti or linguini is too wonderful to just throw away. Here's a solution—one I first tasted for breakfast (!) in Florence, Italy. This won't work if you've made a heavy tomato or primavera and mixed all your pasta with sauce or meat or a large number of vegetables. So, plan ahead occasionally, cook a little extra pasta, and save it for a first course the next night, or an hors d'oeuvre—or breakfast.

*2 cups leftover bow-tie or other
  small fancy-shape pasta or
  linguini or spaghettini
Oil for deep-frying*

*Salt and white pepper
Garlic salt
Grated Parmesan cheese*

Deep-fry the cooked pasta in the oil until golden. Drain and sprinkle with salt, white pepper, garlic salt, and Parmesan cheese.

Serves 2

❧ *Fried Pasta with Anchovies*

*4 tablespoons olive oil
2 cloves garlic, crushed
6 salt-cured anchovy filets,
  rinsed and coarsely chopped
¼ cup chopped fresh parsley*

*Pepper
1 pound pasta (preferably a
  thin variety)
Salt*

Heat the oil in a large, heavy skillet and add the garlic. Cook until lightly browned, then remove the garlic and add the anchovies. Cook until soft and add the parsley and some pepper.

Cook the pasta until it is just al dente in plenty of boiling salted water. Drain well, pour into the skillet and toss with the sauce. Shape the pasta into a flat pancake with a spatula or the back of a fork. Cook until brown underneath, then turn it over and brown on the other side. It should be crisp and brown on the outside and soft on the inside.

Serves 4 to 6

✿ *Fried Noodles with Mixed Meat and Vegetables*

¼ *cup shredded lean pork*
¼ *cup shredded raw chicken*
  breast
¾ *teaspoon cornstarch*
  dissolved in 2 tablespoons
  water
Salt
1 *teaspoon light soy sauce*
6 *ounces thin Japanese noodles*
  (available in specialty
  stores), or I suppose you
  could use angel hair pasta
  dropped in boiling water for
  a minute or so—no more

3 *tablespoons vegetable oil*
¼ *cup shredded canned*
  bamboo shoots
¼ *cup quartered broccoli*
  flowerets
½ *teaspoon dry sherry*
Scant 1 cup chicken broth
2 *teaspoons cornstarch mixed*
  with 1 tablespoon water to
  make a smooth paste
¼ *cup thinly sliced Virginia,*
  Tennessee, or prosciutto ham
  for garnish

Mix the pork and chicken with the ¾ teaspoon cornstarch dissolved in water, a pinch of salt, and the soy sauce and marinate for 15 minutes or so.

Drop the noodles into a pot of boiling water and when the water begins to boil again, pour the noodles into a strainer and rinse under cold running water until separated. Drain well and spread on a cookie sheet to dry.

Heat a wok, add a scant 2 tablespoons of the vegetable oil, and heat to smoking. Add the noodles and stir in the hot oil until golden brown. When they hold together and form a pancake, turn and fry them on both sides until lightly brown and crisp. Remove and place on a very warm serving plate.

Reheat the wok and add the remaining tablespoon of oil. Add the marinated pork and chicken and the bamboo shoots. Stir-fry until the meat changes color, about 1 minute. Remove and set aside. Stir-fry the broccoli for 1 minute, then return the meat and bamboo shoots and add ½ teaspoon of salt, the sherry, and the chicken broth. Stir-fry briefly and bring to a boil. Add the 2 teaspoons cornstarch mixed with water, cover, and cook briefly until the sauce thickens and turns glossy, about 1 minute, stirring occasionally. Pour over the noodles and garnish with the thinly sliced ham.

Serves 6 to 8

❧ *Greek Macaroni Mold*

Two ¾-pound eggplants
Salt
3 quarts well-salted water
3 cups elbow macaroni
3 tablespoons olive oil, or
   more if needed
⅔ cup chopped onion
1 pound ground beef
1½ cups brown stock or sauce
   (if you don't have it, use 1
   cup strong beef or chicken
   stock, add 2 tablespoons
   tomato paste and 1 bay leaf,
   and simmer for 1 hour)

3 eggs, lightly beaten
⅔ cup freshly grated Parmesan
   cheese
½ teaspoon pepper
2 tablespoons chopped fresh
   parsley
Tomato Sauce (page 214)
Parsley or watercress for
   garnish

Peel the eggplants. Cut one into ⅓-inch rounds and slice the other one lengthwise ¼-inch thick. These are for lining your mold. Salt one side. Stand the slices up in a colander until the bitterness is drained off. Pat dry with paper towels.

Bring the water to a boil. Add the macaroni and cook until al dente (8 minutes maximum). Drain, rinse with cold water, and set aside in a large bowl.

Sauté the slices of eggplant in the oil until lightly browned. The thinner ones should be browner on one side than the other—I'll explain why in a moment. Set them aside on paper towels to drain. In the same skillet, sauté the onion, adding extra oil if needed, until softened. Remove the onion, add the beef to the same oil, and brown. Pour off all excess fat. Return the onion to the skillet, add the brown stock, and simmer the mixture for 1 hour. Add to the macaroni. Add the eggs, ⅓ cup of the Parmesan cheese, ½ teaspoon salt, and the pepper. Mix well.

Generously oil or butter a 9-inch round cake pan, 2 inches deep. Place the thinner slices of eggplant, brown side down, on the bottom and sides of the pan. Try to make a regular pattern, overlapping the slices slightly on the sides and meeting in the center—it will be prettier when unmolded.

Chop any remaining eggplant or any irregular thick slices and add it to the beef mixture. Place the beef mixture in the lined mold. Cover with foil and weight with a 2-pound weight (a couple of cans on a pie plate). Put the cake pan in a baking pan, add enough boiling water to the baking pan to reach halfway up the sides of the cake pan, and bake in a preheated 275° oven for 1½ hours.

Remove the weight and foil, invert a heated serving plate over the pan, and invert the mold into the plate. Sprinkle with the remaining ⅓ cup of Parmesan cheese mixed with the chopped parsley. Place under the broiler just until the cheese melts slightly. Serve with the Tomato Sauce on the side, garnished with parsley or watercress.

Serves 6 to 8

❉ Potatoes

The best natural vegetable I know is the potato. There's hardly a way to ruin potatoes—you can tell by the number of recipes I have in here how I feel about them. You can add leftover vegetables, lots of ham, salami, green peppers—you name it, potatoes like it. I heard a well-cooked potato was good for you too, but don't let that bother you.

❉ Steamed Sliced Potatoes

2 potatoes
2 tablespoons olive oil or
  margarine
Salt and pepper

½ cup chicken broth
3 tablespoons chopped fresh
  parsley
1 teaspoon paprika

Thinly slice the unpeeled potatoes, putting them in cold water until ready to use. In a large skillet, heat the olive oil or margarine over medium-high heat. When hot, add the drained potatoes and salt and pepper to taste. When the potatoes are lightly browned on one side, turn and just cover with the chicken broth. Cook over medium heat until the potatoes are tender but not mushy. Sprinkle with chopped parsley and paprika.

For a nice variation, before adding the potatoes, sauté ¼ cup chopped onion until brown.

Serves 4

❊ Skillet Potatoes

I use an iron skillet for this one.

3 potatoes, very thinly sliced (I
   don't peel them but you may
   prefer to)

Salt and pepper
½ to ¾ cup butter or
   margarine, melted

Generously grease the bottom and sides of a cast-iron or oven-proof skillet with some of the melted butter or margarine. Arrange a layer of potatoes in the skillet, then add salt and pepper to taste, and a little melted butter or margarine. Add another layer of potatoes, salt and pepper, and butter or margarine. Continue until you have used all the potatoes. Bake in a preheated 350° oven until the potatoes have turned brown and crisp. Serve with almost any kind of meat.

Serves 4 to 6

❊ Baked Roasted Potatoes

Serve these with roast anything—chicken, lamb, fish. They're a great complement.

6 new potatoes or small
   baking potatoes
½ to ¾ cup butter or
   margarine, melted
Salt and pepper

2 tablespoons fresh chopped
   dill or 2 teaspoons dried
½ cup grated Parmesan cheese
½ teaspoon paprika

Peel the potatoes and slice them almost all the way through, leaving them intact at the bottom. Drizzle with the melted butter or margarine, and generously salt and pepper to taste. (You may want to make foil cups to help keep the potatoes together.) Sprinkle with the dill, making sure it goes in between the slices. Sprinkle with Parmesan cheese and paprika.

Bake in a preheated 400° oven for 35 to 40 minutes, until the potatoes are tender and golden brown.

Serves 6

❋ Crisp Potatoes

3 tablespoons butter or
  margarine, melted
4 large white boiling potatoes,
  peeled and very thinly sliced
Salt and pepper

2 tablespoons chopped fresh
  dill or 2 teaspoons dried
  dillweed or your favorite
  herb
1 cup milk

Line a 9-inch baking dish with foil. Brush with some of the melted butter or margarine. Arrange half the potato slices in the dish, overlapping, and brush with one half of the remaining melted butter or margarine. Sprinkle with salt, pepper, and half the dill. Pour ½ cup of the milk over all. Bake in a preheated 350° oven for 35 to 40 minutes, or until the potatoes are crisp on the outside and tender on the inside.

Prepare a second baking dish in the same manner and place on a second rack of the oven 15 minutes before the first dish is served—you'll need it.

Serves 6

❋ Scalloped Potatoes

3 pounds thin-skinned
  potatoes, such as white rose,
  peeled and thinly sliced
2 garlic cloves, halved
Butter or margarine
8 medium mushrooms, thinly
  sliced

¼ cup finely chopped scallions
Salt and freshly ground pepper
1 tablespoon flour
½ cup half and half
1½ cups milk

Preheat the oven to 325°.

Place the sliced potatoes in a bowl of cold water to keep them from turning brown. Rub a shallow oven-proof baking dish with the cut garlic cloves until the cloves practically disappear. Butter the dish well. Drain the potatoes and arrange a layer of potatoes in the dish, top with a layer of mushrooms and scallions, season with salt and pepper, and dot with butter. Continue layering in this manner until all the potatoes are used.

Mix the flour with the half and half. Pour the milk and half and half over the potatoes and dot with more butter.

Bake in the preheated oven for about 1½ hours. During the last 10 minutes of baking, raise the temperature to 400° to brown the top.

Serves 8

❧ *Herbed New Potatoes*

1½ pounds small new
   potatoes, uniform in size if
   possible
Salt
1 clove garlic, peeled
2 tablespoons olive oil
1 tablespoon butter or
   margarine
1 tablespoon finely chopped
   chives

1 teaspoon finely chopped
   shallots
2 tablespoons finely chopped
   parsley
1 tablespoon finely chopped
   fresh sage

Boil the potatoes in salted water with the garlic clove until just done. In a heavy skillet, heat the olive oil and butter or margarine. Add the chives and shallot and sauté, then sprinkle in the parsley and sage. Add the cooked, drained potatoes and roll them in the mixture until well coated. Serve hot.

Serves 4 to 6

❧ *Roasted Potatoes with Dill*

3 medium-size potatoes, peeled
   or unpeeled, thinly sliced
Butter for the pan
1 teaspoon salt
½ teaspoon pepper

½ cup butter or margarine,
   melted
¼ cup chopped fresh dill or
   parsley

Lay the potatoes in a single layer in a well-buttered pie plate. Salt and pepper them well. Brush with the melted butter or margarine, and sprinkle the chopped dill or parsley over all.

Roast in a preheated 350° oven for about 45 minutes, or until tender. During the last 5 minutes of cooking, increase the oven temperature to 400° to brown and crisp the potatoes.

Turn out carefully with a spatula. Have another pan ready to go in— you'll need it.

Serves 4 to 6

❧ *Potatoes and Dill Baked in Milk*

8 potatoes, unpeeled, thinly
    sliced
Salt and pepper
2 cloves garlic, finely chopped
2 tablespoons chopped fresh
    dill

8 tablespoons butter or
    margarine plus extra for the
    baking dish
1½ cups milk
½ cup chicken broth

    Arrange a layer of potatoes in the bottom of a buttered oven-proof baking dish. Sprinkle the potatoes with salt and pepper, garlic, and dill. Dot with the butter or margarine. Continue layering in this way until all the potatoes are used up. Pour the milk and chicken broth over all.

    Bake in a preheated 400° oven for about 1 hour, until the potatoes are tender and all the liquid is absorbed.

Serves 6 to 8

❧ *Broccoli-Stuffed Baked Potatoes*

2 large baking potatoes
1 small bunch broccoli, stems
    peeled, cut into flowerets
Salt and pepper

2 tablespoons butter or
    margarine, or more if
    desired
Freshly grated Parmesan or
    mozzarella cheese

    Preheat the oven to 400°. Bake the potatoes for 45 minutes, or until they are done.

    Blanch the broccoli in boiling water to which you have added salt and pepper. Cook until tender, but not until the broccoli loses its bright green color. Drain well.

    Slice the potatoes in half lengthwise and scoop out the flesh, leaving ⅛ inch in the shell to keep it firm. Place the potato flesh in a mixing bowl and add salt and pepper to taste. Mash the potatoes until there are no lumps. Add the butter or margarine and broccoli and mash into the potatoes. Taste for seasoning.

    Refill the shells with the potato mixture, piling it as high as you can. Sprinkle with Parmesan or mozzarella cheese and dot with a little butter or margarine if desired. Everything to this point may be done ahead of time.

    Bake in a preheated 350° oven for about 15 minutes, until the potatoes are heated through and the cheese is melted.

Serves 4

❋ *Yesterday's Mashed Potatoes*

Who says you can't reclaim "yesterday's mashed potatoes?"

2 medium potatoes, baked
  (can be leftover)
½ cup low-fat milk, heated
2 tablespoons margarine,
  melted
Salt and pepper
1 teaspoon chopped fresh dill
1 teaspoon chopped fresh
  parsley

½ teaspoon chopped fresh
  marjoram
1 tablespoon chopped walnuts
2 tablespoons grated
  mozzarella cheese
2 tablespoons grated Cheddar
  cheese

Cut the potatoes in half crosswise (not the usual lengthwise). Scoop out the cooked potato and place in a bowl. Set the shells aside.

Add the hot milk to the potatoes, 1 or 2 tablespoons at a time, beating after each addition until the potatoes are fluffy and there are no lumps. Add the margarine, salt and pepper, dill, parsley, marjoram, and walnuts. Mix well. Add the cheeses, reserving some for topping and mix again. Return the potato mixture to the shells and top with the remaining cheese.

Place in a baking dish and bake in a preheated 350° oven until the potatoes are heated through and the cheeses are bubbly.

Incidentally, if you have any leftover crisp bacon, pieces of chicken, vegetables, et cetera—add any one or all of them.

Serves 2

❋ *Potato Pancakes*

6 potatoes
1¼ teaspoons salt
½ teaspoon pepper
1 small onion, minced or
  grated

2 eggs
1½ tablespoons flour
¼ teaspoon baking powder
Oil for the griddle or pan

Peel the potatoes and place them in cold water to soak for several hours. Drain well, dry, and then grate them coarsely. Place in a bowl and add the salt, pepper, and onion; mix well. Stir in the eggs. Mix together the flour and the baking powder. Sift into the potato mixture and stir vigorously until well blended.

Heat a griddle or cast-iron frying pan, oil it lightly, and drop the potato batter from a large spoon or pour it from a measuring cup. Cook until the batter rises and the surface is dotted with holes. Turn and cook the other side until lightly browned. Serve hot, with melted butter or margarine, cold applesauce, or a tart jam.

Serves 4

✿ *Swiss Shredded Potato Pancakes*

1¾ *pounds large boiling*
  potatoes
1 *onion, minced*
4 *tablespoons unsalted butter*

½ *teaspoon salt or to taste*
¼ *teaspoon freshly ground*
  pepper

Peel the potatoes, grate them medium-coarse, and place them in cold water until ready to use. Then drain and dry them thoroughly.

In a bowl, combine the potatoes, onion, 2 tablespoons of the butter, melted and cooled, the salt, and pepper.

In a nonstick 8-inch skillet, heat 1 tablespoon of the butter over moderately high heat until the foam subsides. Add half the potato mixture, tamping it down firmly with a rubber spatula, and cook the potato cake, shaking the skillet frequently, for 7 minutes, or until the underside is golden and crisp. Invert the potato cake onto a flat plate, slide it carefully back into the skillet, and cook it for 7 minutes more, or until the underside is golden and crisp. Make a second potato cake in the same manner with the remaining potato mixture and butter. Cut each cake into wedges.

Serves 4

✿ *Spanish Patatas*

2 *tablespoons vegetable oil*
2 *large potatoes, very thinly*
  sliced, placed in cold water,
  and drained

Salt and pepper
1 *tablespoon chopped pimiento*
6 *eggs, beaten*

Heat the oil in a skillet, add the potatoes, and season generously with salt and pepper. When the potatoes are soft, add the pimiento. Pour the eggs over the potatoes and cook until the eggs are done to the consistency you desire. Serve hot for breakfast.

Serves 6

❀ *Potato Casserole*

Here's another example of the friendly potato combined with many things. First cook it this way and then later, in addition to the recommended ingredients, you can add a layer of broccoli, spinach, or green pepper, or even chopped walnuts. You name it—potatoes like it.

½ *pound country ham or corned beef, cut into small pieces*
2 *medium onions, sliced*
Milk
4 *medium potatoes, thinly sliced*
1 *cup sour cream*
1 *tablespoon Dijon mustard*
1 *teaspoon Worcestershire sauce*

½ *teaspoon Tabasco sauce*
½ *teaspoon sugar (optional)*
Red pepper flakes to taste
2 *tablespoons margarine*
Scant ½ *cup flour*
Salt and white pepper
½ *cup chicken broth*
1 *cup low-fat milk*
¼ *cup grated mozzarella cheese*
¼ *cup grated Cheddar cheese*

Soak the ham or corned beef and the onions in milk to cover for 20 to 30 minutes. Place the sliced potatoes in ice water. Mix together the sour cream, mustard, Worcestershire sauce, Tabasco sauce, sugar (if desired), and red pepper flakes. Drain the potatoes and pat dry.

Lightly oil an oven-proof baking dish. Place a layer of potatoes in the bottom of the dish and spread with the sour cream mixture. Cover with a layer of the drained ham and onions, and dot with some margarine. Sprinkle with flour, salt, and white pepper. Repeat the layers. Pour a mixture of the chicken broth and low-fat milk over all. Sprinkle with the grated cheeses and bake in a preheated 350° oven for 1 hour, or until the potatoes are cooked through and the cheeses are bubbly.

Serves 6

❀ *Artichoke-Potato Casserole*

1 *large artichoke, trimmed, cut into 4 pieces, and choke removed*
Salt and pepper
½ *lemon*

Melted butter (optional)
Mayonnaise (optional)
3 *medium potatoes, sliced as if for French fries*
Butter for the casserole

SAUCE

2 tablespoons margarine

2 tablespoons flour

¾ cup chicken broth

¼ cup milk

Salt and white pepper

Cayenne pepper

Pinch of dillseed

2 tablespoons ricotta cheese

3 tablespoons freshly grated
  Parmesan cheese

3 tablespoons grated Monterey
  Jack cheese

Place the artichoke in boiling water with salt, pepper and the ½ lemon. Cook until the artichoke heart is tender. Remove from the water and cut the heart into chunks. (Use the leaves to garnish your main dish or another vegetable dish, or serve with melted butter or mayonnaise for dipping.) Add the sliced potatoes to the artichoke water and parboil. Do not cook completely. Remove and place in cold water until ready to bake the casserole.

To make the sauce, melt the margarine in a saucepan, and slowly add the flour, blending with a wooden spoon. Slowly add the chicken broth and milk, stirring constantly with a whisk to prevent lumps from forming. Add the seasonings to taste. Blend in the ricotta cheese. Mix the Parmesan and Monterey Jack cheeses together, reserving 3 tablespoons for the topping. Add the Parmesan and Jack cheeses to the mixture and blend well. The sauce should not be too thick.

Butter a 9-inch round casserole dish and layer the potatoes in the dish. Sprinkle the artichoke hearts over the potatoes. Pour the sauce over all. Sprinkle with the remaining cheese and bake in a preheated 350° oven for 30 minutes, or until the potatoes are just tender and the top is crisp and brown.

Serves 4

❧ Potato-Turnip Casserole

1 potato, peeled and thinly
  sliced
1 turnip, peeled and thinly
  sliced
1 small yellow onion, sliced
  crosswise into rings
1 clove garlic, halved and
  mashed
2 tablespoons olive oil
1 pound ground chuck
Salt and pepper
Paprika
Scant 4 tablespoons margarine

2 tablespoons mixed chopped
  fresh dill, tarragon, and sage
1 tomato, sliced
1 small head Chinese cabbage,
  finely chopped, reserving 4 or
  5 whole leaves for top of
  casserole
¾ cup chicken broth
¾ cup tomato juice cocktail or
  V-8
½ cup grated Monterey Jack
  cheese
½ cup grated Cheddar cheese

Place the potato and turnip in cold water. Sauté the onion rings and garlic in the olive oil until soft but not brown. Add the chuck and cook, stirring to break up the lumps, until brown. Sprinkly lightly with salt, pepper, and paprika.

Spread a thin layer of meat-onion mixture in the bottom of an oven-proof casserole. Cover with a layer of turnip. Dot with some margarine, and sprinkle with salt, pepper, and the herb mixture. Then add a layer of potato and tomato, seasoning them the same way, then a layer of meat. Repeat the layers, ending with meat. Then, finally, add a layer of chopped cabbage. Pour the broth and tomato juice cocktail over all. Cover snugly with the reserved cabbage leaves and sprinkle with the grated cheeses. Cover with a lid from a smaller pan, just to hold it down but not to cover too thightly, to let the liquid cook through and reduce a little.

Bake in a preheated 300° oven for 40 minutes, or until the casserole is hot and bubbly and the cheese is melted.

Serves 6 to 8

❧ Rice

Whatever I said about how pleasantly accommodating the potato is holds true for rice too. Long grain, Uncle Ben's, Italian arborio, Oriental, short grain, white, ad infinitum. If I've left any out, forgive me. Add your vegetable, meat, chicken, or fish. Serve it under or on the side of any or all of the above-mentioned "main" dishes, or serve it all by itself. The Risotto (page 236) comes to mind as a first-class main dish.

✤ Rice Casserole

8 cups water
3 cups unconverted long-grain
  white rice
1 teaspoon salt
¾ cup sliced scallions
¾ cup sour cream
½ cup chopped pimiento
½ cup sliced pitted black olives

Two 4-ounce cans green chili
  peppers, drained, seeded, and
  chopped
5 tablespoons unsalted butter,
  cut into bits, plus extra for
  casserole
1¾ cups grated Monterey Jack
  cheese

Bring the water to a boil in a large saucepan. Sprinkle in the rice and salt, and return the water to a boil over high heat, stirring. Boil the rice, stirring occasionally, for 20 minutes. Drain in a colander and rinse under cold water. Set the colander over a pan of boiling water and steam the rice, covered with a dish towel and a lid, for 15 to 20 minutes, or until fluffy and dry.

In a buttered 2-quart casserole, combine the rice with the remaining ingredients, reserving 3 tablespoons of the butter and ¼ cup of the cheese. Dot the top of the casserole with the remaining butter, sprinkle with the remaining cheese, and bake in a preheated 350° oven for 30 minutes.

Serves 8

✤ Italian Rice

This and the next two recipes must be made no more than 45 minutes to an hour before serving. Unfortunately, it just can't sit and wait for a late dinner guest. Oh—it will be okay, but the joy of this is the freshly melting blend of cheeses and butter and rice.

3 quarts water
1 tablespoon salt
1½ cups raw rice (preferably
  Italian arborio)
6 tablespoons butter or
  margarine, cut up

2 tablespoons finely chopped
  fresh basil or parsley
1½ cups coarsely grated
  mozzarella cheese
⅔ cup freshly grated Parmesan
  cheese

Bring the water to a boil, add the salt and the rice, and mix with a wooden spoon. Reduce the heat and cook covered until the rice is tender but firm to the bite. Depending on the rice, this will take 15 to 20 minutes.

Stir occasionally with a wooden spoon. Let the rice sit, covered, for a few minutes, it will absorb some of the moisture but you want some for the mixing. If there is still too much, drain off ½ cup, but save it until you've finished blending and mixing the butter and cheeses.

Place rice in a warm serving bowl. Mix in the butter, add the basil or parsley, and mix well. Add the mozzarella and mix quickly and thoroughly. Stir in the Parmesan and mix lightly. Serve immediately.

Serves 4 to 6

✿ *Risotto*

This is a rare and wonderful delicacy. Some restaurants make it superbly and creamily. Don't mind the twenty-minute wait, it's worth it, but some restaurants don't understand and add a little seafood, mushrooms, or whatever to the rice. That's not risotto—this is!

2 tablespoons olive oil or 1 tablespoon olive oil and 1 tablespoon butter or margarine
1 onion, chopped
1½ to 2 cups Italian arborio rice, rinsed in a strainer to remove the starchy coating

1 cup good dry white wine
5 cups chicken or veal broth
Pinch of ground turmeric
Pinch of powdered saffron
Salt and pepper to taste
Sliced mushrooms for garnish

Heat the oil in a saucepan and sauté the onion until soft. Add the rice and sauté over low heat about 2 minutes, until the rice is coated with oil. Do not brown. Add ½ cup of the white wine and stir. Then add ½ cup of the broth and stir until absorbed, then add the remaining ½ cup of wine and, when absorbed, add 1 cup of broth, stirring frequently. Cook slowly until the broth is absorbed. Repeat the process with the remaining broth, slowly adding ¾ to 1 cup at a time, stirring frequently. With the fourth cup of broth, add the seasonings and taste. Simmer slowly, stirring often, until the broth is absorbed. The rice will be creamy and light.

Serve garnished with sliced mushrooms. This must be served immediately, it really won't wait for guests.

Serves 4 to 6

✽ Creamy Risotto with No Cream

1 cup raw rice (do not use
    quick-cooking—I like the
    Italian arborio)
2 tablespoons olive oil
1 small onion, chopped
1 clove garlic, halved

½ teaspoon salt
¼ teaspoon powdered saffron
3 to 4 cups chicken broth
Freshly grated Parmesan cheese
    (optional)

Place the rice in a strainer and rinse under cold running water until most of the starchy white cover disappears. In a large saucepan, heat the oil over low heat, add the onion, then the garlic, and sauté until the onion is tender. Add the rice and stir to coat it thoroughly with oil. Mix in the salt and saffron. Add 2 cups of the chicken broth and cook uncovered over low heat until the rice absorbs the liquid. The rice will absorb the liquid quickly; add more broth, ½ cup at a time, as needed—this rice really drinks up the broth, but it's worth it. Stir constantly with a wooden spoon, or as often as you can. When tender and cooked through, taste for seasoning. Add a couple of tablespoons of freshly grated Parmesan cheese at the last minute, if you like.

Transfer into a lightly buttered simple ring mold, press down to give the rice its shape, and turn out onto a serving platter.

If you don't want to use a mold, shape it on a warmed plate with a large tablespoon, leaving room in the center for your filling. Mushroom Chicken Livers (page 33) is a fine complement. Actually, on its own this Risotto is as special as any pasta, but it really needs to be timed to coincide with dinner. It's hard to do ahead and have it creamy, *not* soupy or mushy. Flavor and texture are everything with this beautiful dish.

Serves 4 as a first course, 6 as a side dish

�֍*Hearty Fried Rice*

White rice is a must with an Oriental dinner, but I'm not sure the Chinese insist on having fried rice with their dinners. Most Americans I know love it. It's so good on its own.

1 teaspoon cornstarch	*3 cups cooked Chinese or*
2 teaspoons water	*Japanese white rice*
Salt	*¼ cup bean sprouts*
¼ cup uncooked shrimp,	*¼ cup finely chopped*
shelled, deveined, and halved	*mushrooms*
4 tablespoons peanut or	*2 water chestnuts, finely*
soybean oil	*chopped*
¼ cup ¼-inch cubes cooked	*1 scallion, minced (white and*
ham	*green parts)*
¼ cup ¼-inch cubes cooked	*1 teaspoon soy sauce*
chicken	*¼ cup shredded lettuce*
2 eggs, beaten	*Freshly ground pepper*

Mix together the cornstarch, water and ¼ teaspoon of salt. Dip the shrimp in the cornstarch mixture.

Heat a wok over high heat. Swirl in 2 tablespoons of the oil to coat the wok. Add the shrimp and stir-fry for 30 seconds. Add the ham and stir-fry for an additional minute. Add the chicken and stir-fry for another 30 seconds. Transfer all the ingredients to a warm dish.

Add the eggs to the wok and stir gently to scramble. Do not overcook. The eggs should remain soft and runny. Add them to the dish with the shrimp mixture. Wipe the wok clean with paper towels, being careful not to burn yourself.

Swirl in the remaining 2 tablespoons of oil. Add the rice and stir-fry for 2 to 3 minutes, separating the grains. Return the shrimp, ham, chicken and eggs to the wok. Add the bean sprouts, mushrooms, water chestnuts, scallion, soy sauce, and salt to taste. Stir-fry briefly, until the combination is well mixed and the egg is broken into small pieces. Stir in the shredded lettuce and mix well. Season with pepper and serve immediately.

Serves 4 to 6

❊ Pork Fried Rice

2 tablespoons peanut oil
1 egg, lightly beaten
1 slice of ginger, about the size
  of a quarter, left whole
1 clove garlic, finely chopped
2 cups cooked white rice
½ cup cooked roast pork,
  shredded ¼-inch thick

1 scallion, finely chopped
  (white and part of green)
2 water chestnuts, coarsely
  chopped
¼ cup bamboo shoots
2 teaspoons soy sauce

Heat 1 tablespoon of the oil in a wok. Scramble the beaten egg in the wok. Remove and set aside. Add the remaining 1 tablespoon of oil. Stir-fry the ginger and garlic over high heat until the garlic is soft. Remove and set aside. Add the rice and stir-fry, turning quickly and constantly, for about 1 to 2 minutes. Add the pork, scallion, water chestnuts, bamboo shoots, and soy sauce and stir-fry until the scallion is soft, but not brown. Add the scrambled egg, ginger, and garlic and stir-fry to heat thoroughly. Remove from the wok and serve immediately.

Serves 4 as a side dish

❀ *Raisin-Saffron Rice*

2 tablespoons butter
1 cup raw long-grain white
    rice
2 cups boiling water
One 2-inch piece of cinnamon
    stick
½ teaspoon ground turmeric

A *pinch of crumbled saffron
    threads or powdered saffron*
1 teaspoon salt
½ cup seedless raisins
2 tablespoons lightly toasted
    pine nuts (pignolia)
1 teaspoon sugar

In a heavy 2- to 3-quart saucepan, melt the butter over moderate heat. When the foam begins to subside, add the rice and stir until the grains are coated with butter. Do not let the rice brown. Add the water, cinnamon, turmeric, saffron, and salt, and, stirring constantly, bring to a boil over high heat. Reduce the heat to low, cover tightly, and simmer for about 20 minutes, or until the rice is tender and has absorbed all the liquid.

Remove from the heat, discard the cinnamon stick, and add the raisins and pine nuts. Fluff the rice with a fork, stir in the sugar, taste, and add more if you wish. Cut a circle of waxed paper or foil and place it inside the pan directly on top of the rice. Cover the pan with its lid and let it stand at room temperature for about 20 minutes. Just before serving, fluff the rice again with a fork and mound it in a heated bowl or platter.

Serves 4 to 6

❀ *Chinese or Japanese Rice*

Madam S. T. Wong is a great, charming lady who writes cookbooks and teaches classes. I learned a little simple trick in cooking perfect Chinese rice from her.

2 cups raw Chinese or Japanese
    rice

⅔ teaspoon salt

Wash the rice many, many times until the water is clear. Put the rice in a heavy saucepan for which you have a well-fitting lid. Pour in enough water to cover the rice up to the first joint of your index finger. Add the salt.

Let the water come to a full boil. Lower the heat and simmer until the water appears to disappear. Cover, remove from the heat, and let the rice sit for 15 to 20 minutes. *Do not peek.*

If you plan to use this for fried rice, it is better, for some reason, if you cook the rice the day before.

Serves 4 to 6

❀ *A Curried Rice Pilaf*

*4 tablespoons butter or
  margarine*
*1 cup raw long-grain white
  rice*
2 cups chicken broth
¾ teaspoon fresh curry powder
¾ teaspoon salt

*Freshly ground white pepper to
  taste*
*½ cup seedless white raisins
  (optional)*
*½ cup pecans, toasted in a
  preheated 325° oven for 15
  to 20 minutes or until crisp*

In a saucepan with a tight-fitting lid melt the butter or margarine over medium-high heat. Add the rice and coat with the butter or margarine. Cook for about 5 minutes, or until the rice is pale straw colored and every grain is moistened with butter or margarine. Add the broth, curry powder, salt, pepper, and raisins (if desired). Bring to a boil, reduce the heat to low, cover, and cook for 15 to 17 minutes (without peeking). Check after 17 minutes. If the liquid is not completely absorbed, cover and cook for another 2 or 3 minutes.

When the liquid is absorbed, remove the saucepan from the heat. Place a clean dish towel over the saucepan. Replace the lid and fold the ends of the towel over the top of the pan. Let sit until ready to serve. The cloth will absorb all the extra moisture. Fold in the toasted pecans.

Serves 4 to 6

Breads, Pancakes, Waffles, Muffins, and Fritters

If I hadn't already confessed on at least five occasions that *this* was my downfall—pasta . . . beans . . . potatoes . . . soups . . . certain desserts come to mind—I'd expect you to believe me when I tell you that *this* chapter could really do it. Especially the breads. I could trip down the ladder to obesity joyously on just the sound and smell of breads cooking, and I have a large number of people who'd go along with me with little or no persuasion. Well, just think about it—warm breads . . . cold butter . . . a great tart jam . . . golden honey—it has kind of a rolling euphony of sound and image, a basic rhythm, et cetera, et cetera, et cetera. Gee, I'm hungry.

❈ Russian Pancakes (Tvorozhniki)

These are lovely for breakfast, brunch, lunch, or even a light supper entrée.

1 pound (2 cups) small-curd
  cottage cheese
2 large egg yolks
2 teaspoons sugar
½ teaspoon vanilla extract
1 teaspoon finely grated lemon
  rind

¾ cup flour, plus a little extra
3 tablespoons unsalted butter
Powdered sugar
Sour cream

Combine the cheese, egg yolks, sugar, vanilla, and lemon rind. Then add the flour and stir until well combined.

Flour a piece of waxed paper lightly. Form the cheese mixture into a long thin loaf or log. Roll it in the waxed paper and chill for at least

1 hour, or overnight if you have time. Just before cooking, cut the log into 1-inch-thick slices.

Melt the butter in a large, heavy skillet over moderate heat. Place the rounds in the butter and brown them gently but crisply on one side and then the other. Turn only once. Serve with powdered sugar and sour cream on the side, or crushed, lightly sugared fresh fruit if you like, but you don't need it—the Tvorozhniki are enough.

Serves 4 to 6

❋ *Carolina Corn Pancakes*

1½ cups fresh or thoroughly thawed frozen corn kernels
2 cups low-fat milk
½ cup flour
¼ cup cornmeal
1 teaspoon salt
1 teaspoon sugar
½ teaspoon freshly ground black pepper

Scant 1 teaspoon baking powder
2 eggs, separated
1 tablespoon margarine or butter, melted
1 tablespoon peanut oil
Maple syrup and honey, warmed

Cook the corn in the milk for about 10 minutes, or until just tender. Drain, reserving the cooking liquid.

Mix together the dry ingredients. Beat the egg yolks and add them to the dry ingredients along with the corn, 1 cup of the cooking liquid, and the margarine or butter. Mix well. If the batter seems too stiff, add a little more cooking liquid.

Beat the egg whites until they stand in peaks. Mix 2 tablespoons of egg whites into the batter and then gently fold in the remaining egg whites.

Drizzle the oil over a *very hot* griddle or skillet. It has to be hot or these delicate little things will stick and tear apart. Drop the batter from a ladle or measuring cup onto the hot griddle. When the pancake is golden on one side, turn it over and turn down the heat a little to let it cook through. Slip the pancake off the griddle onto a very hot plate and drizzle lightly with a mixture of warmed maple syrup and honey. Have "them" waiting at the table—the corn cakes can't.

Serves 4

❖ Beer Waffles

1 envelope active dry yeast
¼ cup warm water (115°)
One 12-ounce can of beer
1 egg
¼ cup vegetable oil
1 teaspoon lemon juice
1 tablespoon grated lemon
  rind

½ teaspoon vanilla extract
2 cups flour
2 tablespoons sugar
½ teaspoon salt
Unsalted vegetable shortening
  (Crisco) for waffle iron

Dissolve the yeast in the warm water. When the yeast is bubbly, pour it into a large bowl or the bowl of a food processor. Add all the other ingredients except shortening and beat until smooth (not too long). Cover and let stand in a warm place until the batter is bubbly, about 15 to 20 minutes.

Brush both sides of a waffle iron with the unsalted vegetable shortening. Preheat the waffle iron until it registers between the B and the A of the bake section. If on the high end of the bake section, allow it to cool a little before pouring on the batter. Pour 1 to 1¼ cups of batter into the center of the waffle iron and close it. (If your waffle iron is not electric and you are using the stove, turn the waffle over after 30 to 45 seconds.) Allow the waffle to bake for 2 to 3 minutes, or until it stops steaming and is brown. Gently remove the waffle with the aid of a fork.

If you are not using an electric waffle iron, before baking the next waffle determine which side of the first waffle is browner, always beginning with the hotter side down.

Serves 4

❖ Corn Waffles

Have the Chili Butter ready—the hot waffle with the cold piquant butter is great, but also have a little syrup or honey and butter ready for the unadventurous.

1 cup unbleached flour
2 teaspoons sugar
2 teaspoons baking soda
¾ teaspoon salt
1½ cups cornmeal
2 eggs, lightly beaten

1½ cups buttermilk
⅓ cup vegetable oil, plus extra
  for waffle iron
1 cup fresh cooked corn
  kernels (optional)
Chili Butter (see below)

Combine all the dry ingredients. Add the remaining ingredients and mix to a smooth batter.

Lightly grease both sides of a waffle iron with oil. Pour about 1¼ cups of batter into the center of the waffle iron. Cook until the batter stops steaming, about 2 or 3 minutes. If it's a Belgian waffle made on top of the stove, turn it over and let it cook on the other side until it's brown; it will slip right out.

Serve with Chili Butter.

CHILI BUTTER

4 tablespoons unsalted butter, softened

2 teaspoons ancho chili powder (or any mild chili powder)

2 teaspoons chopped fresh cilantro (coriander)

1 serrano chili, seeded and finely chopped

Pinch of salt

Mix all the ingredients well and spread on the hot waffles.

Serves 4 carefully, 2 perfectly

❉ Corn Fritters

¾ cup fresh corn kernels
¼ cup milk
2 tablespoons cornmeal
2 tablespoons flour
2 tablespoons sweet butter, melted
2 eggs
¼ teaspoon salt
¼ teaspoon pepper

2 tablespoons chopped fresh chives
Nonstick cooking spray for skillet
Butter or margarine for skillet
Olive oil for skillet
Sour cream or plain low-fat yogurt

Place the corn kernels in the bowl of a food processor and process only long enough so that the kernels are broken up but not pureed. In a bowl, combine the kernels with the milk, cornmeal, and flour.

In a separate bowl, mix together the melted butter, the eggs, salt, pepper, and 1 tablespoon of the chives. Combine both mixtures and mix lightly, don't beat.

Preheat a griddle or skillet. When a drop of water dances and evaporates on the surface, it's ready. Spray lightly with nonstick cooking spray and then grease with butter or margarine and olive oil mixed together.

Drop enough batter to make fritters about 2 inches in diameter onto the hot griddle. Fry about 2 minutes on each side until golden brown. Serve with sour cream or yogurt mixed with the remaining tablespoon of chopped chives.

Serves 4

❖ *Dinah's Beer-Apple Fritters*

The only reason for the possessive Dinah etc. is that I've been making them for so long, and often nobody else will take the blame or credit— depending on how you like the fritters.

BATTER
2 cups sifted all-purpose flour	1 pint (2 cups) beer, at room temperature

FRITTERS
5 medium-size tart cooking apples	Vegetable oil for deep-frying
1 cup sugar	Confectioners' sugar
1 tablespoon ground cinnamon	

Make the batter early (aren't you glad?), as it must sit for 2 to 3 hours. Sift the flour into a deep mixing bowl and make a well in the center. Slowly pour in the beer and stir gently, gradually incorporating the flour. Continue to stir until smooth, but *do not* beat or overmix. Set the batter aside to rest at room temperature for 2 to 3 hours.

Fifteen minutes before making the fritters, peel and core the apples. Cut them crosswise into ⅓-inch-thick rounds. Combine the sugar and cinnamon. Sprinkle the mixture evenly on both sides of each apple round, or dip each slice into the sugar mixture.

Preheat the oven to its lowest setting. Line a large shallow baking dish or jelly-roll pan with a double thickness of paper towels. Set the pan in the middle of the oven. Pour the vegetable oil into a deep fryer, a large saucepan, or an electric wok to a depth of about 3 inches. Heat the oil to 375°.

With tongs, dip each coated apple slice in the batter. When well coated on both sides, drop it into the oil. Deep-fry 3 or 4 slices at a time for 4 minutes, turning them occasionally, until evenly browned. As they brown, transfer the slices to the paper-lined pan in the oven, while coating and deep-frying the remaining slices.

Arrange the fritters on a heated platter, and sprinkle lightly with the confectioners' sugar just before serving. Serve at once while hot.

Set these down and get out of the way—these go fast.

Serves 4 to 6

❋ *Corn Muffins with Jalapeño Peppers and Fresh Dill*

*1 medium ear corn or ½ cup
    frozen corn, thawed
10 tablespoons unsalted butter,
    melted
3 small jalapeño peppers,
    seeded and finely chopped
1½ teaspoons chopped fresh
    dill
1 cup cornmeal*

*1 cup flour
2 tablespoons light brown
    sugar, packed
1½ teaspoons baking powder
1 teaspoon salt
1 egg
¾ teaspoon baking soda
1½ cups buttermilk*

Preheat the oven to 425°.

Cut the kernels from the ear of the corn and set them aside. Brush 12 medium-size muffin cups with some of the butter and set them aside. Add the jalapeño peppers to 1½ tablespoons of the butter and cook slowly for 1 minute. Remove from the heat. Add the corn and the dill to the pan with the peppers and set it aside.

Mix together the cornmeal, flour, sugar, baking powder, and salt. Add the egg and baking soda to the buttermilk. Add the egg, baking soda, and buttermilk to the cornmeal mixture and lightly mix. Add the slightly cooled melted butter and then the jalapeño and corn mixture. Mix lightly—it doesn't matter if it's slightly lumpy. Spoon the batter into the muffin cups until they are no more than three quarters full and bake the muffins for 18 to 20 minutes. When the muffins are done, a toothpick inserted in the center of one will come out clean. Let the muffins sit in the tins for a minute or two before removing them.

One nice tip to use for these or any other type of corn bread is to put ½ teaspoon of butter, margarine, or any other shortening in each cup and place the muffin tin in the preheated oven for a couple of minutes while you're mixing the batter. Pour the batter into the hot cups and immediately put the muffin tin back in the oven. The muffins will rise more than you anticipated.

Makes 12 medium-size muffins

✽ *Walnut Wheat Muffins*

1 cup unbleached white flour
1 cup whole wheat flour
2¼ teaspoons baking powder
½ teaspoon salt
3 tablespoons wheat germ
1 whole egg
1 cup milk

1 tablespoon honey
4 tablespoons butter or
   margarine, melted and
   cooled
1 cup chopped lightly toasted
   walnuts

Preheat the oven to 400°.

Mix together the flours, baking powder, and salt. Add the wheat germ. Beat the egg, milk, and honey together. Add the liquid ingredients to the flour mixture and stir until just combined. Don't overmix. Fold in the walnuts.

Spoon the batter into 12 buttered muffin cups and fill three quarters full. Bake in the middle of the preheated oven for 20 minutes, or until puffed and brown. Turn out onto a rack to cool a little. Serve hot with butter and honey.

Makes 12 muffins

✽ *Jack Daniel's Bran Muffins*

This is really healthy and lusty. (The Jack Daniel's takes care of that.)

½ cup chopped pitted prunes
¼ cup Jack Daniel's whiskey or
   bourbon or brandy
2 soft bananas, mashed
One 10.5-ounce package Oat
   Bran Muffin Mix

½ cup low-fat milk
⅓ cup pecan pieces
1 whole egg or 2 egg whites

Preheat the oven to 400°.

Soak the prunes in the Jack Daniel's for 30 minutes.

Mash the bananas into the muffin mix. Add the prunes and all the other ingredients and mix; don't worry if there are lumps. Butter 8 to 10 muffin cups well or line them with muffin papers. Fill the cups two thirds full and bake in the preheated oven for 15 to 20 minutes, or until a toothpick or sharp knife inserted in the center of a muffin comes out clean. Serve warm for breakfast or tea or for noshing all day.

Makes 8 to 10 medium-size muffins

❋ *Banana-Nut Rum Bread*

2 cups unbleached flour
1 teaspoon baking soda
½ teaspoon salt
⅓ cup milk
1 teaspoon lemon juice
3 ripe bananas
8 tablespoons butter, plus
  extra for the pan

8 tablespoons margarine
1 cup sugar
2 eggs
¾ cup coarsely chopped
  walnuts
3 tablespoons light rum

Preheat the oven to 350°.

Mix the dry ingredients and set aside. Mix the milk and lemon juice (the mixture will curdle a little but not to worry) and set aside. Mash the bananas and set aside.

With a hand mixer, cream the butter and margarine until a little fluffy. Add the sugar gradually, then the eggs one at a time, beating after each addition. Then alternately add the flour mixture and the milk-lemon mixture. Fold in the bananas, then the walnuts. Add the rum and mix well.

Pour the batter into a well-buttered 9-x-5-x-3-inch loaf pan and bake for 1 hour. Bread is done when it is golden on top or a knife or toothpick inserted in center comes out clean. Don't overcook.

Serves 6

CLOCKWISE FROM TOP: Tony's Filet Mignon of Tuna
p. 161 Linguini with Smoked Salmon p. 212
Chopped Tomato Salad with Bruschetta p. 29
Scallop Pasta p. 220 Cannelloni with Lump Crab
Meat p. 208

CLOCKWISE FROM TOP: Pineapple Upside Down Skillet Cake p. 269 Chess Tarts p. 280 Pecan Carmel Chocolate Chip Ice Cream p. 290 Teatime Pecan Pie Cookies p. 295 Thinnest Brownies p. 298 Coconut Cream Pie p. 278 Hot Fudge Pudding Cake p. 267 Sweet Potato–Praline Pie p. 278 Tennessee Trifle p. 270 Amber Glass Custard p. 285

CLOCKWISE FROM TOP: Gloria's Shrimp Cocktail p. 18 Santa Fe Chicken p. 130 Red Tomato Salsa p. 83 Chicken Rolls with Chilies and Cheese p. 120 Salad Sonora p. 73 Sweet Onion Parmesan Bread p. 260

❈ Banana Date Pecan Bread

I have never used a mix, but when I went back to Nashville and Winchester on this last trip home, I found the land of "cooking from scratch" had converted to a mix occasionally. I succumbed. It works and is delicious!

One 16.6-ounce package Date Bread Mix	1 egg
1 cup water	3 ripe bananas, mashed
1 tablespoon vegetable oil	Generous ½ cup chopped pecans

Preheat the oven to 350°. Butter the bottom of a 9-x-5-inch loaf pan.

Combine the date bread mix with the water, oil, and egg. Beat with a wooden spoon until well blended. Add the bananas and nuts and mix well.

Pour the batter into the pan and bake for 40 to 50 minutes, or until a toothpick inserted in the center comes out clean. Cool in the loaf pan on a rack for 15 minutes. Remove from the pan and cool completely before serving.

Makes one 9-x-5-inch loaf

Variation: Add ¼ cup Jack Daniel's whiskey or brandy and ¾ cup water instead of 1 cup water.

❀ *Spiral Bread*

DOUGH

2 envelopes active dry yeast
1 cup warm water (115°)
1 cup scalded milk
2½ teaspoons salt
2 tablespoons sugar
¼ cup shortening (butter, margarine, or oil), plus extra for bowl
7 cups unbleached white flour, slightly warmed in the oven (try your favorite variations. If you like, add ¼ cup wheat and/or rye flour to your unbleached white flour; just be sure it comes out to the 7 or so cups recommended.)
Melted butter or margarine
1 egg, beaten

FILLINGS

Cinnamon and sugar
Chopped walnuts
Chopped raisins and dates (nice if you want a sweet bread)
Melted butter (very good in the center)

Dissolve the yeast in the warm water in a slightly warmed large mixing bowl. Set it aside while you mix the milk, salt, sugar, and shortening in another bowl. Spoon the milk mixture into the yeast-water mixture and stir. Slowly add flour by cupfuls. Mix well until the dough is smooth and satiny.

Turn the dough out onto a lightly floured board and knead for 12 minutes. Shape into a ball and place it in a buttered bowl. Turn to coat on all sides. Cover with a clean cloth (I use a heavy bath-type towel over the bowl to be sure it is draft-free) and set it in a warm place for 45 minutes, until doubled in bulk.

Punch down the dough and turn it out onto a lightly floured board once more. Let the dough rest while you grease two 9-x-5-x-3-inch bread pans. Cut the dough in half and roll it into balls, then shape it into rectangles (using a rolling pin if you like), ¼ to ½ inch thick and the length of the pan. Brush with melted butter or margarine and with the beaten egg.

Spread the desired filling over the rectangles and roll them up jelly-roll fashion from the long side. Seal the edges, and place sealed side down in the pans. Brush the tops with more melted butter or margarine and cover with a clean cloth. Place a large roasting pan over the dough to give it plenty of room to rise and to be sure it's draft-free. Let the dough rise for nearly 1 hour.

Bake in a preheated 400° oven for 1 hour. Turn out on racks to cool, or serve warm.

Makes 2 loaves

❉ *Buttermilk Corn Bread*

I like to see the steam rising from this as it's served hot from the oven. An occasional "ouch" from the diners picking it up warms my soul.

Scant 2 tablespoons butter or margarine for bottom of baking pan
1 cup flour
1 cup cornmeal
2½ teaspoons baking powder
¾ teaspoon salt
1 tablespoon sugar, more if you like

1½ cups buttermilk mixed with ½ teaspoon baking soda
2 eggs, beaten
4 tablespoons butter or margarine, melted and cooled

Preheat the oven to 400°.

Place a scant 2 tablespoons of butter or margarine in an 8-inch square pan and place the pan in the preheated oven for a few minutes while you are mixing the batter.

Place the dry ingredients in a mixing bowl. Mix the buttermilk, eggs, and melted butter in a large measuring cup and pour into the dry ingredients. Mix all the ingredients together; don't overmix—lumps are okay.

Pour your lumpy batter into the hot pan and bake for 25 minutes, or until done.

Serves 6 to 8

Variation: To make Sweet Milk Corn Bread, use whole or low-fat milk instead of the buttermilk and eliminate the baking soda. Proceed as directed.

✲ *French Baguettes*

1 tablespoon sugar
¾ cup warm water (110°–
   115°)
2 teaspoons active dry yeast
1 tablespoon butter or
   margarine, melted and
   cooled

1¾ cups unbleached flour,
   warmed slightly in the oven
1 teaspoon salt
Oil for the bowl
1 egg white mixed with a little
   cold water
Sesame or poppy seeds

Mix the sugar with the water, sprinkle in the yeast, stir briefly, and set aside to proof for about 5 minutes. Add the melted butter or margarine.

Place the flour and salt in the bowl of an electric mixer fitted with a dough hook. When the yeast mixture is bubbly, pour it into the flour, turn the mixer to medium, then high, and knead until the dough forms a soft ball. Turn the dough out onto a floured board (flour your hands a little too) and knead by hand for about 5 minutes or more if you feel like it. If the dough sticks to the board, sprinkly a little more flour on the board, it will be a light lovely dough. Place the dough in a lightly oiled bowl, cover, and set in a draft-free place to rise until doubled in bulk, about 35 to 40 minutes.

Remove the dough from the bowl and cut it in 2 equal pieces. Knead each one to remove air bubbles and form each into a neat ball. Put the balls back into the oiled bowl to rise again, about 10 minutes. When doubled in bulk, remove to a floured board and shape each ball into a flat rectangle with a rolling pin or your palms. Roll up tightly from the long side, pinch together to seal well, and taper the ends. Place the loaves on a greased baking sheet, cover, and let rise until nearly doubled in bulk, about 50 to 60 minutes.

Brush with a little cold water and make 3 neat diagonal cuts on each loaf. Use a razor blade or sharp-pointed scissors, or the point of your sharpest knife—these have to be neat—you don't get a second crack at it without messing up your loaves. Brush with the egg white and water mixture and sprinkle with sesame or poppy seeds. Bake in a preheated 375° oven for 20 to 25 minutes. When gorgeously golden, remove from the baking sheets and set back in the oven to crisp the bottoms too. Set on racks to cool.

Makes 2 small baguettes

✽ French-style Bread with Greek Olives

I was trying to demonstrate to Shirley Secretary how really easy it is—and fun—to bake yeast bread. She had shied away from it all her cooking life. . . . I think I created a monster. She baked Raisin Pumpernickel, Italian or Greek Kalamata olive loaves, and was well on her way to kasha rye, Swedish limpa, French sourdough baguettes, but it was getting dark with no more rising time. Try the Greek Kalamata—it has a superb crisp crust, lovely texture, and the flavor—uuuumm. And while you're at it, the pumpernickel with or without the raisins (page 261) is great for sandwiches or toast. Caraway seeds make a nice addition to the pumpernickel.

1½ envelopes active dry yeast
1 tablespoon sugar
2 cups warm water (110°–115°)
1 tablespoon salt
5 to 6 cups flour

1 cup pitted and coarsely chopped Kalamata or Greek olives
Butter for bowl
3 tablespoons yellow cornmeal
1 tablespoon egg white mixed with 1 tablespoon cold water

Combine the yeast with the sugar and warm water in a large bowl and set aside to proof. Mix the salt with the flour and mix it into the yeast mixture, a cup at a time, until you have a stiff dough.

Remove to a lightly floured board and knead until the dough is no longer sticky, about 10 minutes, adding flour as necessary. While you are kneading the dough, knead in the olives as evenly as possible. Place the dough in a buttered bowl and turn to coat the surface with butter. Cover and let rise in a warm place until doubled in bulk, 1½ to 2 hours. After the first rising, remove the dough from the bowl, punch it down and knead it again for 5 to 10 minutes. Return to the bowl, cover, and let rise again. When it has doubled in bulk, shape into 2 long French-style bread loaves and place seam side down about 1 or 2 inches apart on a baking sheet sprinkled with the cornmeal. Cover and let rise for 30 minutes.

Make 3 diagonal slashes ¼ to ½ inch deep in each loaf with a razor or sharp knife. Brush with the egg white and water, and place in a cold oven set for 400°. Bake until nicely browned and hollow sounding when the tops are tapped, 35 to 45 minutes

Makes 2 long loaves

❧ *Sesame–Poppy Seed Ring*

I tasted something like this at a great restaurant in St. Louis called Tony's. His pasta is on page 220 (Vincent Bommarito's Pasta Primavera from Tony's) and his tuna is on page 161 (Filet Mignon of Tuna). If I had known how great these would be, I wouldn't have filled up on this reasonable facsimile of his bread.

2 envelopes active dry yeast
1 tablespoon sugar
1 cup warm water (110°–115°)
⅓ cup butter, cut into small
  pieces, plus extra for baking
  sheets
1 to 1¼ cups hot water
1½ teaspoons salt
6 cups flour, warmed slightly
  in the oven
1 egg
1 egg white

2 tablespoons finely chopped
  fresh dill
Cornmeal
1 egg, lightly beaten with 2
  tablespoons water (for loaf
  number one)
½ cup water, combined with
  1½ teaspoons cornstarch and
  ½ teaspoon salt (for loaf
  number two)
Poppy seeds
Sesame seeds

In a small bowl, mix the yeast with the sugar and warm water and let stand for about 5 minutes, until bubbly and doubled in size. While your yeast is proofing, melt the butter in the hot water and let it cool to lukewarm. Add the salt and combine with the yeast mixture.

Place the flour in the large bowl of your electric mixer. Make a well in the center of the flour, and add the egg and the egg white. Stirring vigorously with a wooden spoon, add the yeast-butter-water mixture and the chopped dill. Use your dough hook now, if you have one, and mix until the dough comes away from the sides of the bowl and clings to the dough hook. It will be a little sticky. Turn the dough out onto a lightly floured board. Using a baker's scraper or a large spatula, scrape under the flour and dough, fold the dough over, and press it with your free hand. Continue until the dough has absorbed enough flour from the board to make it easy to handle. Knead for 5 minutes or so. Be sure to keep your hands well floured, since the dough may still be a little sticky. When the dough is smooth and elastic, let it rest for 5 to 6 minutes. Divide the dough into 2 equal pieces.

LOAF NUMBER ONE

Slightly flatten the dough and cut it into 6 equal pieces. Shape each piece into a ball. Butter a round baking sheet and sprinkle with the cornmeal. Place the balls, seam side down and just touching one another, in a circle on the baking sheet. Cover the dough balls with plastic wrap and a large tea towel and place in a warm, draft-free place to rise until more than doubled in bulk, 50 to 60 minutes. I cover my loaves with the lid of a large roasting pan to give the dough plenty of room to rise.

Preheat the oven to 425°. Brush the dough with some of the beaten egg wash and sprinkle with the poppy seeds. Bake for 10 minutes, reduce the heat to 350°, brush again with the beaten egg wash, and bake for another 25 to 30 minutes, or until the bread is a rich, golden color and makes a hollow sound when you tap the crust, top and bottom, with your knuckles.

LOAF NUMBER TWO

Roll the dough into a ball and flatten it slightly. Using two fingers, make a hole in the center of the dough, twirl the dough in a circular motion with your fingers until the hole becomes larger and the dough forms a ring 9 to 10 inches in diameter. Try to keep it as even as you can by shaping it with both hands from time to time. Butter a pizza brick or a baking sheet and sprinkle with the cornmeal. Place the ring on the prepared surface. Cover with a large bowl, the well-known roasting pan, or anything to give it plenty of rising room. Place in a warm, draft-free place to rise until more than doubled in bulk, 50 to 60 minutes.

Meanwhile, cook the water, salt, and cornstarch mixture, stirring until clear but thick. Preheat the oven to 425°. Just before baking, brush some of the cornstarch mixture over the ring, and sprinkle with the sesame and poppy seeds in alternating pie-shaped wedges, the narrow point in center, widening at the outer edges.

Place the ring on the upper shelf of the oven and splash water in the bottom of the oven to create a little steam. Bake for 5 to 10 minutes, then reduce the heat to 325°. Brush once again with the cornstarch mixture and bake for another 35 to 40 minutes, or until the bread is a rich, golden color and makes a hollow sound when you tap the crust, top and bottom, with your knuckles. If the bottom isn't as crusty as you like, remove the ring from the baking sheet and place it directly on the rack of the oven for the last 5 minutes of baking.

Makes 2 rings

✳ *Tecate Bread*

The Golden Door is one of the first Fat Farms or Pamper Palaces to which I retreated after writing a cookbook to get back into shape for golf and tennis and television. They serve this great Tecate Bread there. It is so nutritious it can't hurt. They gave me the recipe ages ago and I misplaced it. I found it later, but I'd been making my own version for so long and I'd gotten used to it. I rather like it better. You can mix almost any kinds of flours and grains, but I especially like this combination. Mix the dough and then step back—it rises fast and persuasively. I was going to tell you how well it keeps or how you can freeze a loaf or so at a time, but after you've baked it, it disappears pretty fast at home, and when friends go out with one under each arm, you're torn between desperation and pride. Have no fear, it's easy to bake and—remember— it's good for you.

4 cups warm water (110°– 115°)
¼ cup vegetable oil*
¼ cup honey
2 packages active dry yeast
8 cups unbleached flour
2 cups whole wheat flour
½ cup buckwheat (if available; if not, use another ½ cup of either of the above flours)

1 heaping cup Miller's Bran (available at health food stores)
2 teaspoons sea salt
1 cup walnuts, coarsely chopped
3 tablespoons cornmeal

Pour the water, oil, and honey into a large, slightly warmed mixing bowl. Sprinkle the yeast over the water mixture and mix well. Let the water-yeast mixture sit as you mix the flours, bran, salt, and walnuts. When the yeast is bubbly, add 3 to 4 cups of the flour mixture and mix well, using the dough hook of your mixer or a large wooden spoon. Add the remaining flour a cup at a time and mix until the dough is stiff and clings to the dough hook. Remove the dough to a lightly floured board and knead well until the dough is smooth and satiny, about 5 to 7 minutes. Roll the dough into a ball. Butter or grease a large, clean rising bowl. Place the dough in the rising bowl and turn to coat on all sides, placing the seam side down. Cover the dough with plastic wrap and place in a warm, draft-free place. Cover the dough with dish towels to insure it. Check the dough in about 1½ hours. Your dough will have risen to more than double its size; it may be pushing at the shelves above the counter if you don't punch it down. A couple of good punches with your fist will get the bubbles out for the second rising. The second rising isn't absolutely necessary if you want to shape your loaves at this point. Have ready 3 good-sized baking tiles or bricks (mine are about 13 inches in diameter), or use round pizza pans or cookie sheets. Sprinkle the center of each surface with 1 tablespoon of cornmeal. After slapping the dough against the board a few times, cut the dough into 3 equal pieces. Roll the pieces into balls and set, seam side down, on the cornmeal in the center of the cooking sheets. With sharp-pointed scissors, cut a cross in the center of the dough, about 3 to 3½ inches long, and sprinkle each loaf with a teaspoon or so of flour. Cover each loaf with a bowl (use the rising bowl for one since it's already greased). It's not absolutely essential, but lightly grease the sides of the 2 other bowls so the dough won't stick. Let the loaves rise another 30 minutes. Bake in the center of a preheated 350° oven for 1 hour and 15 to 20 minutes, until the loaves are dark-golden and gorgeous.

Makes 3 loaves

*Measure honey in the same cup you used to measure the oil. This way, the honey won't stick.

❋ Sweet Onion Parmesan Bread

While working on this chapter I was really into breads. I must have been. I woke up one morning with this one all worked out in my mind— measured, mixed, baked, tasted with butter melting on the first luscious slice.

2 envelopes active dry yeast
1 tablespoon sugar
1 cup warm water (110°–115°)
5⅓ tablespoons butter or
  margarine, cut into small
  pieces, plus extra for baking
  sheets
¾ cup hot water
2 teaspoons salt
5½ cups flour, warmed a bit in
  the oven

Generous ¾ cup thinly sliced
  sweet onions (If the onion
  isn't sweet, sprinkle a little
  sugar on it.)
¾ cup freshly grated Parmesan
  cheese
Cornmeal
1 egg, lightly beaten with 2
  tablespoons water

In the bowl of your electric mixer, proof the yeast with the sugar and warm water for about 5 minutes, or until bubbly and double in size. While your yeast is proofing, melt the butter in the hot water and cool to lukewarm. Add the salt and combine with the yeast mixture. Add the cooled butter-water mixture. Stirring vigorously with a wooden spoon or a dough hook, add the flour, 1 cup at a time, until the dough almost comes away from the sides of the bowl. It will be a little sticky.

Turn the dough out onto a lightly floured board. Using a spatula, scrape under the flour and dough, fold the dough over, and press it with your free hand. Continue until the dough has absorbed enough flour from the board and is easy to handle. Knead for 2 minutes. Add the onions and cheese and continue kneading for 2 more minutes, being sure to keep your hands well floured because the dough is still sticky. When the dough is soft and smooth, let it rest for 5 to 6 minutes.

Divide the dough in 2 pieces. With a rolling pin, roll each half into a rectangle about 12 x 8 inches. Cut two ½-inch strips from the long side of each rectangle and set aside. Starting at the wide end, roll each rectangle up gently, pinching the seams at both ends of the loaf as you roll. Roll each ½-inch strip of dough in your hands until it is slightly longer than each loaf. Place them on top and down the center of each loaf of bread, pulling the ends over and pressing them gently onto the underside of loaves to hold them in place while the dough is rising.

Butter 2 baking sheets well and sprinkle with cornmeal. Place the loaves seam side down on the baking sheets. Cover with plastic wrap and a large tea towel and place in a warm, draft-free place to rise until more than doubled in bulk, 50 to 60 minutes. I cover my loaves with the lid of a large roasting pan to give the dough plenty of room to rise.

Preheat the oven to 425°. Brush the top and sides of each loaf lightly and thoroughly with the beaten egg wash and bake for 40 minutes, or until the loaves are a rich, golden color and make a hollow sound when you tap the crust, top and bottom, with your knuckles. Cool on a rack. Serve warm with cold butter.

Makes 2 loaves

✳ *Raisin Pumpernickel Bread*

This is a good and heavy, crusty rye bread. From the directions it looks like it takes forever, but it doesn't. It's just that from time to time in the course of the day you go back to check it out and work with it a little. Just serve it with butter—maybe a little cream cheese and maybe warm it again, wrapped in foil in the oven (not the microwave) before serving.

1 envelope active dry yeast
1 tablespoon sugar
1¼ cups warm water (110°– 115°)
2 tablespoons molasses
2 tablespoons vegetable oil or butter, plus extra for bowl and pan
1 tablespoon salt

1 cup white unbleached flour, more if necessary
1 cup whole wheat flour
2 cups rye flour
½ cup cornmeal
¾ cup raisins
1 egg beaten with 2 tablespoons water

Combine the yeast, sugar, and ¼ cup of the warm water in a large mixing bowl, and let proof for 5 minutes. Add the molasses, the oil or butter, and the salt and mix well. Add the remaining cup of water. Mix the flours and cornmeal together, and add, a cup at a time, to the yeast mixture, beating it in until you have a fairly stiff but workable dough; it will be sticky, heavy, and difficult to blend.

Turn out onto a floured board and knead, adding more flour as necessary, until the dough becomes smooth and fairly elastic. While you are kneading the dough, knead in the raisins as evenly as possible. It will take at least 10 minutes of kneading and possibly longer until the dough is only slightly sticky. (It will not be completely resilient, and it is apt to seem extremely heavy but that's the nature of this dough.) Shape into a ball, put into a large buttered bowl, and turn to coat on all sides. Place smooth side up. Cover with a heavy dish towel, maybe two, and let rise in a warm, draft-free spot until doubled in bulk, about 2 to 2½ hours.

Punch down the dough and shape into a loaf that will fit a well-buttered 8-x-4-inch tin. Cover and let rise to the top of the pan, another 2 to 3 hours.

About ¼ inch from the edge of the dough, with a sharp knife or clean kitchen shears, cut a slit about ¼ inch deep all around the sides of the bread in order to let the air out. Brush with the beaten egg wash. Bake in a preheated 375° oven for 35 to 45 minutes, or until the loaf sounds hollow when tapped on the top and bottom. Cool thoroughly on a rack before slicing.

Makes one 8-x-4-inch loaf

❧ *Cottage Cheese Corn Bread Pudding*

Susan Meredith found this luscious spoon bread–type recipe in Dallas. I don't know whether it's meant for dessert or a side dish, or a great brunch dish with a salad. We tried it all three ways and it passed each occasion with flying colors.

¾ *cup fresh white or yellow corn kernels*	1½ *cups cottage cheese*
2 *tablespoons butter or margarine, melted, plus 2 tablespoons at room temperature*	2 *eggs, beaten*
	1¾ *cups buttermilk*
	½ *teaspoon baking soda*
	2 *boxes corn muffin mix, 7 ounces each*

In a large skillet, cook the corn kernels slightly in the 2 tablespoons of melted butter or margarine. Preheat the oven to 400°.

Mix the cottage cheese, eggs, buttermilk, and baking soda together and blend well. Add the corn muffin mix to the cottage cheese mixture and mix well. Add the corn and butter from the skillet.

Place a large oven-proof casserole in the preheated oven with the 2 tablespoons of butter or margarine at room temperature. Melt the butter or margarine and tilt the casserole to make sure the sides and bottom are well covered. Pour in the batter and bake in the center of the oven for about 30 minutes, or until golden brown. (Don't let it overcook, please.) Serve it warm.

Serves 8

❧ Old World Hot Cereal

I play golf, as you may have gathered, with a lot of great friends. One of them happens to be a very low handicapper. His wife will be one soon and his son has just turned pro. It runs in the genes, I guess, but the low handicapper is named Mike Starkman. He is in the brokerage business and gets to play golf after the market closes in New York.

Early, early in the morning he breakfasts at a famous restaurant out here called Old World. Long before it was "in," the restaurant was known for being health-food conscious. This cereal is one of its most famous, healthiest, and most delicious. You won't find the makings for this on your neighborhood market shelves. Mike persuaded—maybe conned is a better way of putting it—the owners to give me the recipe for our book. The amounts were staggering—15 pounds of oats, 12 cups of wheat germ, 12 tablespoons of cinnamon, 9 gallons of milk, et cetera. We broke it down, copied it (as did the lady in the health-food store when we asked her for the ingredients), cooked it—and it worked!

1¼ cups wheat berries	*1 tablespoon ground*
2½ cups rolled oats	*cinnamon*
1 cup wheat germ	*2½ tablespoons vanilla extract*
¾ cup bulgur wheat	*3 quarts milk*

Cook the wheat berries in boiling water to cover for approximately 30 minutes, or according to package directions.

Cook the oats, wheat germ, and bulgur wheat in boiling water to cover, with the cinnamon and vanilla, for about 30–35 minutes, or until almost done. Mix with the cooked wheat berries. Add the milk and cook over low heat for approximately 10 more minutes, or until the cereal is done.

Serve with raw or brown sugar and milk. Also, you may serve it with raisins if you like. It really doesn't need much.

Serves 12

Desserts

Well, here we are again—I've stated often, and I still believe, I'm not a "sweets" person, but this chapter gives the lie to my conviction. You should see the recipes I agonized over leaving out. This is kind of a cross section of desserts in our country. Well, perhaps it's weighted a little in favor of my native Tennessee favorites, where it all started for me. My mother used to say, "Now save a little something to take the sweet taste out." Meaning, save a bite of your favorite piece of chicken and mashed potatoes to counter the meltingly delicious taste of the dinner capper—the dessert. It kept me from craving the sweet snack, but after I'd "taken the sweet taste out" there were times when I wanted another smidgen of that sweet to take the salt taste out, to be immediately followed by a little something to take the sweet taste out, and on and on. I was a skinny little kid with a strong set of teeth, so I could continue this ad infinitum (and still do).

❋ Chocolate Cake with Pureed Raspberry Sauce

4 tablespoons butter or
  margarine, plus extra for
  cake pan
One 8-ounce package
  semisweet chocolate
5 eggs, separated
2 tablespoons flour
¾ cup sugar plus 1 tablespoon

Pinch of salt
Confectioners' sugar (optional)
Pureed Raspberry Sauce (see
  below)
1 cup whipped cream
Fresh raspberries, if in season,
  for garnish, or reserve a few
  frozen berries from the sauce

Preheat the oven to 325°. Butter and flour a 10-inch cake pan.

In a double boiler melt the 4 tablespoons butter or margarine and the chocolate. In a large bowl, combine the egg yolks, flour, and ¾ cup sugar and beat thoroughly. Fold in the chocolate mixture. Beat the egg whites until firm, add the 1 tablespoon of sugar and the salt, and beat until the egg whites form peaks. Carefully fold the egg whites into the batter.

Pour the batter into the prepared cake pan and bake for approximately 1 hour, or until a toothpick inserted in the center comes out clean. If desired, sprinkle the cooled cake with confectioners' sugar. Place some of the raspberry sauce on a plate. Top with a wedge of cake. Top with whipped cream, and drizzle a little of the sauce over the cream. Garnish with raspberries.

PUREED RASPBERRY SAUCE

One 16-ounce package frozen raspberries, defrosted
2 tablespoons sugar

2 tablespoons orange-flavored liqueur

Place all the ingredients in a blender or food processor and puree.

Serves 8 to 12

❋Decadent Chocolate Fudge Cake

1¼ pounds semisweet chocolate, broken into squares, or chocolate bits
6 eggs, separated, plus 2 egg whites
12 tablespoons unsalted butter, at room temperature, cut into 1-inch pieces, plus extra for pan

½ cup sugar
¾ cup coarsely chopped pecans
Crème Anglaise (see below)

Butter a 9-inch springform pan and set aside.

Melt the chocolate in the top of a double boiler, over boiling water, stirring until smooth. Set aside to cool. Whisk the egg yolks in the top of another double boiler until slightly cooked and lighter in color, about 2 minutes. Remove from the heat and whisk until cool, about 2 minutes. Cream the butter in a large bowl until light and fluffy. Fold in the cooled melted chocolate and then add the egg yolks.

Beat the 8 egg whites in a large glass bowl at medium speed until soft peaks form. Gradually beat in the sugar, 1 tablespoon at a time, and continue beating at high speed until the meringue forms stiff peaks but is not dry. Fold the meringue into the chocolate mixture.

Pour into the springform pan. Sprinkle chopped pecans over the top and press them lightly into the batter. Place in the refrigerator covered with plastic wrap for 3 hours, or until set. Remove from the pan, cut into wedges, and serve with Crème Anglaise.

CRÈME ANGLAISE

3 egg yolks
⅓ cup granulated sugar
1¼ cups hot milk

2 teaspoons vanilla extract
1 tablespoon butter

Beat the egg yolks in a stainless-steel saucepan until thick and sticky (1 minute). Gradually beat in the sugar, then beat in the hot milk by droplets. Place the saucepan over moderately low heat and stir with a wooden spoon until the sauce thickens enough to coat the spoon. (Do not let the sauce come near the simmer or the egg yolks will curdle.) Remove from the heat and stir in the vanilla and butter. Serve warm or cool.

Serves 12

❧ Hot Fudge Pudding Cake

In June 1989 I gave the commencement address at the Hershey School in Hershey, Pennsylvania. Facing those eager, enthusiastic young people was inspiring. It went well and as a reward the next day they took me through the Hershey kitchens! Talk about turning a termite loose in a lumberyard—I went crazy and I'm not all that hung up on sweets (she keeps saying). This was one of the recipes they gave me to try at home. I did. It's great.

1¼ cups sugar
1 cup flour
7 tablespoons unsweetened
   cocoa
2 teaspoons baking powder
¼ teaspoon salt
½ cup milk

⅓ cup butter or margarine,
   melted
1½ teaspoons vanilla extract
½ cup light brown sugar,
   packed
1¼ cups hot water
Chopped pecans or walnuts for
   garnish

Heat the oven to 350°.

In a medium mixing bowl combine ¾ cup of the sugar, the flour, 3 tablespoons of the cocoa, the baking powder, and salt. Blend in the milk, melted butter, and vanilla. Beat until smooth.

Pour the batter into a square pan, 8-x-8-x-2 or 9-x-9-x-2 inches.

In a small bowl combine the remaining ½ cup of sugar, the brown sugar, and the remaining 4 tablespoons of cocoa; sprinkle the mixture evenly over the batter. Pour the hot water over the top; do not stir. Bake for 40 minutes, or until the center is almost set. Remove from the oven and let stand for 15 minutes; spoon into dessert dishes, spooning sauce from the bottom of the pan over the top. Garnish with chopped nuts.

8 to 10 servings

❧*Lee's Aunt's Chocolate Pound Cake*

Lee is LeElla Moorer. A great, longtime friend transplanted from Alabama to L.A. She claims she can't—or won't—cook a lick, but after much persuasion she was drafted into helping us test a few—very few recipes. She came up with the Alabama pecans for many of the recipes in the book and this great recipe from her Aunt Clara. She says it serves sixteen normal slices, ten to twelve for people who appreciate the cake the way Lee does.

½ cup vegetable shortening	*½ teaspoon salt*
8 tablespoons butter or	*½ teaspoon baking powder*
margarine	*4 tablespoons unsweetened*
3 cups sugar	*cocoa*
5 eggs	*1 cup milk*
3 cups flour	*1 teaspoon vanilla extract*

Preheat the oven to 325°.

Cream the vegetable shortening and butter or margarine together until very fluffy. Add the sugar and beat very well until smooth and fluffy. Add the eggs, one at a time, beating after each addition. Sift together the dry ingredients. Add to the butter-sugar mixture, alternating with the milk. Stir in the vanilla.

Turn the batter into a 9- or 10-inch pound cake pan or a 9-x-5-inch loaf pan, and bake for 1 hour and 20 minutes, or until a toothpick inserted in the center comes out clean. Cool on a rack in the cake pan.

Serves 10 to 12

✽ Pineapple Upside Down Skillet Cake

I've loved Pineapple Upside Down Cake since Mother made it for special holidays when I was a child. Hers was great! I tried to improve on perfection by adding the second layer, but I think you'll like it.

16 tablespoons butter or
   margarine
2¼ cups light brown sugar,
   packed
⅓ cup plus 1 teaspoon
   amaretto liqueur
Two 20-ounce cans sliced
   pineapple, drained
2 cups plus 3 tablespoons
   sliced toasted almonds

3 eggs, separated
¾ cup white sugar
2 cups flour
2 teaspoons baking powder
¼ teaspoon salt
⅓ cup milk
1 cup heavy cream, whipped
   with 1½ teaspoons
   confectioners' sugar

Melt half the butter or margarine in a 10-inch pan or cast-iron skillet at least 2 inches deep. Stir in 2 cups of the brown sugar and ⅓ cup minus 1 tablespoon of the amaretto liqueur. Mix well. Remove half the mixture and set aside.

Sprinkle the pineapple slices with the 1 tablespoon of amaretto. Sprinkle 1 cup of the almonds over the brown sugar mixture remaining in the pan. Layer half the pineapple slices over the almonds on the bottom of the pan.

Beat the egg yolks. Cream the remaining 8 tablespoons of butter with the remaining ¼ cup of brown sugar, the white sugar, and the beaten egg yolks. Combine the flour with the baking powder and salt. Blend into the creamed mixture alternately with the milk. Beat the egg whites until stiff but not dry. Fold into the mixture.

Carefully spoon half the mixture in an even layer over the almonds and pineapple slices. Then layer the reserved brown sugar–butter mixture over the cake mixture. Sprinkle with another 1 cup of almonds and layer the other half of the pineapple slices over the almonds. Add the remaining cake mixture carefully in an even layer over the pineapple slices.

Bake on the middle rack of a preheated 350° oven for 40 to 45 minutes, or until a knife inserted in the center comes out clean. Cool for a few minutes, then invert onto a waxed-paper-lined rack. Cool 15 minutes more. Serve with whipped cream flavored with confectioners' sugar and the remaining 1 teaspoon of amaretto. Sprinkle with the remaining 3 tablespoons of almonds. Serve either warm or cold.

Serves 10 to 12

✻ *Tennessee Trifle*

Franklin County is my home. It encompasses Winchester, Tennessee, and all the lovely, lovely people around it. There is a brand new Dinah Shore Boulevard there that goes from the town square in front of where my father's store used to be straight through to Decherd. On the day we celebrated this wonderful event, amidst the tears and cheers we had a luncheon at the Franklin County Country Club. Ms. Jean Shurdick supervised and cooked the most spectacular meal. In all the excitement, naturally, I still couldn't help noticing the food. This Tennessee Trifle is one of the reasons why. The Coconut Cream Pie (page 278) is another. The Fudge Cake is only sensational.

4½ ounces vanilla instant pudding and pie filling
2½ cups milk
2 cups apricot preserves
¼ cup cherry-flavored liqueur
Fudge Cake (see below)
One 15½-ounce can pitted dark cherries, drained
1 cup heavy cream
1 teaspoon vanilla extract
2 teaspoons confectioners' sugar
½ cup sliced toasted almonds

Prepare the pudding according to the package directions, using the milk. Chill for 30 minutes, or until slightly thickened.

Combine the preserves and liqueur and set aside. Split the Fudge Cake horizontally into 2 layers. Spread 1 layer of cake with some of the preserve mixture and place the other layer on top. Cut the cake into 2-inch squares.

Place a third of the pudding in the bottom of a large glass bowl with straight sides or a glass soufflé dish and then layer with the cake squares, pressing them down slightly. Add a layer of cherries and a layer of mixture. Then another layer of pudding, cake, cherries, and preserves, ending with a layer of pudding. Cover and chill overnight.

Just before serving, whip the cream with the vanilla and sugar and spread the whipped cream on top of the trifle. Sprinkle with toasted almonds.

Serves 6 to 8

FUDGE CAKE

1 cup plus 2 tablespoons flour
3 tablespoons unsweetened
* cocoa*
1 cup sugar
½ teaspoon baking soda
½ teaspoon salt

⅓ cup vegetable oil, plus extra
* for pan*
1 egg
¾ cup water
1 teaspoon vanilla extract

Preheat the oven to 350°.

Stir together the dry ingredients. Add the moist ingredients. Beat on low speed until well blended, then beat on medium speed for 2 minutes.

Pour the batter into a greased and floured 9-inch baking pan and bake for 30 to 35 minutes or until toothpick inserted in center comes out clean. Cool in the pan on a rack.

Serves 6 to 8

❈ *Pecan Coffee Cake*

¾ cup dark brown sugar,
* firmly packed*
6 tablespoons unsalted butter,
* at room temperature, plus*
* extra for pan*

¾ cup pecan pieces
¼ cup orange juice
1 teaspoon vanilla extract
Refrigerator Dough (see below)
Oil for plastic wrap

Grease a 9-inch round cake pan and set it aside. Use the metal blade of a food processor or an electric mixer to cream together the brown sugar and butter. Process or mix for about 20 seconds, stopping once or twice to scrape down the sides of the bowl. Add the pecans, orange juice, and vanilla, and turn the machine on and off 6 to 8 times, or until well mixed. Spread the mixture over the bottom of the prepared pan.

Divide the Refrigerator Dough into 26 to 28 equal pieces and roll each into a smooth ball about 1¼ inches in diameter. Set the balls on the pecan mixture in one layer, leaving a little space between them. Cover with oiled plastic wrap and set to rise in a warm place (75°–80°) for about 1½ hours or until doubled in bulk.

Preheat the oven to 350°. Bake for 25 to 30 minutes, or until lightly browned. Cool in the pan for 5 minutes and then invert onto a plate. Scrape any remaining pecan mixture from the pan over the top and cool a few minutes more before serving.

REFRIGERATOR DOUGH

1 envelope active dry yeast
1½ tablespoons sugar
¼ cup warm water (110°–115°)
3¼ cups unbleached flour or 3 cups plus 2 tablespoons bread flour
4 tablespoons unsalted butter, at room temperature, plus extra for bowl

2 tablespoons solid vegetable shortening, at room temperature
1 teaspoon salt
2 large eggs
⅓ cup cold milk
Oil for plastic wrap

Stir the yeast and sugar into the warm water and let stand for 5 to 10 minutes at room temperature.

Use the metal blade of a food processor or an electric mixer with a dough hook to process or mix the flour, butter, shortening, and salt for 20 seconds. With the machine running, add the eggs and yeast mixture through the feed tube or to the mixing bowl and then pour in the milk in a steady stream as fast as the flour mixture will absorb it. Process or mix for 30 seconds.

Scrape the dough into a well-greased 3-quart mixing bowl. Cover *tightly* with oiled plastic wrap and refrigerate until the dough has doubled in bulk, about 4 to 6 hours. Punch down the dough, and, if you are not using it immediately, cover it tightly and refrigerate for up to 4 days. Punch the dough down just before use.

Serves 8

❧ *Pie or Tart Crust*

1¾ cups flour
10 tablespoons cold unsalted butter or 5 tablespoons butter and 5 tablespoons lard or 5 tablespoons cold, unflavored, unsalted, rendered chicken fat

1 teaspoon salt
2 to 3 tablespoons ice-cold water

Put all the ingredients except the water in a food processor fitted with the metal blade. Process until the mixture has the texture of coarse cornmeal. With the motor running, add the water a tablespoon at a time, very gradually. Do not overprocess. Remove from the bowl, wrap loosely in waxed paper, flatten slightly, and chill in the refrigerator for 30 minutes or up to 2 hours.

FOR TARTS

Preheat the oven to 375°.

Place the unwrapped dough on a floured board and whack it with a rolling pin. Roll the dough out about ⅛ inch thick. Cut in circles large enough to fit into your tart pans or muffin cups. Bake for 10 to 15 minutes. Cool before filling.

FOR PIECRUST

Preheat the oven to 375°.

Place the unwrapped dough on a floured board and whack it with a rolling pin to flatten. Roll out the dough to about ¼ to ⅛ inch thick and a good 2 to 3 inches larger than your pie plate.

Flour the rolling pin. Loosen the dough on the board with a spatula and lift the end nearest you onto the rolling pin. Roll the dough over the pin gently, place it over the center of the pie plate, and unroll. Crimp the edges attractively with your fingers. Lift the pie plate and, with a sharp knife, trim all the excess dough.

For a baked pie shell (to be used only when specifically called for in a recipe), prick the dough all over with the tines of a fork. Cover the dough with waxed paper and put beans or pie weights on top of the waxed paper to keep the shell from puffing up or collapsing. Bake for 10 minutes, then remove the paper and the weights carefully (stop here if the recipe calls for a partially baked pie shell). For a completely baked shell, continue to bake until the shell is golden, about 10 minutes longer.

Makes 1 crust

❧ *Maple Sugar–Nut Pie*

2 tablespoons butter, softened
½ cup dark brown sugar, packed
3 eggs, lightly beaten
1 cup pure maple syrup
½ cup light cream
2 teaspoons vanilla extract
2 tablespoons flour
Pinch of salt

1 cup chopped nuts (a combination of pecans, walnuts, and almonds)
One 9-inch unbaked Pie Crust (page 272)
1 cup heavy cream
2 teaspoons confectioners' sugar

Preheat the oven to 350°.

Cream together the butter and brown sugar, then beat in the eggs, maple syrup, light cream, 1 teaspoon vanilla, flour, and salt until well blended. Fold in the chopped nuts. Scrape the filling into the pie shell.

Bake for 45 to 55 minutes, or until a skewer inserted into the center of the pie comes out clean. Cool the pie on a rack. Whip the cream; add 1 teaspoon of vanilla and the confectioners' sugar and blend well. Serve at room temperature with plenty of whipped cream.

Makes one 9-inch pie

✽ *Mocha Butter Crunch Pie*

PIECRUST

1 cup flour
¼ teaspoon salt
⅓ cup brown sugar
⅓ cup butter
3 tablespoons chopped
  semisweet chocolate

¾ cup chopped walnuts
4 to 5 tablespoons water
2 teaspoons vanilla extract

Preheat the oven to 350°.

In a bowl, mix together the flour, salt, and brown sugar. With a pastry blender cut in the butter. With a fork, stir in the chocolate, walnuts, 2 to 3 tablespoons of the water, and 1 teaspoon of the vanilla. After mixing, add 2 more tablespoons of water and 1 more teaspoon of vanilla. The mixture will be crumbly.

With floured fingers, press the dough into a shallow 9-inch pie plate. It is important to push the dough up and onto the rim of the plate so that it will not shrink down the sides while baking. Bake for 15 to 20 minutes. Cool.

FILLING

16 tablespoons unsalted butter
1 cup brown sugar
4 teaspoons instant coffee
2 teaspoons vanilla extract

3 ounces unsweetened
  chocolate, melted and cooled
4 eggs, separated

Cream the butter until very fluffy and completely smooth. Add the brown sugar, instant coffee, and vanilla; cream very well. When completely smooth, add the cooled chocolate. Whisk the egg yolks in the top of a double boiler until pale and slightly cooked, about 2 minutes. Cool, then add the unbeaten whites to the yolks. Add ¼ of the eggs at a time to the chocolate, beating 3 to 5 minutes after each addition. Pour the filling into the baked pie shell and chill for several hours.

TOPPING

1 cup very cold heavy cream	*¼ cup confectioners' sugar*
1 tablespoon plus ½ teaspoon instant coffee	*Grated chocolate*

Beat the cream with the coffee and sugar until stiff enough to hold its shape. Spoon the whipped cream into a pastry bag fitted with a large star tip. Pipe large whipped cream rosettes over the entire surface of the pie. Garnish with grated chocolate.

Serves 8 to 10

❋ Butterscotch Chocolate Pie

3 ounces unsweetened chocolate	*One 9-inch unbaked pie shell (page 272)*
2 cups light brown sugar	*1 cup heavy cream*
8 tablespoons butter, softened	*2 teaspoons confectioners' sugar*
3 eggs	
2 teaspoons vanilla extract	*Grated semisweet chocolate*
½ cup half and half	

Preheat the oven to 350°.

In a heavy saucepan or a double boiler, melt the chocolate, stirring from time to time. In the bowl of a food processor, process the brown sugar and butter until light and fluffy. With the processor running, add one egg at a time through the feed tube and blend until well mixed. Add the melted chocolate and blend well. Add 1 teaspoon of the vanilla and the half and half and blend until just mixed.

Pour the mixture into the pie shell. Bake for 45 minutes, or until the filling has set and a knife blade inserted in the center comes out clean. When the pie has cooled, whip the cream; add 1 teaspoon of vanilla and the confectioners' sugar and mix well. Top the cooled pie with whipped cream, and, to be really disgusting, grate semisweet chocolate over the top.

Makes one 9-inch pie

❧ Buttermilk Pie

This is light and airy and thoroughly delicious. I'd forgotten how wonderful it was until I tasted it again during my homecoming to Winchester. It brought back all kinds of warm memories.

6 tablespoons unsalted butter,
  softened
1½ cups sugar
2 eggs, separated
3 tablespoons flour
1½ cups buttermilk
2 teaspoons fresh lemon juice,
  strained

1 teaspoon grated lemon rind
One 9-inch pastry shell,
  partially baked and cooled
  (page 272)
¼ teaspoon grated nutmeg

Preheat the oven to 350°.

In a deep bowl, cream the butter and sugar together until the mixture is light and fluffy. Beat in the egg yolks, one at a time and, when thoroughly incorporated, beat in the flour. Still beating, pour in the buttermilk in a thin stream, then stir in the lemon juice and rind.

In a large mixing bowl, beat the egg whites with a wire whisk or an electric beater until they are firm enough to stand in stiff peaks. With a rubber spatula, stir a few tablespoons of the egg whites into the batter, then scoop the remaining batter over the whites and fold together gently but thoroughly. Pour the filling into the pie shell and sprinkle the top evenly with the nutmeg. Bake in the center of the oven for 40 minutes, or until the filling is firm. Cool to room temperature before serving.

Makes one 9-inch pie

❧ Virginia Martin's Old-fashioned Lemon Meringue Pie

Nobody gets off scot-free around here. Howard Martin innocently came out to the house to wallpaper a bedroom in the middle of tasting and testing. He happened to mention that his mother had been a fabulous cook and that her recipes had been left intact to his sister and to his wife, Virginia. It was a mistake on his part. My eyes lit up; my ears perked up, and there was a definite lightness of foot after that. The next morning he came in with his wife's Old-fashioned Lemon Meringue Pie. It was gorgeous! It was as delicious as it looked. It made a perfect breakfast dish. I know because I think between us we finished it off. We all shared because at the time I was testing the Spanish Patatas (page 231). He loved it. There is nothing like a midmorning snack—lemon meringue pie and egg fried potatoes!

1½ cups sugar
3 tablespoons cornstarch
3 tablespoons flour
Dash of salt (optional)
3 large egg yolks
⅓ cup lemon juice

½ teaspoon grated lemon rind
1½ cups hot water
1 to 2 tablespoons butter or
 margarine
One 9-inch fully baked pie
 shell (page 272)

Off the heat, mix the sugar, cornstarch, flour, and salt in a saucepan until well blended. Set aside.

Mix the egg yolks, lemon juice, and lemon rind together. Set aside.

Add the hot water to the dry ingredients and cook over medium heat, stirring constantly so the bottom won't burn, until the mixture starts to bubble and thicken. It will look thick and cloudy. Add the egg mixture gradually, while stirring, and bring back to a bubble, stirring constantly. Remove from the heat and add the butter. Stir until the butter is melted. Cool for about 10 minutes and then pour into the baked pie shell.

MERINGUE

3 egg whites, at room
 temperature
¼ teaspoon cream of tartar
6 tablespoons confectioners'
 sugar

1 teaspoon lemon juice
 (optional) or 1 teaspoon
 vanilla extract
Grated lemon rind (optional)

Beat the egg whites with an electric mixer until foamy. Add the cream of tartar. Continue beating until the whites form soft peaks. Add the sugar and lemon juice or vanilla and continue beating until stiff peaks form.

Spread the meringue on top of the pie and sprinkle with the grated lemon rind.

Bake in a preheated 350° oven for about 12 to 15 minutes, or until golden brown. Cool, then refrigerate until ready to serve.

Makes one 9-inch pie

❋ *Sweet Potato–Praline Pie*

Doris McNew is a friend from Mt. Juliet, Tennessee, which is close to Nashville. That's all the proof I need that Doris knows and cooks great food. This is her Sweet Potato–Praline Pie. Try it—you'll see what I mean. If you don't have the pumpkin pie spice called for, make your own with 1 teaspoon cinnamon, ½ teaspoon freshly grated nutmeg, ¼ teaspoon ground allspice, ¼ teaspoon ground cloves, ½ teaspoon ground ginger, and ½ teaspoon salt. This will make more than you'll need for this recipe, but keep it on hand for spice cakes and other pies.

8 tablespoons butter or
    margarine
1 cup chopped pecans
1 cup mashed, cooked sweet
    potatoes
3 eggs, beaten
½ cup brown sugar, firmly
    packed
1 cup dark corn syrup

1 teaspoon pumpkin pie spice
2½ teaspoons vanilla extract
2 tablespoons bourbon
    (optional)
1 unbaked 9-inch pie shell
    (page 272)
1 cup heavy cream
2 teaspoons confectioners'
    sugar

Preheat the oven to 425°.

Melt the butter in a large heavy saucepan; add the pecans and cook over low heat, stirring constantly, until the butter is golden brown and the pecans are toasted. Remove from the heat. Stir in the mashed sweet potatoes, eggs, brown sugar, dark corn syrup, pumpkin pie spice, 1½ teaspoons of vanilla, and the bourbon. Mix well.

Pour the mixture into the pastry shell and bake for 10 minutes. Reduce the oven temperature to 325° and bake for an additional 45 minutes, or until set. Cool on a wire rack.

Whip the cream; add the confectioners' sugar and 1 teaspoon of vanilla; mix well. Top the cooled pie with whipped cream before serving.

Makes one 9-inch pie

❋ *Coconut Cream Pie*

1½ cups sugar
4 tablespoons cornstarch
¼ teaspoon salt
2½ cups milk
4 egg yolks, lightly beaten

2½ cups flaked coconut
1 teaspoon vanilla extract
1 fully baked 10-inch pie shell
    (page 272)

MERINGUE

4 egg whites
½ teaspoon cream of tartar
½ cup sugar

1 teaspoon vanilla extract
2 tablespoons flaked coconut

Preheat the oven to 425°.

Off the heat, combine the sugar, cornstarch, and salt in a saucepan. Gradually add the milk and heat, stirring, to just below the boiling point. Beat a small amount of the filling into the egg yolks and add this back into the filling. Cook, stirring constantly, until thick and smooth. Remove from the heat and cool. Stir in the coconut and vanilla. Pour the filling into the baked pie shell.

Beat the egg whites until light and frothy. Add the cream of tartar and continue beating until the whites are stiff enough to hold a peak. Gradually beat in the sugar and continue beating until the meringue is stiff. Add the vanilla.

Pile the meringue on the cooled pie filling, spreading it until it touches the edges of the pastry to prevent the meringue from shrinking. Bake in the oven until the top is brown, about 5 to 6 minutes. Cool on a wire rack. Sprinkle with the coconut.

Makes one 10-inch pie

✽ Blackberry Pie

One unbaked 9-inch piecrust
* (page 272)*
4 cups blackberries
1½ to 2 cups sugar
¼ cup flour
1½ tablespoons lemon juice

2 teaspoons quick-cooking
* tapioca (optional—use only*
* if the fruit is very juicy)*
1 to 2 tablespoons butter
Glaze (optional), see below

Make the pastry as directed and fit half into a 9-inch pie pan. Do not trim the edge. Roll out the top crust, cut slits in the center, and set it aside, covered with a dish towel, while you make your filling.

Sprinkle the blackberries with sugar, flour, lemon juice, and tapioca if necessary to thicken a bit, and stir gently until well blended. Let stand for 15 minutes.

Preheat the oven to 450°. Pour the blackberry mixture into the pie shell and dot with the butter. Brush the pastry rim with cold water, and fit the top crust over the fruit. Trim, seal, and crimp the edges. Apply the optional glaze, if desired. Bake for 10 minutes, reduce the heat to

350°, and bake for about 45 minutes more, or until the pie is golden brown.

GLAZE (Optional)

1 tablespoon milk or cream
1 tablespoon sugar

Before placing the pie in the oven, brush the top crust with milk and sprinkle it with sugar.

Makes one 9-inch pie

✽ *Chess Pie or Tarts*

From time to time—from recipe to recipe—I've heard this referred to as Jefferson Davis Chess Pie. I don't know if he created it or if it was created for him, but legend has it that he was a dedicated chess player and never wanted to interrupt his concentration to go to the kitchen for a little something or other. The kitchen staff kept a generous supply of chess tarts at his elbow during a hot chess match. The tarts were small, didn't crumble all over the chess board, and provided enough energy to keep him alert and, of course, perceptive. Fact or fiction, it's a nice picture, isn't it? Boy, do I love these over a hot Chinese checker game. I tasted five different chess pies after returning home from Nashville. Carolyn Dodson's from Herbert's Barbecue in Franklin, Tennessee, was the best and most uncluttered, it seemed to me.

1 tablespoon apple cider vinegar
1 tablespoon white or light Karo syrup
1 teaspoon vanilla extract
8 tablespoons butter or margarine, melted
1 cup sugar
4 eggs, lightly beaten
8 unbaked tart shells or one 9-inch unbaked piecrust (page 272)

Preheat the oven to 350°.

Add the vinegar, syrup, and vanilla to the melted butter. Set aside. Place the sugar in a large mixing bowl. Add the butter-vinegar mixture and stir until the sugar is blended. Add the beaten eggs and mix well. Pour the mixture into the pastry-lined 9-inch pie plate or 8 pastry-lined tart pans.

Bake the pie for 35 to 40 minutes, or until a knife inserted in the center comes out clean. If making individual tarts, bake them for 25 to 30 minutes.

Place the pie or tarts on a wire rack to cool. Don't forget the pie keeps cooking a minute or two after coming out of the oven, so don't overcook it.

Makes one 9-inch pie or 8 tarts

✿ *Apple Tarts*

Shirley Schroer tested this one one evening—tried and tested is a better way of putting it. She tried three versions. We had to sample all three. (It's a tough chore, but somebody had to do it.)

3 tablespoons butter or
  margarine, melted
1 sheet frozen puff pastry (half
  a 17¼-ounce package),
  thawed
1 pound small Granny Smith
  apples, peeled, quartered,
  and cored

3 tablespoons confectioners'
  sugar
2 tablespoons brown sugar
3 tablespoons coarsely chopped
  walnuts

Place the oven rack in the center of the oven. Preheat the oven to 425°. Lightly grease a 17-x-14-inch cookie sheet with a small amount of the melted butter.

On a lightly floured surface, roll out the pastry to a 16-x-11-inch rectangle. With a small sharp knife, carefully cut out six 5-inch circles of pastry. (I used a 5-inch floured saucer as a guide.) Arrange the circles about 1 inch apart on the prepared cookie sheet. Prick at 1-inch intervals with a fork.

With a thin sharp knife, slice the apples wafer-thin (the slices should be almost transparent). Arrange the apple slices overlapping in pinwheel fashion on the pastry circles, leaving a ¼-inch border of pastry. Gently brush with the remaining butter. Dust the tops with the confectioners' sugar stirred through a small strainer. Bake for 10 minutes. Reduce the oven temperature to 325°. Remove the tarts from the oven and sprinkle with the brown sugar and walnuts. Bake 10 minutes longer, or until the edges are golden brown. Remove the tarts to a wire rack to cool.

Makes 6 tarts

�֍ *Peach-Nectarine Tart*

3 ripe peaches, peeled and
   sliced
3 ripe nectarines, peeled and
   sliced
One 10-inch unbaked tart shell
   (page 272)
3 tablespoons finely chopped
   blanched almonds

3 tablespoons unsalted butter
4 tablespoons sugar
2 egg whites
1 tablespoon flour
¼ cup Apricot Glaze (see
   below)

Preheat the oven to 400°.

Place a layer of sliced peaches and nectarines on the bottom of the pastry-covered tart pan. Sprinkle with 2 tablespoons of the chopped almonds. Arrange the remaining sliced peaches and nectarines decoratively on top. Cut 2 tablespoons of the butter into small pieces and distribute them over the top. Sprinkle with 2 tablespoons of the sugar. Bake for 45 minutes.

Melt the remaining 1 tablespoon of butter and put it in a small mixing bowl with the remaining tablespoon of almonds, 2 tablespoons of sugar, the egg whites, and flour. Beat the mixture with a fork for a few seconds, until it is slightly frothy. When the tart has baked for 45 minutes, pour the mixture over the top and bake for 15 to 18 minutes more, until the top is nicely browned. Remove from the oven and cool on a wire rack.

When the tart has cooled slightly, spoon and brush the Apricot Glaze over the top. Cool to room temperature on the rack.

Serves 6 to 8

APRICOT GLAZE

One 12-ounce jar apricot
   preserves

1 or 2 teaspoons kirsch or
   Cognac (optional)

Strain the preserves through a sieve or the finest disc of a food mill. Stir in the kirsch or Cognac, if used. To make spreading easier, you may heat the mixture to lukewarm over low heat before brushing it on the tart.

Makes about ¾ cup

✽ Pear Tart

Pears start coming in in abundance during the fall season. This is a beautiful way to use them. If you fall in love with the result and can't live without your Pear Tart until the next September, use canned ones in the spring.

One unbaked 9-inch tart crust (page 272)

Line a 9-inch tart mold (with removable bottom) with this pastry dough. Line the pastry with waxed paper and fill with dried beans. Cook at 350° to 375° for 20 minutes, or until a golden color. Remove from oven and lift out the beans and paper.

FILLING

½ cup sugar
3 cups water

Peel of ½ lemon
8 fresh pears

Combine the sugar, water, and lemon peel, and cook over low heat until the sugar dissolves completely. Peel the pears and poach them in the sugar syrup until just softened. Drain, cool, and slice the pears. Arrange them over the pastry.

A CREAMY CUSTARD

½ cup sugar
5 to 6 egg yolks
¼ cup flour

1½ cups scalded milk
¼ teaspoon vanilla extract
Finely ground almonds for topping

Mix the sugar and 3 to 4 eggs yolks until pale yellow. Beat in the flour and scalded milk flavored with the vanilla, and cook, stirring constantly, over low heat until it reaches the boiling point. Remove from the heat and continue to stir until cooled. Beat in 2 more egg yolks and pour the mixture evenly over the pears to cover. Top with the almonds and bake at 325° for 45 minutes. Unmold to serve, either warm or cold.

Makes one 9-inch tart

❀ *Chocolate-Strawberry Tarts*

*6 squares (6 ounces) semisweet
    chocolate
8 tablespoons butter
⅔ cup confectioners' sugar
2 eggs*

*Generous ½ cup chopped pecans
1 teaspoon vanilla extract
6 unbaked tart shells (page 272)
    6 to 8 large strawberries, thinly
    sliced crosswise*

Melt the chocolate in a double boiler, stirring, over boiling water. Set aside to cool.

Whip the butter in a food processor or use an electric beater, add the sugar and eggs, one at a time, and process until well blended. Scrape down the sides of the bowl as needed. When the chocolate has cooled, add it to the butter mixture. Blend in a double boiler over low heat, then add the chopped pecans. When the mixture has cooled, add the vanilla and mix well. Spoon into the tart shells and bake for 15 minutes in a preheated 350° oven, or until the tart shells are just brown.

Layer the sliced strawberries in an attractive pattern over the chocolate filling.

Makes 6 tarts

❀ *Raspberry Cobbler*

A true old-fashioned down-home cobbler. If you want it au courant, *use a piecrust (page 272) with vents cut in the top, but this one is great and nostalgic.*

*1 pint fresh raspberries or 2
    cups frozen, thoroughly
    defrosted and drained
1 cup flour
2 teaspooons baking powder
1 cup sugar
2 eggs*

*¾ cup milk
1 teaspoon vanilla extract
1 teaspoon grated lemon rind
1½ cups heavy cream, chilled
2 tablespoons confectioners'
    sugar*

Preheat the oven to 350°.

Wash the raspberries, discarding any stems or blemished fruit. Spread the fresh or defrosted berries on paper towels and pat them dry with additional paper towels. Pour the berries into a 2-quart oven-proof mold or soufflé dish and set aside.

Sift the flour and baking powder into a large mixing bowl and drop in the sugar, eggs, milk, vanilla, and lemon rind. Beat well with a wooden spoon until the ingredients are thoroughly combined. Pour the batter over the berries and bake in the center of the oven for 1 hour, or until the top is crusty brown.

Beat the cream until it foams. Then beat in the confectioners' sugar and continue to beat until the cream forms soft peaks when the beater is lifted out of the bowl. Serve the cobbler hot, accompanied by a bowl of the whipped cream.

Serves 6 to 8

✿ *Amber Glass Custard*

This sounds lethal. It isn't. It's only a crunchy and marvelous dessert.

½ teaspoon butter
⅔ cup plus 2 tablespoons
   sugar
1 cup water
2 eggs plus 2 egg yolks
2 cups milk

1 cup heavy cream
1 teaspoon vanilla extract
2 pints fresh strawberries,
   raspberries, blueberries, or
   mangoes, or whatever fresh
   fruit you like

With the ½ teaspoon butter, lightly grease an 8-inch square baking dish or glass casserole and a 1-quart soufflé dish and set both dishes aside.

Mix ⅔ cup of the sugar with the water and heat in a heavy saucepan over medium heat. After about 20 to 25 minutes of cooking, the sugar water will start to darken a little. Stir to even the color and continue cooking until the caramel turns a dark amber, about 15 minutes more. (Watch carefully as it can burn.)

Pour half the caramel mixture into the soufflé dish and rotate the dish to coat the bottom. Pour the remainder into the 8-inch baking dish and spread the mixture to coat the bottom of the dish evenly. Set aside to cool.

Preheat the oven to 350°. Whisk the eggs and yolks in a large mixing bowl until creamy and set aside. In a double boiler, heat the milk and ½ cup of the heavy cream with the remaining 2 tablespoons of sugar. When the custard begins to simmer, remove from the heat and slowly whisk in the egg mixture. (I usually take a couple of tablespoons of the custard and whisk them into the egg mixture; then whisk the egg yolks into the custard.) Add the vanilla and pour into the soufflé dish.

Set the soufflé dish in a larger oven-proof pan and set the soufflé on the middle shelf in the oven. Pour boiling water into the larger oven-proof pan until it reaches halfway up the sides. Bake for 45 minutes, or until a knife inserted in the center comes out clean. Cool and refrigerate.

Carefully shatter the cooled caramel in the baking dish into random-size pieces. Place the caramel pieces in the refrigerator until ready to serve.

When ready to serve, whip the remaining ½ cup of cream and set it aside. Sprinkle the shattered caramel pieces over the custard in the soufflé dish. Cover with a portion of the fruit and serve with the remaining fruit and the whipped cream on the side.

Serves 6

❊ *Chocolate Bread Pudding*

Many trials and many errors ago we had the idea that a chocolate bread pudding could be even better than a bread bread pudding. I tested this on the Sinatras when they first became enchanted with beach living. I like to think this contributed to their seduction. It would to mine.

12 slices French bread (not sourdough), cut into ½-inch cubes

2 cups half and half or milk

8 ounces semisweet chocolate

8 tablespoons butter or margarine, plus extra for baking dish

⅓ cup sugar

3 eggs, lightly beaten

2 teaspoons vanilla extract

1 tablespoon Kahlúa

1 cup coarsely chopped pecans

Kahlúa Sauce (see below)

Preheat the oven to 325°.

Place the bread cubes in a well-buttered 2-quart baking or soufflé dish. Combine the half and half or milk, chocolate, butter, and sugar in a saucepan. Cook, stirring, over low heat until the chocolate and butter are melted. Remove from the heat, then beat with a wire whisk until the mixture is smooth. Beat in the eggs, vanilla, Kahlúa and pecans. Pour the chocolate mixture over the bread cubes.

Place the baking dish in a larger pan and pour 1 inch of boiling water into the outer pan. Bake for 40 to 45 minutes, or until a knife inserted in the center comes out almost clean. Unmold onto a flat platter. Serve warm or cool, with Kahlúa Sauce.

KAHLÚA SAUCE

1½ cups sugar
12 tablespoons butter or
 margarine
½ cup Kahlúa

⅓ cup water
1 teaspoon cornstarch

Combine all the ingredients in a saucepan. Simmer, stirring constantly, until slightly thickened.

Pour half the sauce over the unmolded pudding and serve the remainder warm in a sauceboat.

Serves 8

✿ Pears with Crème de Menthe

2 large pears, cored and sliced
 into equal wedges (I use an
 apple corer that cores and
 slices)
Juice of 1 lemon
2 tablespoons butter or
 margarine

2 tablespoons olive oil
1½ tablespoons brown sugar
4 whole sprigs fresh mint
2 tablespoons crème de menthe
 liqueur

Sprinkle the pears with a little lemon juice. In a hot skillet, melt the butter or margarine and olive oil. Add the pears in a single layer, if possible, and sauté, flipping the pan to cover all the pieces with butter and olive oil. Cover the pan for a minute or two. Mix the remaining lemon juice with the brown sugar and sprinkle over the pears. Flip the pan or turn the pears to be sure they are equally coated. Cook for 3 or 4 minutes (depending on the ripeness of the pears) covered part of the time. Turn the pears often.

Add the mint and crème de menthe. Flip the pan or turn the pears with a spatula to make sure they are completely coated with sauce. Taste the sauce, you may need a little more brown sugar and lemon.

Serve warm on warm plates. It can be served as a side dish with the main course, but it's even better as a light dessert.

Serves 2 as a dessert, 4 as a side dish

✻ *Cherry Dessert*

One 6-ounce can grapefruit
   juice or 6 ounces juice from
   canned cherries
2 tablespoons sugar, or more
   to taste
3 tablespoons Boggs cranberry
   liqueur
10 to 12 fresh cherries (don't
   remove the stems) or canned
   white and red cherries

Scant 1 teaspoon cornstarch
Two 2-inch slices pound cake
Shredded coconut (optional)
Slivered toasted almonds
   (optional)

Heat the grapefruit juice and sugar or the juice from the cherries and the sugar. Add the cranberry liqueur and boil until the alcohol is boiled away, about 1 minute. Add the cherries and cook over medium heat until the cherries begin to soften; don't let them cook until mushy. Two minutes should do it. If using canned cherries, drop them in just long enough to heat through. Place the cornstarch in a small cup and add 2 tablespoons of sauce. Mix well to form a paste. Pour this paste into the sauce, and rinse the cup with extra liquid to get it all. Cook for 1 or 2 minutes, until the sauce is thickened and glossy.

Pour the sauce over the cake slices and sprinkle with the coconut and almonds, if using them. This dessert can be served elegantly at the table. Even try to light it if you dare—I didn't because I'd already boiled away the alcohol.

Serves 2

✻ *Baked Figs in Strawberry Sauce*

9 fresh ripe figs
6 whole cloves
10 to 12 fresh strawberries,
   halved
2 tablespoons sugar
1 tablespoon butter

1 whole cinnamon stick
2 tablespoons lime or lemon
   juice, or to taste (the sauce
   should be slightly tart)
¼ cup Grand Marnier liqueur
¼ cup Cognac

Place the figs, stems up, in 3 individual soufflé dishes, 3 figs per dish. Place a clove or two in the bottom of each dish.

Cook the strawberries, sugar, butter, cinnamon, lime or lemon juice, and the remaining cloves in a small saucepan and cook until the strawberries are soft and cooked through, about 12 minutes. Add the Grand Marnier and Cognac (reserving 2 tablespoons of each) and mix well.

Pour the sauce over the figs. Deglaze the pan with the reserved liqueurs, increase the heat, and flame the liqueurs (be careful, turn your face away). Spoon equally over the figs. Bake in a preheated 350° oven for 20 or 25 minutes. Serve with crème fraiche, whipped cream, or sour cream.

Serves 3

✾*Lemon Snow with Raspberry Sauce*

One evening when I was tired of cooking I asked dear friends to bring over their favorite diet dish. Art Buchwald was the guest of honor that night and agreed dieting was a fine idea as long as there was plenty of food. There was. Bee Korshak, a dear friend, was given the chore of bringing a delicious dessert that wasn't simply cut-up fruit. She came up with this. Were we delighted!

2 envelopes unflavored gelatin
1 cup cold water
6 eggs, separated
1 cup sugar
Juice of 2 lemons
Grated rind of 1 lemon

Have all ingredients ready as this sets quickly.

Soften the gelatin in the cold water and dissolve over hot water. Set aside to cool to lukewarm. Beat the egg yolks with the sugar until light and almost white. Add the lemon juice, lemon rind, and cooled gelatin. Beat the egg whites until stiff and fold into the gelatin mixture. Do not pour into the mold until the mixture holds its shape when stirred with a spoon. Pour into a 1½ quart oiled mold and chill until set.

Serves 8

RASPBERRY SAUCE

One 10-ounce package frozen raspberries, thawed, reserving juice
1 tablespoon Chambord (raspberry liqueur)
2 teaspoons fresh lemon juice
2 teaspoons sugar (more if needed)

Puree the raspberries in a blender along with the juice. Add the liqueur, lemon juice, and sugar to taste. Serve with the Lemon Snow.

❧ *French Vanilla Ice Cream with Fresh Fruit*

2 cups milk
1 cup sugar
5 large egg yolks
2 cups half and half
2¼ cups fresh fruit (2 nectarines, 2 plums, 2 bananas), peeled, chopped, and pureed

Juice of ½ lemon, to squeeze over fruit before pureeing
1 teaspoon vanilla extract

Beat the milk and sugar together with a wire whisk. Add the egg yolks. Place the mixture in a double boiler over hot, not boiling, water and stir (in one direction) constantly until thickened. The custard should coat the back of a spoon. Don't overcook it. Remove from the heat and cool a little. Add the half and half, then the fruit, and vanilla. Chill for a couple of hours before putting in an ice cream maker. Freeze according to the directions for your ice cream maker.

Makes about 1½ quarts ice cream

❧ *Pecan Caramel Chocolate Chip Ice Cream*

This is properly sinful as a good ice cream should be. Accept it and enjoy.

½ cup white sugar
½ cup water plus ⅛ cup very hot water
5 eggs
2 cups milk
½ cup brown sugar

2 cups half and half
1 cup lightly toasted pecan pieces
¾ cup semisweet chocolate chips
1 teaspoon vanilla extract

In a heavy saucepan, cook the white sugar and ½ cup water over low heat, stirring constantly. When the sugar is melted and straw colored, *very slowly* add the ⅛ cup hot water to make the syrup heavier. Remove from the heat.

Beat the eggs with a wire whisk, then add the milk and brown sugar. Cook in a double boiler, stirring, until the mixture thickens and coats the back of a spoon. Remove from the heat and stir in the half and half and caramelized sugar, then the pecans. When cooled a little, add the chocolate chips and vanilla.

Chill the mixture thoroughly in the refrigerator, then pour into the freezer can of your ice cream maker and follow the instructions that come with your machine.

Makes about 1 quart

❊ *I've Never Been to Cuba—But*

4 bananas
8 teaspoons half and half
8 teaspoons dark rum

Coffee ice cream or frozen
   yogurt (vanilla or coffee)

Cut the bananas into 2-inch pieces. Carefully place them in a large flat glass dish and marinate them in the half and half and rum for an hour or so.

Place a scoop of ice cream or frozen yogurt in the bottom of a large, stemmed red wineglass or a pretty fluted glass bowl if you have it. Cover generously with the banana mixture.

If you're doing this ahead, place in the freezer until you're ready to serve it. The glass, the ice cream—almost everything is frosty but the rum.

Makes 4 servings

❊ *Oat Bran–Chocolate Chunk Nut Cookies*

4 tablespoons margarine,
  softened
2 tablespoons butter, softened,
  plus extra for cookie sheet
6 tablespoons brown sugar,
  packed
6 tablespoons white sugar
½ cup flour
½ cup rolled oats
2 tablespoons all-bran

¼ teaspoon salt
½ teaspoon baking powder
1 egg
1 teaspoon vanilla extract
⅔ cup coarsely chopped
  walnuts or pecans
4 ounces sweet or semisweet
  chocolate, cut into good-size
  chunks

Preheat the oven to 375°.

Place the margarine, butter, brown sugar, and white sugar in the bowl of a processor or use an electric beater and process or mix until creamy.

Mix together the flour, oats, All-Bran, salt, and baking powder. Add this to the butter-sugar mixture and process or mix until well blended, scraping down the sides of the bowl as needed. Add the egg and vanilla and process until blended. Fold in the nuts and chocolate.

Drop by teaspoonful (make sure there are nuts and chocolate in each cookie) onto a greased cookie sheet at least 2 inches apart. Bake for 8 to 10 minutes.

Cool on a rack.

Makes about 2 dozen cookies

✤ Chocolate-Oatmeal Crisps

6 squares (6 ounces) semisweet chocolate
8 tablespoons butter or margarine
½ cup sugar
1 teaspoon vanilla extract
1 egg

1 cup less 1 tablespoon sifted flour
1 teaspoon baking powder
½ teaspoon salt
½ cup quick-cooking oats

Melt the chocolate in a double boiler over hot, not boiling, water, and cool. Cream the butter or margarine and sugar in a food processor or use an electric mixer. Add the vanilla, egg, and melted chocolate. Mix well. Sift together the flour, baking powder, and salt. Add this to the butter mixture along with the oats. Mix well.

Form the dough into a long roll about 1½ inches in diameter. Wrap in waxed paper and chill for 1 hour. Slice the dough into cookies ⅛ inch thick and bake on an ungreased cookie sheet in a preheated 375° oven for about 10 minutes. Watch carefully: They burn easily. Remove from the oven, cool slightly on the sheet to set their shape, then place on a wire rack to crisp.

Makes about 2 dozen cookies

�֍ *Chocolate Drop Cookies*

Butter for cookie sheets
2 squares (2 ounces)
   unsweetened chocolate
1²/₃ cups flour
½ teaspoon salt
1 teaspoon baking soda
1 cup sour cream

1 cup brown sugar
1 egg, beaten
1 teaspoon vanilla extract
1 cup seedless raisins
½ cup chopped pecans or black
   walnuts
Mocha Frosting (see below)

Preheat the oven to 350°. Butter 2 cookie sheets.

Melt the chocolate in a double boiler over boiling water, and set aside to cool. Combine the flour, salt, and baking soda in a 2-cup measuring cup or a small bowl and stir with a fork.

Beat the sour cream and the brown sugar together until they are light and fluffy. Add the beaten egg, the chocolate, and the vanilla. Stir in the dry ingredients and continue to stir until they have been completely incorporated into the sour cream mixture. Add the raisins and nuts.

Drop the batter by teaspoonsful onto the greased cookie sheets. Bake for 10 minutes. Cool on racks and then frost with the Mocha Frosting.

MOCHA FROSTING

2 tablespoons butter
4 tablespoons strong black
   coffee

2 teaspoons unsweetened cocoa
2¼ cups confectioners' sugar

Combine the butter, coffee, and cocoa in a small saucepan and heat, stirring, until the butter is completely melted. Remove from the heat and add the sugar by half cups, beating after each addition.

Makes about 4 dozen cookies

❋ *Thumbprint Cookies*

Wanda Myron is very well known around here, not only because she is Shirley Secretary's (Schroer's) sister, but because when we need a new cookie recipe fix Wanda comes to the rescue. Here's a sample.

4 tablespoons each butter and margarine, softened and mixed together
¼ cup brown sugar
1 egg, separated
½ teaspoon vanilla extract

1 cup sifted flour
¼ teaspoon salt
¾ cup finely chopped pecans
Semisweet chocolate bits
A clear jelly

Preheat the oven to 375°.

Place the butter and margarine in a mixing bowl. Mix in the brown sugar, egg yolk, and vanilla. Sift the flour and salt together and stir into the brown sugar mixture.

Roll the dough into 1-inch balls. Dip the balls into slightly beaten egg white and roll in the nuts. Place the balls about 1 inch apart on an ungreased baking sheet. Bake for 5 minutes.

Remove from the oven and quickly press a thumb on top of each cookie. Place the semisweet chocolate bits in the thumbprints and return the cookies to the oven to bake for 8 minutes longer. Cool.

If you do not want to use chocolate bits, when you remove the cookies from the oven the second time, place a bit of sparkling jelly in each thumbprint.

Makes about 30 cookies

❋ *Date Nut Sugar Cookies*

1 cup flour less 2 tablespoons
⅔ cup coarsely chopped pecans
8 tablespoons butter or margarine, at room temperature, cut into pieces, plus extra for sheet
Pinch of salt

½ cup sugar
½ teaspoon vanilla extract
1 tablespoon Grand Marnier liqueur
½ cup (or less) chopped pitted dates
Confectioners' sugar

Preheat the oven to 300°.

Mix ¼ cup of the flour with the pecans. Place the butter or margarine, salt, sugar, vanilla, and Grand Marnier in the bowl of a food processor and process for 20 seconds or so. Add the pecan mixture, the dates, and the remaining flour, and pulse a few times until well blended.

Form the dough into walnut-size balls and place them 2 inches apart on a lightly greased cookie sheet. Bake in the lower third of the oven for 15 to 20 minutes. Don't let the cookies get brown.

Transfer to a wire rack to cool. Sift confectioners' sugar over the warm cookies.

Makes about 25 cookies

✤ *Teatime Pecan Pie Cookies*

This is another of Wanda's wonders (see page 298 for another). They're tiny, little, irresistible one-bite pecan pies.

One 3-ounce package cream
  cheese, softened
9 tablespoons butter or
  margarine, softened, plus
  extra for muffin tins
1 cup sifted flour

1 egg
¾ cup brown sugar
1 teaspoon vanilla extract
1 teaspoon maple flavoring
¼ teaspoon salt
⅔ cup coarsely broken pecans

Cream the cheese with 8 tablespoons of the butter. Stir in the flour and mix until the dough forms a soft ball. Wrap the dough in wax paper and chill in the refrigerator for about 1 hour.

Shape the dough into two dozen 1-inch balls. Place the dough balls in well-buttered 1¾-inch muffin tins or cups, pressing it into the bottom and sides of the tins.

Beat together the egg, sugar, remaining 1 tablespoon butter, the vanilla, maple flavoring, and salt until just smooth. Divide half the pecans among the pastry-lined tins; add the egg mixture and top with the remaining pecans.

Bake in a preheated 325° oven for 25 minutes, or until the filling is set. Cool and remove from the tins.

Makes 2 dozen cookies

❀ Lemon Butter Cookies

8 tablespoons unsalted butter,
   room temperature, plus extra
   for sheets
½ cup sugar
1 egg yolk
¼ cup fresh lemon juice

1½ teaspoons grated lemon
   peel
Pinch of salt
14 tablespoons sifted flour
Confectioners' sugar

Preheat the oven to 375°. Grease 3 baking sheets.

Using an electric mixer, cream the butter and sugar until light and fluffy. Mix in the egg yolk, lemon juice, lemon peel, and salt. Fold in the flour.

Drop the batter by teaspoonsful onto the prepared baking sheets, spacing them 2 inches apart. Bake until the edges of the cookies begin to brown, about 10 minutes. Cool slightly on the baking sheets.

Transfer to a rack, dust with the confectioners' sugar, and cool completely.

Makes about 3 dozen cookies

❀ Pecan Meringue Kisses

2 egg whites
⅛ teaspoon cream of tartar
⅛ teaspoon salt
1 teaspoon vanilla extract

⅓ cup confectioners' sugar
½ cup brown sugar, firmly
   packed
1 cup coarsely chopped pecans

Preheat the oven to 300°.

In the bowl of an electric mixer beat the egg whites until foamy. Add the cream of tartar and salt and beat for an additional 30 seconds. Add the vanilla and beat for 30 seconds more. Sprinkle in the confectioners' sugar, 1 tablespoon at a time, beating for 30 seconds after each addition. Sprinkle in the brown sugar, 1 tablespoon at a time, beating for 30 seconds after each addition. Beat the meringue for 2 minutes and fold in the chopped pecans.

Drop heaping teaspoons of the meringue on a baking sheet lined with parchment paper and bake the meringues for 30 minutes or less, until just brown. Turn off the oven and let the meringues sit for 1½ hours or more, until crisp.

Remove from the oven, slide the parchment off the sheet, and let the meringues cool for about 10 minutes. Transfer the meringues with a spatula to a rack and let them cool completely. Store in an airtight container.

Makes about 2 dozen meringues

✿ *Coconut Bars*

Shirley Secretary-Chef tells me I've had these bars dozens of times in dozens of places. I find it hard to believe unless, like love, it's ever new. I love them. They have all the good-bad things for you, but my darling sister, Bessie, gave me the recipe years ago and she swears by it—and don't forget, she's the one with the sweet tooth—I've got the ones that protrude.

CRUST
8 tablespoons butter

1 cup flour

½ cup brown sugar

Mix all the above ingredients into a crumbly mixture. Pat into a 9-x-9-inch pan, making a layer ¼ to ½ inch thick. Bake in a preheated 375° oven for 10 minutes. Set aside and cool.

FILLING
2 eggs

¼ teaspoon salt

1 cup brown sugar

1½ cups flaked coconut

1 teaspoon vanilla extract

1 cup chopped pecans or walnuts

2 tablespoons flour

½ teaspoon baking powder

Beat the eggs, sugar, and vanilla. Mix the flour, baking powder, and salt. Combine the coconut and nuts and sift the dry ingredients over them. Add to the egg mixture, and mix well.

Pour over the baked crust and bake for 20 minutes in a preheated 375° oven. Cool and cut into squares

Makes eighteen 2-inch squares

❈ *Wanda's Nutty Bars*

For a few words about Wanda see page 294.

1½ cups flour
¾ cup brown sugar
10 tablespoons butter, softened,
   plus extra for pan
½ cup light Karo syrup

1 cup butterscotch chips
1 tablespoon water
One 13-ounce can mixed
   salted nuts (preferably with
   not too many peanuts)

Preheat the oven to 350°.

Place the flour, sugar, and 8 tablespoons of the butter in a food processor fitted with a steel blade. Process with several on/off turns until the dough forms a soft ball. (This may also be done by hand, using a wire pastry blender.)

Press the dough over the bottom of a well-greased jelly-roll pan, 15½ x 10½ x 1 inch. Bake for 10 to 15 minutes.

Place the Karo syrup, butterscotch chips, water, and the remaining 2 tablespoons of butter in a double boiler over medium-high heat and cook, stirring constantly, until all the ingredients are melted and the mixture is smooth. Pour over the baked crust. Spread the nuts over the top and press them into the filling with a spatula.

Cool and cut into squares with a pizza cutter.

Makes thirty-five 2-inch squares

❈ *Thinnest Brownies*

This is another one of those gems that happened out of necessity in Malibu. I needed a dessert for a new neighbor's welcome. I wasn't given much notice and this was quick, easy, light, and luxurious. I liked it— so did the company.

5 tablespoons unsalted butter,
   plus extra for waxed paper
¼ cup unsweetened cocoa
½ cup sugar
1 large egg, lightly beaten
¼ cup flour

½ teaspoon vanilla extract
Pinch of salt
¼ cup walnuts, chopped
¼ cup semisweet chocolate
   chips
Confectioners' sugar

Preheat the oven to 350°. Line a 9-x-9-inch baking sheet with well-buttered waxed paper.

In the top of a double boiler, melt the butter with the cocoa and stir until smooth. Remove from the heat and stir in the sugar. Beat in the egg and stir in the flour, vanilla, salt, nuts, and chocolate chips. Spread the batter on the baking sheet and bake in the middle of the oven for 10 to 15 minutes, or until the cake pulls away from the sides of pan and is just firm to touch.

When cool, dust with the confectioners' sugar. Cut into 2-inch squares and serve with a small ball of vanilla ice cream with shaved semisweet chocolate over all.

Makes eighteen 2-inch squares

❧ *A White Butter Cake*

4 egg whites
2½ cups sifted flour, plus extra
  for cake pans
2 teaspoons baking powder
½ teaspoon baking soda
½ teaspoon salt

1½ cups sugar
8 tablespoons butter, softened,
  plus extra for cake pans
1 cup sour cream
1 teaspoon vanilla extract

Preheat the oven to 350°. Thoroughly grease two 8-inch cake pans and sift a little flour over each.

Warm the egg whites or have them at room temperature. Mix together the flour, baking powder, baking soda, and salt. Beat the egg whites at high speed until foamy. Beat in ¾ cup of the sugar a little at a time, beating well after each addition until the egg whites hold soft peaks. In the large bowl of a mixer or food processor, cream the softened butter with the remaining ¾ cup of sugar until light and fluffy. Add the flour, alternating with the sour cream, a little at a time, ending with the flour. Mix well. Stir in ½ cup of the egg whites to soften the mixture. Then fold in the remaining egg whites and the vanilla. Stir until smooth.

Pour the batter into the prepared baking pans and bake for 30 to 35 minutes, or until the cake springs back when gently pressed with your fingertip. Cool in the pans for 10 minutes. Remove from the pans and cool thoroughly on a rack.

Spread with Caramel Frosting Number 1 or 2 (see the following recipe), or your favorite coconut or chocolate icing—I'm easy. The cake is light and wonderful.

Serves 8 to 10

✻ *Caramel Icings for White Cake*

NUMBER 1

1½ cups brown sugar, firmly packed
½ cup white sugar
1 cup milk
1 tablespoon butter
1 teaspoon vanilla extract

Boil both sugars and the milk together to the soft-ball stage (a drop of the mixture will form a soft ball when dropped into cold water), then add the butter. Cool to lukewarm, add the vanilla and beat until thick, creamy, and of spreadable consistency.

Makes enough for one 9-inch layer cake

NUMBER 2

2 cups sugar
1 teaspoon baking soda
1 cup buttermilk
1 tablespoon butter
1 teaspoon vanilla extract

Combine the sugar, baking soda, and buttermilk in a saucepan and boil to the soft-ball stage (see above). Add the butter and vanilla and beat until creamy. If the icing gets too hard while you are spreading it, add a little sweet cream.

Makes enough for one 9-inch layer cake

Index

All-year-round vegetable soup, 46–47
Almonds
    almond soup, 56
    braised celery with almonds, 181–82
    crunchy almond shrimp, 22
    orange and almond salad, 72–73
    trout amandine, 160
Amber glass custard, 285–86
Anchovies, fried pasta with, 222
Appetizers
    apples with cheese on sourdough, 30
    Cheddar cheese turnovers, 27–28
    chilaquiles, 30–31
    chopped tomato salad with bruschetta, 29
    cold scallops dressed with garlic-chive
      sauce, 25
    crunchy almond shrimp, 22
    eggplant, peppers, and cucumber spread,
      35–36
    green tomatillo sauce, 39
    hot artichoke dip, 39
    mushroom chicken livers, 33
    mushrooms Provençale, 32
    nopales strips, 32
    peppery stuffed crab, 23
    phyllo pillows, 14
    piroshki, 15–16
    pot stickers, 17–18
    quiches, 26–27
    Roman spiced artichokes, 34–35
    salmon dip, 37
    sautéed mushrooms, 34
    savory cheese spread, 29
    Sho's cheese olives, 28
    shrimp balls, 20
    shrimp cocktail, 18–19
    shrimp in a cloud, 21
    South American black bean dip, 38
    spicy deviled crab meat, 22
    spring rolls, 16–17
    stuffed dates, 37
    stuffed deviled crabs, 24
    tapenades, 36–37
    See also Pizzas
Apples
    apples with cheese on sourdough, 30
    apple tarts, 281
    Dinah's beer-apple fritters, 247–48
    veal scallopini with cream, Calvados, and
      apples, 108
Apricot glaze, 282
Artichokes
    artichoke-potato casserole, 232–33
    hot artichoke dip, 39
    Roman spiced artichokes, 34–35
    shrimp-and-crumb-stuffed artichokes, 144–
      45
Arugula
    arugula and spinach salad with white wine–
      honey vinaigrette, 71–72
    arugula pizza, 9
Asparagus
    asparagus crepes, 174
    asparagus soup, 47
    baked asparagus Parmesan, 173
    chicken with asparagus and bean sprouts,
      125–26

Bacon, escarole with, 186
Baguettes, 254
Balsamella sauce, 210
Bananas
    banana date pecan bread, 251
    banana-nut rum bread, 250
    I've never been to Cuba—but (ice cream
      dish), 291

301